Exploring
Wisconsin
Trout Streams

Exploring Wisconsin Trout Streams

The Angler's Guide

SECOND EDITION

Steve Born, Jeff Mayers,
Andy Morton, and Bill Sonzogni

THE UNIVERSITY OF WISCONSIN PRESS

The University of Wisconsin Press
1930 Monroe Street, 3rd Floor
Madison, Wisconsin 53711-2059
uwpress.wisc.edu

3 Henrietta Street
London WC2E 8LU, England
eurospanbookstore.com

Printed in the United States of America

Illustrations on pp. 8, 20, 30, 48, 62, 63 (bottom),
65 (bottom), 80, 99 by Stephen Di Cerbo.
Copyright 1995 by Stephen Di Cerbo.
Illustrations on pp. 1, 16, 29, 38, 40, 43, 47, 49,
50, 53, 54, 61, 63 (top), 64, 65 (top), 72, 87,
92, 94, 109, 111 by Richard Berge.
Maps by Susan Hunt.

Library of Congress Cataloging-in-Publication Data
Born, Stephen M., author.
Exploring Wisconsin trout streams : the angler's guide /
Steve Born, Jeff Mayers, Andy Morton, and
Bill Sonzogni. — Second edition.
        pages   cm
First edition published in 1997.
Includes bibliographical references and index.
ISBN 978-0-299-30004-3 (pbk. : alk. paper)—
ISBN 978-0-299-30003-6 (e-book)
1. Trout fishing—Wisconsin—Guidebooks. 2. Fly fishing—
Wisconsin—Guidebooks. 3. Wisconsin—Guidebooks.
I. Mayers, Jeff, 1959–, author. II. Morton, Andy, author.
III. Sonzogni, Bill, author. IV. Title.
SH688.U6E96 2014
799.12'409775—dc23
2013046016

Contents

Illustrations

Photographs

Figures

Foreword

Trout fishing has always been a passion for me. At age four I was casting into the mud puddles in front of the house. By six I was exploring the local trout streams with vigor. At eleven I was inspired to take up flyfishing by the writings of Joe Brooks, Al McClane, Ted Trueblood, the young Ernest Schwiebert, and other flyfishing writers of the time. It has been a full-time and fast-paced pursuit ever since.

Over the years I have been blessed with an agenda that has taken me around the world to some of the best trout fishing that can be found: the hallowed chalk streams of England, the crystalline streams and lakes of New Zealand, the swift little mountain brooks and spring creeks of South Africa, the tundra rivers of Alaska, the freshwater lagoons of Tasmania, the brawling salmon rivers of Russia, and many others.

In all this, I have come to see the common threads in the complex fabric of flyfishing; the strands that run through trout fishers, the fish they so lovingly pursue, the environs that make this sport possible, and the impact that humankind has had on this fragile resource. It has become evident to me that the cold, clean water that harbors trout is a rare commodity on this planet. In fact, scientists have calculated that less than one millionth of one percent of the world's water actually flows in trout streams at any one time.

Because they are so rare, such waters are easily degraded by the activities of man—farming, road construction, housing developments, waste disposal, even recreational activities, all take their toll. And so it is, that when one finds a state well blessed with trout water, such as Wisconsin, one can be assured that it is no accident—that it must be a carefully husbanded resource.

The truth is that the history of Wisconsin has been one of intense overuse of the forest and agricultural resources, followed by an intense, conservation-based ethic that has restored the pristine quality of many of the state's lakes and streams. True, the vast forests of huge white pines are gone, but Wisconsin's currently well-managed forest cover contributes strongly to its healthy water-sheds, and consequently to its healthy fisheries. True, the sweeping acreages of tall-grass prairie have disappeared beneath the plow, but the farmers of Wis-consin now are among the most conservation-minded of this nation. Ours is a state that tries hard to reconcile its human resources with its natural resources.

And the natural resources are many. In the north of the state, the heavy forest cover of mixed hardwoods and conifers invites logging and pulp cut-ting, and the land lies covered with a patchwork of uneven-age forest stands. Injected into this vast woodland are a myriad of streams, curving first this way and then that. They are the home of brookies, browns, and rainbows, and in sequestered areas of the back-country watersheds, these fish can at-tain sizes that make the angler gasp in appreciation.

Still mostly pure, these freestone streams offer an excellent selection of insects and other food items to the trout. Mayflies still emerge in abundance, and caddis hatches can cloud the sky. Midges and stoneflies abound. Add to these the alderflies, fishflies, hellgrammites, beetles, waterbugs, terrestrial insects, crustaceans, forage fish, and leeches, and the trout have an almost endless array of food items to feed upon. Yes, the fishing can be quite good!

The center of the state forms a giant bowl that once held the meltwater lake that out-flowed from the glaciers. Here are Aldo Leopold's beloved "sand counties," intensively farmed for potatoes, peas, sweet com, and other truck crops. The forest land is more open than in the north, with oak savannas dotting unfarmed openings between the more classically wooded low hills.

The streams of the sand counties perfectly fit the classic definition of a meadow stream, meandering strongly and gouging out deep corner pools between shallow runs where the sand bottom continually shifts its footing. Daytime fishing in these streams can be productive, but at night they come alive, especially during the Hex hatch of June. These are prime waters for the giant mayflies, and truly large rainbows and browns are taken here each year as the insects complete their life cycles. Other nights a huge streamer or skated mouse can bring solid results. For those who ply the velvet darkness in solitary pursuit of large browns, this is the stuff dreams are made of.

The southern fertile crescent stretches from Madison to the Mississippi, and then north along the "Father of Waters" to just beyond Hudson. This is the land of wood-lot farms and coulee streams, the Driftless Area that the glaciers did not touch. It's a land of steep-sided hills and narrow little valleys, each filled with its own spring creek. Nourished by the abundant minerals in the underlying limestone, these streams are immensely rich and can harbor truly huge trout.

The fish are shy in the thin, clear water of these streams. The fisher is chal-lenged to just get close enough to cast, and often the first cast sends the fish dashing for cover. It's a challenge, but many consider it the best fishing the state has to offer: the hatches are outstanding, the fish are outstanding, the scenery is outstanding. Three out of three ain't bad!

The Lake Michigan shore offers a unique fishery, one that has sprung up like magic and that feeds the fire within every fisher with the lure of gigantic browns, rainbows, brookies, king salmon, and coho salmon. These fish were introduced into the short, often seasonal streams of the dairy-farm coast, and provide migratory fisheries. The fishing is early and late in the season, extending the angler's opportunities in both directions. When conditions are right, the fisher can take the Wisconsin grand slam: all five species from the same stream in the same day. There's nothing quite like it.

Yes, ours is indeed a unique fishery, and this is a unique fishing book. It offers far more than a quick fix on what to use to catch fish in Wisconsin. And it's not guilty of being a kiss-and-tell book, either. Like its authors, its pages reveal a broad-ranging knowledge of Wisconsin's landscape and its fisheries; information that's not only useful for increasing catch rates but also placates the curiosity beast within us—you know, the one that causes every four-year-old to ask incessantly, "But why?" It's a book that creates awareness in the angler, a book that speaks to the whole person.

This is also the story of a strongly conservation-based history that has molded a lovingly kept resource. It is also a book of warnings: the resource doesn't exist in a vacuum. The resource is molded by man for better or worse, and without constant vigilance, the worse always seems to win. If we fish, we need to be sure that our voice is heard on the right side of the issues.

Read this book with a discerning eye. Don't merely skim its pages in search of trout; dig deep, and let it reveal to you the interplay between the fisher and the husband of resources inside you. Find all its treasures. You won't be sorry you did.

GARY A. BORGER, 1997

Preface

The air is still and dripping with humidity as the sun dips below the rounded hills on the horizon. Mosquitoes are buzzing around your ears and biting through your paint-stained long-sleeved shirt. Your nostrils are filled with the pungent combination of cigar smoke and bug dope. Your body is tense with excitement and anticipation for what's to come. Suddenly your eyes are focused on the single mayfly that emerges from the oozing silt bank below your feet. Before this almost hummingbird-sized creature reaches tree-top level, it is snatched from the air by a swooping red-winged blackbird. More mayflies follow, despite the fate of the leader. It is nature's way.

The hatch is on, and before you know it trout—big trout—are slurping, Blup. Blup. Blup. The once-still waters at one of your favorite corner pools on your "home" trout stream are disturbed by rippling, concentric circles emanating from the rises. You begin to make your cast, focusing on the biggest fish of the bunch, the one you've missed several times this year. It's night now, and you're casting to a sound in the dark. Your big mayfly imitation hits the water with a splat. You watch it float to the target and then . . .

This is just a taste of what Wisconsin trout fishing has to offer. You can experience it, too, if you have the curiosity to explore the world of Wisconsin trout.

Thousands of anglers found the first edition of *Exploring Wisconsin Trout Streams* a way to satisfy at least some of their curiosity.

The success of the first book encouraged us to tackle a second edition that we hope will be just as satisfying. And some seventeen years after that first edition, we are proud to say the vast majority of the stories and information we chronicled the first time around remain current, though we and others worry that the Wolf River is in danger of becoming a warmwater fishery. Where possible, we eliminated out-of-date information.

We also enhanced the offerings by adding:

- **A new introduction in the form of an essay on the future of Wisconsin trout streams explaining how fishing opportunities have improved since the mid-1990s as well as the looming threats to coldwater fisheries;**

- **Many new photos;**

- **And an updated "Fishing the Web" section providing our choice of the best links for trout anglers.**

The good news is all these years later you're still never very far from a trout stream in Wisconsin. But this easy access to trout and their environs is a mixed blessing. Trout, because of their clean, cold water requirements, are a fragile resource made even more fragile by the inevitable intervention of humans.

Can we stop these pressures? Not any more, not even in a midwestern farm state like Wisconsin. Today, conservationists must do more than wring their hands about the "way things used to be"; thankfully, in Wisconsin many are. Cold-water resource advocates—professionals at state and local agencies and various educational institutions as well as volunteers from every walk of life—are constantly at work protecting trout and the rich fishing heritage these beautiful creatures symbolize.

To these conservationists, we dedicate this book. We chronicle, and in the process celebrate, their efforts to preserve the state's treasured trout streams. We hope others will follow their lead.

When we first undertook this book, we knew we wanted to do more than compile a guide to the state's best fishing. As anglers, we're very sensitive to the "kiss-and-tell" style of travelogue that leads to crowded conditions and too much pressure on the fishery—especially on our smaller streams. So we chose to highlight a group of already well-known rivers around the state, taking care to omit specific directions to the "honey hole," or to the little feeder stream that should be discovered through countless hours of exploring and wading, not from your easy chair.

Yes, we could have told you a bunch of secret places to fish—places we've discovered over our accumulated 100 years of angling experience. But instead we embarked on a broader effort, focusing on the history, the conservation, and the *feel* of Wisconsin trout fishing. Consequently, you'll get a lot more than just fishing information.

Trout fishing in the Badger State is a rich privilege that offers endless variety and challenge. We aim to celebrate this privilege and share it with you. Our book will help the novice angler get started, and will provide the experienced angler with a tidy package of information to explore even more trout waters. We'll point you in the right direction, so if you're curious and do some exploring, you'll catch more than your share of trout.

Spreading this information isn't harmful. On the contrary, we think trout and their rivers need all the friends they can get these days. Helping people discover their favorite prime waters should form a solid constituency to push for the kind of protective measures trout need to survive.

The pressures are inexorable. Nevertheless, the fishing is actually getting better in some places. For that we can thank environmental regulation, progressive-thinking biologists, the hard work of cold-water conservationists, and thousands of cooperative, conservation-minded anglers. We hope this book will help those efforts by telling the story of Wisconsin trout fishing. Along the way, of course, we know you'll find information here that will enrich your fishing experience in the Badger State.

Acknowledgments

We owe a great deal to many people who gave us their time, their insight, and their support throughout the writing of the first book and now the second edition. First, a special thanks to our families who took up the slack at home. We also acknowledge the assistance of the many dedicated fisheries and resources management personnel at the Wisconsin Department of Natural Resources—some now retired (such as Larry Claggett, Dave Vetrano, and Max Johnson) and others still hard at work for trout and their habitat.

The book is richer for all of those who contributed graphics and photographs, especially Dick Berge and Steve DiCerbo, who lent their artistic skills to our project, and Susan Hunt, who did a superb job in preparing our maps. We also thank our many friends who contributed photos for the first and second editions. We drew from Dr. Stan Szczytko and Jeff Dimmick, University of Wisconsin–Stevens Point, and Dr. Gary Borger, professor emeritus University of Wisconsin Center–Marathon County for entomological information. We also want to thank Dave Graczyk, United States Geological Survey, who helped us compile hydrologic information; SallyWhiffen, who passed along historical tidbits about her beloved Bois Brule River; and Mindy Schlimgen-Wilson, for Prairie Dells Dam historical information. Thanks also must go to those who reviewed our work, providing sound and constructive criticism. Among them: Jim Bartelt, Sara Johnson, Harold "Bud" Jordahl, Lee Kernen, Tim Kinzel, Jeff Smith, and John Thurman. Judy Holmes gave us timely and immeasurable help in pulling together the manuscript.

We are indebted to those at the University of Wisconsin Press who accepted our proposal and encouraged us along the way. Sam Diman, then the associate director, helped get us in the door, and then-director Allen Fitchen resisted showing us out. For the second edition, we were ably guided by Adam Mehring at the Press. Finally, we thank our many angling friends who, over the years, shared with us their knowledge, opinions, theories, conjectures, and especially their love for Wisconsin trout streams and their inhabitants.

Thanks to all!

Introduction

These Are the Best of Times

MORE THAN a decade ago, the first edition of *Exploring Wisconsin Trout Streams* described Wisconsin and much of the Upper Midwest as "flyover country"—that part of the United States that traveling anglers see from the air on the way to someplace else. No longer. Thanks to dedicated stewardship of trout habitat, magazine stories, flyfishing film festivals, and word-of-mouth among anglers fueled by the Internet revolution, our region has a growing legion of admirers that make the state and its 13,000 miles of trout waters a destination in its own right.

In fact, the "good old days" of trout fishing are NOW. These are the best of times for trout anglers based on fish populations, size of the trout, and increasing opportunities.

One of the reasons is Wisconsin's leadership in natural resource management and protection—and its great influence on the national conservation movement. It is this historical and continuing commitment to conservation that is key to the future sustainability of our coldwater trout streams—more in need of protection than ever, given threats such as climate change. Trout require year-round cold water to survive, and in many parts of the state nutrient-rich creeks fed mostly by cool spring water provide some of the most treasured haunts for trout and anglers.

Climate change looms large for anglers and those managing fisheries. Data for long-term ice cover show Wisconsin lakes are freezing later and breaking up earlier. (On Lake Mendota near our Madison-area homes, ice fishers are lamenting the loss of about one month of their icefishing season!) Research compiled by the Wisconsin Initiative on Climate Change Impacts (WICCI), a consortium led by the University of Wisconsin–Madison's Nelson Institute for Environmental Studies and the Wisconsin Department of Natural Resources (WDNR), indicates that our average annual temperature has risen 1.1 degrees Fahrenheit since 1950, precipitation has increased by

10 percent, and extreme events have become more common. Using modified international climate computer models, projections show that temperatures in Wisconsin will warm by 4 to 9 degrees Fahrenheit by the middle of the twenty-first century.

Few species are more sensitive to changes in their environment than trout. Work by UW and WDNR researchers suggests that, under the most extreme summer warming conditions projected by the models, water temperatures would increase by over 7 degrees; under that scenario brook trout may not survive in Wisconsin, and brown trout populations could decrease by more than 80 percent. The researchers note that even under more moderate conditions of thermal change (less than a degree Fahrenheit in water temperatures), brook trout distributions might shrink by 44 percent and brown trout populations by 8 percent.

Some think this could be a factor in explaining why the Wolf River, still featured in this edition, is now a more marginal trout fishery; other factors such as habitat degradation, stocking changes, and watershed practices could also play a role. Given this inexorable warming, the experts are studying strategies that could lessen the impact on trout, such as prioritizing resources to coldwater streams where fish are most likely to succeed and emphasizing the need for a holistic management approach.

If past is prologue, conservation heroes will emerge to address the challenge. The legendary John Muir walked through Wisconsin long before he discovered the vistas of California's Yosemite Valley. Aldo Leopold researched the state's wonderful land and water resources and formulated a comprehensive way of thinking about the earth's riches long before the term "ecologist" came into everyday use. Gaylord Nelson was governor and created a trend-setting land and water protection program here years before he became the father of Earth Day while serving in the U.S. Senate in 1970. Dedicated university and government researchers have contributed many ideas and discoveries that have played major roles in understanding, preserving, and protecting trout species and their environs.

And local literary figures such as Gordon MacQuarrie have chronicled the sport and its appeal with rare style. "Trout fishing is not like drinking beer. It's more like sipping champagne," MacQuarrie once wrote. "You take a tiny leetle bit and smack your lips. So with trout. You want to get the stage all set. You look ahead and figger out every move. You will not be rushed. You are not after a pail of fish."

In the pages ahead, you'll get to know more about these Wisconsin-based conservation figures, the state's highly regarded environmental programs, and a trout resource enjoyed by more than 140,000 people who buy fishing licenses and inland trout stamps each year.

Wisconsin's natural heritage is a treasure with an abundance of challenging opportunities to hook naturally reproducing trout. There are rich "limestoners" in the unglaciated Driftless Area of Wisconsin, Minnesota, and Iowa that rival those in England and central Pennsylvania. There are miles and miles of remote brook trout water in the glaciated and heavily forested northern part of the state. There are remnant populations of the great native Lake Superior brook trout hanging onto a niche in the largest of the Great Lakes. There are big, tumbling freestone rivers like the Namekagon in northwest Wisconsin. There are natural spring ponds in northern Wisconsin reminiscent of beaver ponds in New England. There are trout-rich brooks bubbling through the Central Sands region that Leopold called home and knew so well. There are a few especially fragile trout streams in the rapidly suburbanizing Kettle Moraine hills of eastern Wisconsin, a part of the state where stream restoration by forward-looking landowners and conservation volunteers has resulted in excellent trout fishing in the Onion River drainage and in tiny brooks less than an hour from downtown Milwaukee. About the only place you don't find many trout streams is along the Lake Michigan shore. But there, because of man's ingenuity and intervention, steelhead and salmon move up the Lake Michigan tributaries each spring and fall, the product of an elaborate stocking operation by the Wisconsin Department of Natural Resources (you'll need to buy a special Great Lakes trout and salmon stamp to pursue this fishery).

Along with all this good fishing is a diverse and subtly beautiful landscape, ranging from Superior's rugged lakeshore and the Appalachian-like setting of the Baraboo Hills to the unique coulee country of southwestern Wisconsin and the neighboring bluff country of Iowa and Minnesota. En route, you'll find lovely prairies, sheltered spring ponds, and serene wetlands. Wisconsin lacks mountains, but it has enough big hills to provide plenty of splendid views. We'll steer you to some of these special places and tell you about the natural heritage through the use of reliable, scientifically based information.

My coauthors and I are all flyfishers now, having pursued this graceful pastime for decades. But we all started as bait and spin anglers. The information here will help every angler, not just those who cast hand-tied imitations of trout food. Some of you may want to try flyfishing after reading this book, but we're not trying to convert you. We do hope you'll follow the fishing regulations and consider releasing most of your catch so the trout can grow and be caught again. That said, we catch and kill the occasional trout for a memorable meal; when done within the framework of trout fishing regulations—outside of designated "catch-and-release" areas—there is no evidence that limited harvest is harmful to the resource.

Young woman flyfishing, ca. 1930. Wisconsin Historical Society, WHi-76966.

The "Getting Started" chapter will give you the basics to get going in the sport of flyfishing for trout. About half of the estimated seven million trout anglers in the U.S. are flyfishers (thanks in part to the popularity of Norman Maclean's novella *A River Runs Through It* and the 1992 movie adaptation by Robert Redford in which Wisconsin's own Jason Borger served as a casting double for Brad Pitt). Long the domain of men—in 2006 four out of five trout anglers nationally were males—participation by women in trout fishing in Wisconsin and beyond is growing. The national Recreational Boating and Fishing Foundation indicates women made up more than 25 percent of flyfishers in 2010, a percentage that increased to 30 percent by 2013. We suspect more Wisconsin women are also joining our ranks.

Women have a long history as anglers—after all, Dame Juliana Berners' *A Treatyse of fysshynge wyth an angle* was written in 1496, and the mother of flyfishing became the central figure in a wonderful historical novel, *Profound River*, by former Wisconsinite John Gubbins. Along with greater participation in trout angling, more and more women are joining and leading fishing clubs and organizations at local, state, and national levels—a very positive sign for river conservation. Today there are trout fishing seminars, retreats, books, and equipment targeted to this growing female audience.

Enthusiastic participants at a women's flyfishing clinic. Photo by Susan Fey.

A happy Wisconsin trout angler. Photo by Jim Bartelt.

While the number of trout anglers in Wisconsin has been stable over the past several years (around 140,000 trout stamps sold annually), a number of dedicated trout anglers (as measured by multiple years of buying trout stamps) have stopped trout fishing. A 2011 WDNR survey of "lapsed anglers" found that the major reason many anglers stopped participating was time constraints in their personal lives. Many of this cohort expressed a low level of commitment to trout fishing versus other outdoor activities; not surprisingly, flyfishers did not make up a significant part of the "lapsed angler" population. Only 12 percent of those surveyed blamed complex inland trout fishing regulations as the main reason they stopped participating. Of special note, more than eight in ten former trout anglers still rated their trout fishing experiences as satisfactory.

Beginners and veterans alike will want to experience some of our "don't miss" trout-fishing opportunities. That means traveling with us to famous waters such as the Bois Brule and Namekagon, to delicious Driftless spring creeks where an afternoon mayfly hatch can cure what ails you, and to remote night-time locations where fishing the Hex hatch can border on a spiritual experience. We concentrate on inland trout, but we couldn't leave out Wisconsin's magnificent "sea-run" salmonids. Sure, our seas are filled with freshwater, but the fish are big and fight as hard as their cousins on the West Coast. And when the inland trout season closes in Wisconsin, you can extend the season in Iowa and Minnesota after the end of September as well as pursue steelhead and salmon on the tributaries of Lakes Michigan and Superior. Some of these streams are in the midst of major urban areas, but the chance of catching a big, pulsing salmonid will provide more than a respite from the cityscape.

Happily, the good news is that all of this fishing is very accessible. Wisconsin, because of its strong Public Trust doctrine that ensures public access to all navigable waters, is a place where you don't have to belong to a private club to catch the big one or simply have a quality fishing experience. All the streams and rivers we feature in the book have numerous access points. The best water can be yours—as long as you have the required fishing license and trout stamp, and obey the regulations that help maintain healthy fisheries. Use our maps, WDNR's website and informative regulations pamphlet, and a plethora of guide, club, and fly shop websites to plan your fishing adventures. See a partial list of such websites in the "Fishing the Web" section at the back of this new edition.

At the same time, we're not pretending to give you a comprehensive guide to all of the state's 13,000 miles of trout streams—up some 800 miles from about a decade ago. That would be impossible and downright threatening to some streams. We believe some trout waters are too fragile, too precious, or too small to be discovered in a book like this (though some of our fishing friends think we presented too much information in the first edition!). Our regional tours of some of our best-known trout waters will help you find your own fishing spots. Selecting which streams to feature was difficult. We chose streams that are already well known, big enough to withstand pressure, and possessing a good conservation story. Our featured streams represent a diverse array of trout waters around the state—from the meandering spring creek to the whitewater-filled freestoner.

One other noteworthy change in trout fishing over the past few decades is the professional help now available to anglers. Trout fishing guides were few in number twenty years ago; now there are a significant number of professional guides working in Wisconsin and the tri-state Driftless Area. These are experienced anglers, excellent teachers, and often great chefs! Some are independent operators; others are tied to one of the many fine fly shops that can provide current information about fishing conditions and gear to meet any need. A quick check of websites will get you started. For beginners, a day with a guide can advance your fishing knowledge and skills dramatically; for veteran anglers, a good guide can show you unfamiliar water and perhaps acquaint you with some new techniques.

In the first edition, we looked ahead through an environmental prism at the challenges facing the future of Wisconsin trout fishing. Two WDNR goals were positive forces: strengthening environmental programs through watershed-based integrated management, and increasing involvement of local interests and non-governmental organizations in environmental stewardship. If watersheds are healthy and sustainably managed, the trout fisheries will flourish.

While WDNR's organizational structure has changed, watershed-based management is still being practiced, especially on waters impacted by point and non-point source pollution. That bodes well for trout.

The second goal has been pursued aggressively and successfully by the agency and local partners, both within and out of government. One spectacular example of this is the Driftless Area Restoration Effort (DARE). DARE, spearheaded by Trout Unlimited (TU), was launched in 1995, building in part upon TU's Home Rivers Initiative in the Kickapoo Valley. It is a geographically focused, locally driven, consensus-based effort to protect, restore, and enhance rivers and streams for fish and other aquatic life throughout the 24,000-square-mile Driftless Area. A broad coalition of federal, state, and local governments, landowners, academic institutions, conservation organizations, sports groups, and other interested parties is working together to prioritize watershed focus areas and projects; implement actions with measurable successes; build new partnerships and strengthen existing ones;

leverage additional funds; and raise public awareness about Driftless Area natural resources through outreach and education. Moving beyond local efforts to restore a reach of stream on a one-at-a-time basis, the DARE effort looks at the stream systems as part of a regional landscape. Under the DARE banner, the partnership has launched a wide variety of projects and assessments in Driftless Area states aimed at addressing habitat degradation and alteration of coldwater streams. The activities are evident throughout the Driftless region, and anglers are prime beneficiaries. The list of projects completed and in progress is stunning (see www.darestoration.com for details of individual stream projects). And the focus on the Driftless as a region rather than individual streams has prompted WDNR to undertake a master planning project for all its trout stream efforts in the Driftless Area. No wonder the Driftless has become a national trout angling destination.

Additionally, local land trusts and TU chapters, sports and conservation clubs, and others have worked closely to obtain conservation and access easements from landowners on streams across the state and beyond. This is a natural partnership that has been fostered by agency commitments to engage local interests in stewardship of their natural resources.

Longstanding pioneering programs, like the Trout Habitat Stamp program in Wisconsin, continue to produce great outcomes for Wisconsin trout fisheries. Started in 1977, that program—supported by more than140,000 trout stamp purchases by trout anglers every year—annually brings in more than $1.2 million of funding for habitat restoration and improvements and related work. While many other states are fighting to maintain their coldwater resources, in the past decade Wisconsin has added more than 200 streams to its portfolio of trout streams. Seen over a longer time horizon, the state went from having 2,677 classified trout streams totaling 9,562 miles in 1980 to 2,869 trout streams with 13,175 miles of trout fishing opportunities in 2013.

Trout fishing has never been better in the Badger state. Since our first edition, WDNR fisheries biologists have aggressively continued the wild trout program, using the offspring of naturally reproducing trout for repopulating streams. The wild trout have flourished. A 2004 study by WDNR fisheries researcher Matt Mitro found that trout with parents born in the wild had a survival rate two to four times better than those with parents from a domestic hatchery. The genetic makeup of these wild trout also has led to better natural reproduction. Thus, the natural environment, rather than man's expensive hatcheries, is producing more sustainable fisheries. Stocking has its place—for urban fisheries where natural reproduction is limited or impossible because of warm water or lack of habitat, for example—but Nature's way is better and more cost efficient. The wild trout program involves both

Representative of many exciting Driftless Area stream restoration projects, the 2013 restoration of lower Black Earth Creek. Photo by Steve Born.

Following the decommissioning of an old dam, the lower Black Earth Creek has been returned to its former meandering channel with habitat enhancements, erosion control, and reconnection to the stream's natural floodplain. Photo by Steve Born.

A beautiful brookie—Wisconsin's only native salmonid. Photo by Jim Bartelt.

brown and brook trout. Brookies, our only native salmonid, are the focus of wild trout restoration activities in those watersheds where good habitat exists and the influx of competing brown trout can be limited.

Good land management and land use, along with habitat and water quality improvement, are key to the future of trout populations. U.S. Geological Survey studies, particularly in southwestern Wisconsin, have documented significant improvements in baseflow to streams and some decrease in flood peaks. These positive changes are attributed in part to changing farming practices and land use—the decline in grazing on steep slopes subject to erosion, for example. The past decade has also seen some shifts in habitat management approaches. Large-scale efforts to restore prairie stream conditions in some watersheds have been undertaken by extensive removal of streamside, non-native trees—a shock to some anglers when they visit familiar waters but a long-term bonus for trout and the environment. At the same time, instream habitat enhancement is on the rise, resulting in greater use of "rootwads" and logs in stream restoration projects; this trend has been accompanied by more selective use of the seemingly ubiquitous "lunker structures" in habitat improvement projects, and the wider use of weirs and other new engineering designs that accomplish habitat improvement, bank stabilization, and flow management goals with a more natural look and feel.

But the land use challenges facing trout streams are unending. In some urbanizing watersheds, more pavement and rooftops—even with responsible stormwater management—threaten both habitat and groundwater inflows to trout waters. Trout water thus can only be sustained if growth is managed with natural resource protection in mind.

Economic activities like mining are a part of Wisconsin's heritage, starting with lead-zinc mining in the southwestern part of the state in the 1820s. In our first edition, we noted the potential threat to the Wolf River region from a very large planned copper and zinc mine near Crandon. After a multi-decade political and regulatory battle, the mine site was purchased by the Sokaogon Ojibwe and Forest County Potawatomi in 2003, ending the prospect of metal mining in that watershed. But new mining controversies have arisen. In the early 2010s, environmental organizations and tribes sought to block a planned iron mine in the Penokee Hills near Lake Superior. At this writing, Gogebic Taconite had begun the WDNR-monitored application process for a huge open pit iron mine near Mellen amidst controversy similar to the Crandon mine project. And mining for silica sand, which has gone on in Wisconsin for decades, emerged as another mining controversy at about the same time because of a dramatic exponential increase in demand for sand for hydrofracking—a technique used by the petroleum industry to enhance recovery of oil and gas. In 2010, the state had only five frac sand mines and five processing plants. By mid-2013, the number had increased more than tenfold, with western Wisconsin home to more than 120 mines and processing facilities. Western Wisconsin sought to grapple with the "sand rush" as people debated the positive economic impacts versus possible water, air, and land degradation.

The farming community has come a long way toward working with anglers and agencies to better protect coldwater habitats, and much of the land access and conservation easement gains of recent years have involved cooperation of farmers. Nutrient and waste management have improved dramatically in recent years, but fish kills because of poorly timed manure spreading and improper storage can still occur. In addition, farmers must manage the waste from large feeding operations involving thousands of animals. Angler concern remains even though these "concentrated animal feeding operations" must get a WDNR permit that requires no discharge and approved manure spreading plans.

Trout fisheries benefit from sound land use planning, effective runoff management, good regulatory oversight, environmentally sensitive infrastructure (such as culvert replacement at streams' intersections with roads and bridges), ongoing soil resource management and conservation programs, plus the engagement of county conservationists. But success requires consistent implementation and adequate funding—not guaranteed in the future when tax dollars and financial support for conservation cannot be taken for granted. Funding cutbacks, staff reductions, and competing priorities can hurt longstanding resource protection and management efforts, which can all too quickly put vulnerable coldwater resources at risk.

Where does this leave trout? The success of efforts like DARE and WD-NR's wild trout program are cause for optimism. But old threats—agricultural runoff, habitat loss, mining, sprawl development, non-sustainable use of aquifers—along with newer ones—such as invasive species, fish diseases, and climate change—are cause for concern.

These are the best of times for trout anglers. Whether that can be said fifty years from now to some degree depends on us—what we do individually, as members of conservation organizations, as citizens and shapers of governmental decisions, and as leaders in our communities. We hope trout fishers of that future time will look back and say thanks to the many of us who loved and worked to protect this most challenging and rewarding of sports, these most magical of fish, and the special places where they flourish.

We've lost some great conservation heroes since this book was first published—among them WDNR researcher Bob Hunt, Wolf River guardian Herb Buettner, the Kickapoo Valley's Roger Widner, and TU leader and Trout Stamp advocate Dan Flaherty. New leaders and trout advocates must fill their shoes. As you enjoy these "best of times" trout fishing, filled with angling memories and special experiences with friends, consider putting aside a small portion of your time to get involved in ensuring the future of trout and trout angling. And good luck astream!

STEVE BORN
November 2013

PART 1

Before You Go Fishing

1

Wisconsin's Trout-Fishing Heritage

A S TROUT ANGLERS and cold-water conservationists, we are the lucky heirs to a rich heritage that spans more than a century. In North America, that heritage immediately brings to mind New York's legendary Catskill Mountain streams, one of the cradles of American fly-fishing. Or Pennsylvania's limestoners, and the rich literature associated with fishing these challenging waters. Or northern Michigan's tannin-colored rivers, the setting for Robert Traver's wonderful writings, including *Trout Madness and Trout Magic*. Or the magnificent Rocky Mountain trout waters, or Zane Grey's and Roderick Haig-Brown's rivers of the Pacific Northwest. Wisconsin is rarely included in those historic circles, but it has made incredible contributions to the world of trout angling, literature and cold-water conservation.

Of course, the Badger State is justly famous for its fishing, but in most minds Wisconsin's official state fish, the belligerent muskellunge, is clearly king. Other warm-water species, especially walleyes, are major tourism and recreational attractions for those who enjoy Wisconsin's 15,000 lakes and tens of thousands of miles of rivers. Yet our state's many contributions to trout angling, lore, and fishery and environmental science deserve recounting. As you may suspect, we take great pride in our state's cold-water heritage. Here's why.

CONSERVATION LEADERS

Wisconsin's most important gift to the well-being of trout fishing is its role in shaping the nation's conservation ethic. Without conservation of cold-water resources, trout angling simply can't be sustained, and some of our greatest conservationists have spent their formative years—in some cases their entire lives—in Wisconsin.

Few have had greater influence than Aldo Leopold. Born in 1887 in Burlington, an Iowa river town, Leopold spent his boyhood exploring the Mississippi River country with his outdoorsman father. He decided early to become a conservationist, and pursued a career in forestry after graduation from Yale. In 1924, Leopold and several of his colleagues in the U.S. Forest Service succeeded in establishing the nation's first wilderness area, in New Mexico's Gila National Forest. His commitment to things wild and beautiful was always tempered by his training as a forester, which taught him to view forests and ecology in economic and utilitarian terms. Leopold's defining small book, *Sand County Almanac,* continues to provide a conceptual framework and serve as a bible for the modern conservation movement.

Leopold moved to Madison to accept a job with the Forest Products Laboratory. Soon the family acquired land along the Wisconsin River, along with the Leopold "shack," an old chicken coop converted to a weekend cabin. These lands, so carefully managed and studied by the family, have become a national conservation shrine. Leopold, known as "A.L." to his colleagues, literally invented the field of wildlife management, and was the first professor of wildlife management at the University of Wisconsin (or at any university for that matter). He displayed skills vital today in conserving cold-water resources. Leopold's ability to communicate and work with farmers, sportsmen, and landowners made him a very effective champion of conservation. We can think of no more powerful words than Leopold's urging farmers to think of conservation as "the owner's portrait of himself"—an idea highly relevant in addressing trout stream degradation in rural and agricultural areas.

Aldo Leopold was also a trout angler and fishery scientist. We are indebted to his daughter Nina Leopold Bradley, who died in 2011, for bringing to our attention an article entitled "Mixing Trout in Western Waters," published in 1918 in the *Transactions of the American Fisheries Society.* Contemporary ideas about the value of wild fish are reflected in this piece. "Nature, in stocking trout waters, sticks to one species. The Forest Service will do likewise . . . " Leopold writes, and "restock with the best adapted species, the native species always preferred." Leopold, often accompanied by one of his hunting dogs, also did extensive research on erosion problems in the flood-prone coulee country of southwestern Wisconsin, an unglaciated area known for its steep hills. He died of a heart attack on April 21, 1948, fighting a grass fire threatening his land; despite health problems tied to a nervous disorder, Leopold rushed into action to save his pine plantation. But he did live to see the acceptance of *Sand County Almanac,* his book challenging the primary land ethic of the time. Oxford University Press had finally accepted it for publication only a few days before his death.

This conservation giant will be best remembered not as a recreational trout fisher and careful observer, but as arguably the major ethical figure in

Aldo Leopold after a day of trout fishing on Montana's Flathead River, July 26, 1926.
University of Wisconsin Archives, Leopold Collection, negative number (X25)1268.

twentieth-century American conservation. His essays in *Sand County Almanac* and other publications have promoted the emergence of a land ethic that today influences land-use decisions all around the country.

Another conservation figure with strong Wisconsin ties is John Muir. Muir, one of the great preservation-minded conservationists of all time, spent part of his youth and college years in central Wisconsin. Although he moved away—in 1864, Muir bid farewell to his family in Marquette County and Portage to join his brother in Canada—the ideas that underpinned the birth of the Sierra Club and the battle for the protection of wilderness in the West's Sierra Nevada had their roots in Wisconsin.

The influence of his early Wisconsin years is wonderfully revealed in *The Story of My Boyhood and Youth,* published in 1913. He recalls coming to Wisconsin in 1849 from Dunbar, Scotland, with his family. He was eleven at the time the family settled on 160 acres of virgin land next to a little glacial lake in what today is Marquette County. They called their new home Fountain Lake Farm. "Oh that glorious Wisconsin wilderness! Everything new and pure in the very prime of spring when Nature's pulses were beating highest and mysteriously keeping time with our own! Young hearts, young leaves, flowers, animals, the winds and the streams and the sparkling lake, all wildly gladly rejoicing together!" he wrote. Before he left for Canada, he tried unsuccessfully to buy forty acres of lake meadow from his brother-in-law in order to fence the land and keep it untouched. Muir biographers say this project planted the seed for Muir's promotion of a national park system. Muir received a doctor of laws degree from the University of Wisconsin in 1897, and died in California in 1914.

Sigurd Olson will be remembered as an avid conservationist who led the way in preserving what is now the 1.3 million acre Boundary Waters Canoe Area in the Quetico-Superior National Forest of northern Minnesota. But Olson, too, was heavily imprinted by his time in the Badger State. Born in Chicago, Olson was raised in Ashland, on the Lake Superior shore in northwestern Wisconsin, where timber was starting to grow again in the region ravaged by the lumber barons. He attended Northland College (now home to the Sigurd Olson Institute), and graduated from the University of Wisconsin in Madison. He soon accepted a teaching position in Minnesota. Although he left Wisconsin, he never lost interest in the state. Over time, Olson emerged as a successful author and giant in the wilderness preservation movement. Trout anglers enjoying wild places while pursuing their sport might recall his memorable words: "By saving any wilderness, what you are really saving is the human spirit."

Perhaps Wisconsin's most prominent contemporary national conservation figure is Gaylord Nelson, born in Polk County's Clear Lake in 1916.

Nelson, a former Democratic governor and U.S. senator, was a conscience and leader in the conservation movement until his death in 2005. After graduating from Law School at the University of Wisconsin, Nelson went on to dedicate much of his thirty-two-year political career to the natural resources of Wisconsin and the nation. In 1970, he spearheaded the organization of the first Earth Day, an event that inspired millions of young people and elevated concern for the environment to the national political level. Having been on the water with him we have to report that he wasn't a particularly accomplished angler! But trout fishers everywhere can be especially grateful for his leadership in establishing the St. Croix and Namekagon National Wild and Scenic Rivers and the Apostle Islands National Lakeshore.

Warren Knowles is another former Wisconsin governor who left a strong legacy favoring trout. Born in River Falls in 1908 and a Republican who held the state's top elected job from 1965 through the end of 1970, Knowles was an avid fisherman who loved the Bois Brule. He continued the environmental activism started by Nelson—protecting wetlands, implementing water pollution control efforts, expanding parks, and advocating better environmental planning. He died of a heart attack in May, 1993, after a day of fishing at the annual Governor's Fishing Opener, an event he helped found.

The dedication of Nelson and Knowles to good conservation work was later honored through the Knowles-Nelson Stewardship Program, a $250 million land-protection fund that has a goal of setting aside 250,000 acres of prime natural and recreational areas. This fund follows in the footsteps of Nelson's landmark Outdoor Recreation Action Program, which he started in 1961. Today's Stewardship Program is well on its way to ensuring that Wisconsin's diverse natural resources, including its trout-fishing resources, will be preserved for future generations to enjoy.

All of the conservationists we've mentioned so far are members of the Wisconsin Conservation Hall of Fame, which inducted Leopold and Muir as charter members in 1985. The hall is located at the Schmeeckle Reserve Visitor Center at the University of Wisconsin at Stevens Point.

Other seminal figures in the conservation movement had connections to Wisconsin. Charles Van Hise, president of the University of Wisconsin during the first two decades of the century, was a friend of President Teddy Roosevelt and his chief forester, Gifford Pinchot (both accomplished trout fishers, by the way). Together, they organized a national conservation congress in 1908 for the nation's governors. The congress played a key role in the establishment of conservation and fish and wildlife agencies in states across the country. On returning from that pioneering conference, Gov. James O. Davidson appointed Wisconsin's first Conservation Commission.

CONSERVATION ORGANIZATIONS

The largest conservation organization dedicated to protecting and restoring cold-water fisheries and their watersheds is Trout Unlimited. Founded in 1959 on the banks of Michigan's Au Sable River by a small band of trout anglers concerned about deplorable trout management and neglect of habitat, the organization has grown to more than 95,000 members, organized in over 400 local chapters nationwide. Wisconsin was among the early states to organize grassroots chapters; the first, organized in 1967 by Wisconsin fishing legend Cap Buettner, was the Wolf River Chapter. Soon after, Madison attorney Nash Williams and others formed the Southern Wisconsin Chapter. These and other chapters around the state, along with a statewide organization, are active in local stream-improvement work and resource protection.

This sketch of a feeding brown trout was used on a T-shirt sold by the Southern Wisconsin Chapter of Trout Unlimited as a fundraiser for trout stream conservation. Copyright © 1995 Stephen Di Cerbo.

In its formative years, Trout Unlimited produced a now-classic film exemplifying the ideals of the organization and the beauty of trout angling. *The Way of the Trout* was shot in Wisconsin at Seven Pines Lodge. This beautiful and historic lodge, built in 1903, is located near Lewis in the west-central part of the state. Knapp Creek, which flows through the property, contains brookies and rainbows. The rustic, serene setting for the film perfectly frames the message of Trout Unlimited—that trout, and the environs they live in, are intrinsically beautiful and worth protecting.

Other conservation organizations, including the Izaak Walton League, Wildlife Federation, Sierra Club, Federation of Fly Fishers, River Alliance of

Wisconsin, and many local fishing and sports clubs have also been active in protecting the angler's environment. Conservationists from these groups have shaped the resource we enjoy today, and in our stream profiles we often highlight their contributions. We encourage you to find and join a conservation-minded group that fits your philosophy; be an active member and support their all-important stream-preservation projects.

LITERARY FIGURES

Wisconsin has produced some extraordinary regional literature on its outdoors by writers like Gordon MacQuarrie and George Vukelich. There have been other writers, but from our perspective these two deserve special mention.

One of the most entertaining Wisconsin outdoor writers of all time was Gordon MacQuarrie. A native of Superior, MacQuarrie was the *Milwaukee Journal* outdoor editor from 1936 until his death. One hundred twenty-two outdoor magazine articles written between 1931 and his death in 1956 have been attributed to him, many of which appeared in national magazines. The "Old Duck Hunter" stories are his most famous, and several collections of these articles have been reprinted in book form. Most are set in Wisconsin, and vividly describe the Wisconsin of the 1930s and 1940s. MacQuarrie makes you feel as if you're there—on the Bois Brule in northwestern Wisconsin fishing for lake-run rainbows, or hunting partridge in a forest near Hayward. But the real beauty of MacQuarrie isn't the outdoor images he evokes. It's the human images—the emotion, passion, humor, and even sadness that all trout fishers experience. His stories make you laugh, cry, or just plain remember as few stories can. MacQuarrie also played a key role in educating Wisconsin hunters and fishers about the importance of good resource management. Robert McCabe, who worked with Leopold at the University of Wisconsin, wrote that Leopold and MacQuarrie "were on the same wavelength regarding wildlife resources . . . [MacQuarrie] often referred to A.L. as the 'Old Master.' As long as Gordon was able, he continued to crusade, inform and educate his Milwaukee Journal clientele as to A.L.'s position on conservation matters."

Starting his career as a popular disc jockey in the Madison area, George Vukelich (known as "Papa Hambone" to his radio audience) wrote about his native Wisconsin with lyricism and wit. It's quite appropriate that he was once given the Gordon MacQuarrie Award from the Wisconsin Academy of Sciences, Arts and Letters. His regular column, called "North Country Notebook" (also the name of two collections of his essays) ran in a local Madison newspaper and was George's forum for commenting on the issues of the day. He regularly wrote of trout, trout personalities, and trout streams. A series of articles on threats to trout streams from livestock and manure played a key role in prodding government to act. Larger pieces appeared in the *Milwaukee Journal,* and George regarded his lengthy interview with Robert Traver (a.k.a. John Voelker) at his fabled Frenchman's brook trout pond in Michigan's Upper Peninsula as his most fulfilling interview experience. We agree with Gaylord Nelson, who said that "Vukelich writes of those things that commanded the talent and attention of Aldo Leopold, John Muir, Sigurd Olson and many others. Each of them said it eloquently and differently, but no one of them said it better nor any of them with as much wit and humor." George was as good an angler as a writer, and was just getting ready to shift his attention to fly-fishing for trout when he died—much too soon—in 1995.

Mel Ellis, Bill Stokes, Clay Schoenfeld, Steve Hopkins, Dan Small, and others have also contributed significantly to the literature of Wisconsin fishing, often with a focus on trout. But if you haven't spent some time with MacQuarrie and Vukelich, you owe yourself the experience. To get a taste of Wisconsin-based outdoors writing, find a copy of the wonderful 1993 anthology *Harvest Moon,* edited by Ted Rulseh.

ANGLING EXPERTS AND AUTHORS

Wisconsin authors have also been contributors to the "how to" trout-fishing literature. Perhaps the best known Wisconsinite writing in this genre is Gary Borger, who's written our Foreword. Gary has taught millions about fly-fishing through his four clearly written books, numerous instructional videos, many magazine articles, and personal appearances around the world. Gary is indeed one of trout fishing's best educators and best-known personalities.

Born in Pennsylvania, Gary earned a doctorate in botany at the University of Wisconsin–Madison. He then took a job as a professor at the University of Wisconsin Center–Marathon County and has been there ever since. Gary's family members share his love of trout fishing and are business partners in his many angling-related enterprises. His son Jason has illustrated several of Gary's books, and served as a fishing double for the actors in the movie *A River Runs Through It.*

Once touted by Pennsylvania trout-fishing legend Charlie Fox as the best book he ever read, *How to Fish from Top to Bottom* is a unique Wisconsin contribution to trout-fishing literature. Its author, Sid W. Gordon, worked for the old Conservation Department as the supervisor of lake and stream improvement projects in Wisconsin from 1934 to 1941. Through his experience surveying Wisconsin waters and observing anglers on rivers like the Bois Brule and

Namekagon, he wrote a wonderfully practical book that keeps showing up on lists of the best books on trout fishing ever written.

Gordon was one of the first to describe the relationship between water quality and fishing quality. For example, he explained in great detail the relationship between water hardness and fish productivity. He also carried stream entomology, particularly as it relates to trout fishing, to new heights. And he had a philosophy about trout fishing that we endorse: "Today the thinking sportsman puts most of the trout he catches back into the stream. With an eye to preserving this great pastime for many years to come, he fishes mainly for the thrill of outwitting and outplaying the extremely wary trout. It may well be that in our understanding of the trout we may even be tempted, now and then, to regard them as friends instead of foes. Why not? We enjoy our friends who give us good competition at bridge, archery or golf, do we not?" First published in 1955, his book, and his observations about trout streams and lakes, were way ahead of his time. Sid Gordon passed away in the mid-sixties in Superior, Wisconsin.

Helen Shaw is a name recognized by most fly-tiers; she ranks among the greatest tiers in the history of the sport, and any fly tied by her is a collector's item. She is also the author of one of the best books on fly-tying ever written, simply titled *Fly Tying,* and first published in 1963. It presents full-page photographs of the various elements in the construction of the fly—the tail, wing, body, hackle and so forth. Her instruction is clear and basic to all types of tying; for the beginner, it's still about as good a text on fly-tying as you can get.

Helen Shaw was born in Wisconsin's capital, Madison. She began tying flies as a child, learning from local Wisconsin tiers, and by the time she finished high school she was an established pro. After high school she set up a shop in Sheboygan, where her reputation flourished. She met her husband, Herman Kessler, the art director for *Field and Stream,* when he came to Wisconsin to fish. In 1953 she moved with her husband to New York, closing her business in Sheboygan but continuing to build her reputation as one of the greatest fly dressers of all time. In a 1988 magazine interview, Shaw talked about the clients of her shop, calling them "true sportsmen who appreciated the art and craft of fly-tying, and fished purely for the love of it. They rarely killed trout, just a few for the pan now and then."

Of the many trout-fishing gurus and characters we have known over the years, none compares to Wisconsin native and spring creek magician Tom Wendelburg. As he once told George Vukelich in an interview, "if you described me as a 'trout fishing bum,' that would be pretty accurate." Born in Milwaukee, Tom earned his journalism degree from the University of Wisconsin in 1965. He went on to publish prolifically—more than 100 articles in leading outdoor magazines. His work, much of which is collected in his book *Catching Big Fish on Light Fly Tackle*, presents some of the most sophisticated observations, techniques, and innovative fly designs in the "how-to" angling literature. In our opinion, Wendelburg is one of our best technical writers. He's also a masterful fisherman, as good as any we have seen. When nothing is hatching and nobody is catching fish, Wendelburg will hook trout—sometimes through very unconventional means. Let's just say he's not above using a panfish popper on occasion. Tom is also an artist when it comes to tying flies. Not only are his flies works of art; they also catch fish. Wendelburg is perhaps best known for the Wendelburg Scud, an all-fur imitation tied with cream hare's mask and a yellow head.

We first met Wendelburg many years ago while he was living streamside out of his car. More than a few stories and fly patterns were born in Tom's old Ford Pinto! His whole existence was focused on tying flies and fishing for trout. He has escaped the work-a-day world for years, eking out a living by selling flies, publishing an article now and then, and serving as an occasional guide or event speaker. He is known for his ability to think and talk trout to the virtual exclusion of all other topics. Modest he is not, as many a Wisconsin angler can attest. "I don't think I can be out-fished by too many people in the world with a fly rod," is a statement often uttered by the incorrigible Mr. Wendelburg. In our experience, Wisconsin's very own "trout bum" may just be right. Tom's writing legacy on how to fish spring creeks, tie innovative fly patterns, and preserve trout streams guarantees him a place in our "expert" hall of fame.

More than a fair share of today's angling writers have a Wisconsin connection, and an emerging group of them are contributing to Wisconsin's trout-fishing heritage. They include: Rich Osthoff, backpacker and wild-country explorer extraordinaire; John Beth, Great Lakes tributary fishing pioneer (who teamed with Gary Borger to record *My Madison,* a unique combination of prose and music that captures the sense and beauty of Montana's Madison River; all of the music was composed and performed by John); Jim Humphrey, born and raised in Madison, a prolific author and contributor to national fishing magazines who co-authored *Wisconsin and Minnesota Trout Streams: A Fly-Angler's Guide;* and Ross Mueller, whose fine, self-published book, *Upper Midwest Flies That Catch Trout and How to Fish Them,* brilliantly capsulizes forty years of Midwest fishing experience. Names now regularly appearing in the trout-angling journals include Dave McCarty, John Holt, Mike Dry, and Ted Leeson—all with ties to Wisconsin. Leeson, who learned his trout skills in southwestern Wisconsin before moving west to Oregon, has written a dandy account of his passion for rivers and trout in *The Habit of Rivers,* a must-read for dedicated anglers. These individuals and others continue to develop Wisconsin's trout-fishing heritage through the written word.

RESOURCE PROFESSIONALS AND SCIENTISTS

Wisconsin has also produced a number of professionals who have made important contributions to trout fishing. Professor Arthur Hasler served as director of the University of Wisconsin-Madison's limnology program for many years. Hasler was heir to the legacy of the University of Wisconsin's Edward Birge and Chancey Juday, the two individuals generally credited as being the fathers of the science of limnology—the study of lakes. In addition to his many scientific accomplishments related to lakes, fisheries research by Hasler uncovered olfactory imprinting in stream-spawning salmon. In other words, salmon find their home waters partly through their sense of smell. This discovery had great consequences for salmonid management world-wide, and led to the successful salmon-stocking program in Lake Michigan (detailed in our chapter on Great Lakes tributary fishing). We love this gentle scientist's recounting of how he happened upon the idea. The incident occurred in 1946 during a vacation to the Wasatch Range of the Rockies in Utah, where he had grown up. Hasler and his family were walking along a mountain path he hiked in his youth. During this hike, his childhood memories rushed back when he noticed the smells associated with a mountain meadow and waterfall. He wondered if salmon used their noses to find their way back home; later, he and his research associates did experiments confirming that they do.

Hasler also mentored many students who have gone on to illustrious careers in the aquatic sciences. Ray White is one of the most influential with regard to trout fishing. He has become a national expert on trout stream habitat and the overall management of trout streams and trout. His controversial two-part article on "Why Wild Fish Matter" in *Trout* magazine brought to a new level the awareness of the negative effects of stocking trout. As White will tell you, his professional fishery management roots are firmly planted in Wisconsin. Ray still counts Black Earth Creek, Lawrence Creek, and the Mecan River (all profiled in this book) among his personal home waters.

Some other scientists deserve mention. Bill Willers from the University of Wisconsin–Oshkosh wrote *Trout Biology—An Angler's Guide,* one of the few modern books aimed at educating fishers about the scientific aspects of a trout as a living organism. William Hilsenhoff, a professor of entomology at the University of Wisconsin–Madison, developed a widely used indexing technique to assess the environmental quality of a trout stream based on collecting stream organisms. Bob Hunt, another graduate of the University of Wisconsin–Madison and a long-time researcher with the Wisconsin Department of Natural Resources, wrote *Trout Stream Therapy* after he retired; it synthesized years of research on trout stream habitat improvement by Hunt and his colleagues at WDNR. This partial listing should suggest that Wisconsin scientists have made major contributions to our understanding of trout and their environs, and thus, indirectly, to the quality of trout fishing.

THE ANGLING "INDUSTRY"—SOME NOTEWORTHY PRODUCTS

Though probably more often thought of as the home of hand-crafted musky lures, Wisconsin has a proud history of fly-tying. In fact, during the 1930s and 1940s, Stevens Point was the world capital of fly-tying: about ten million flies were produced there annually in the forties! This industry was started by Carrie J. Frost, a hunter and fisher and the daughter of a trout fisherman, who marketed flies under the name of the C.J. Frost Co. Then came Weber Lifelike Fly, The Worth Co., and other firms. At its height about 500 tiers, mostly women, were employed in the industry. Sadly, Wisconsin's great tying operations began to decline after World War II because of the overseas competition that brought an end to so many labor-intensive American businesses, and the introduction of spinning equipment that spurred many anglers to trade in their fly rods.

While such commercial fly production companies have slipped into obscurity, one big maker of artificial spinning lures keeps hooking more and more customers. One of the great spinning lures of all time—the Mepps—is manufactured in Wisconsin. Mepps is an acronym for Manufacturier D'Engins de Précision pour Pêches Sportives, or, "Manufacturer of Precision Equipment for Sport Fishing." Sheldons', Incorporated, located in Antigo near the Wolf and the Eau Claire rivers, produces an amazing variety of Mepps spinners, some of which are among the best trout lures ever invented. The company even makes a spinning lure called the Thunder Bug (a dragonfly nymph), that looks and acts like an insect, enabling spin anglers to "match the hatch."

The Sheldons' success story is pure serendipity. A. L. "Todd" Sheldon owned a retail sport shop in Antigo, and after World War II he was given some French Mepps spinners by an ex-GI. They lay in his tackle box tarnishing until the day nothing was working on the Wolf; out of desperation he tried the French lure and caught trout. He was so impressed he started selling the lure at his store. The ex-GI he knew, Frank Velek, struck up a pen-pal relationship with a French woman, who sent spinners in exchange for nylon stockings. But the lures were selling too fast for that arrangement, so Velek worked out a supply line to the French factory. Eventually, Sheldon acquired the North American distribution rights to Mepps lures. In 1972 he purchased Mepps

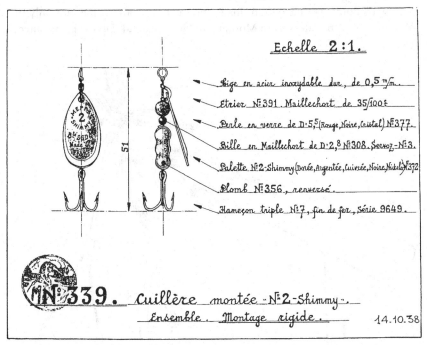

The original design for the MEPPS spinner. Courtesy of Sheldons' Inc.

France. Todd Sheldon died in 1995 at the age of eighty-one, but the business is still in the Sheldon family and going strong, employing 120 people in the town of 8,000. One of the most popular Mepps spinners has squirrel tail tied over the treble hook. If you drive through Antigo you'll see a sign that says "Squirrel Tails Wanted." This sign is authentic; Sheldons' will either pay cash or trade Mepps lures for the tails. It's not too surprising, then, that squirrels are hard to find around Antigo.

During the period when Wisconsin dominated the commercial fly-tying world, a number of flies emerged to become classics. The Hornberg, a unique streamer with large mallard feathers for wings, was named after Stevens Point area game warden Frank Hornberg. The pattern continues in use today and is considered by many, including us, to be one of the top attractor patterns for Wisconsin waters (for any water, for that matter). Another fly designed about the same time (1938) is the Pass Lake. Fished either as a wet or dry fly, the Pass Lake consists of a combination of a black body, a white wing, and brown hackle. It was designed by a minister from Clintonville, a small town just east of Stevens Point. We have seen this fly produce time after time, not only in Wisconsin but in waters from Montana to New Zealand. Divine providence, perhaps?

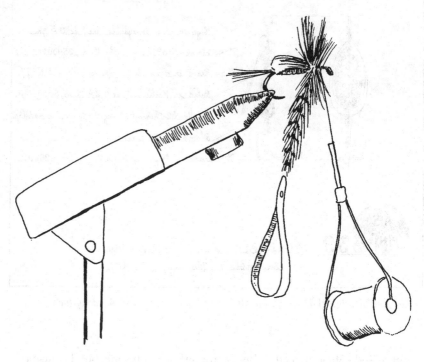

Since Wisconsin's golden fly-tying era before and during World War II, a number of Wisconsin fly-tiers have made their mark. Gary Borger and Helen Shaw, of course, are probably the most famous. However, many other outstanding tiers have links to our state. Royce Dam of the Milwaukee suburb of Wauwatosa —described by some as the best fly-tier in the world today—is a master tier and tying educator who won the 1994 Buz Buszek Award from the Federation of Fly Fishers. This award is given annually to recognize the professional or amateur who has made a significant contribution to the art of fly-tying. Borger credits Royce with the idea for Gary's well-known Strip Nymph, a fly that features a thin strip of animal hide, with the fur still on it, tied to the rear of the hook. Fly-tying and fly-fishing were his passions, and by 1953 he was selling his flies to tackle shops. Many have commented on Royce's big hands, wondering how he could so skillfully dress any fly. But the former factory worker has shown an unsurpassed skill in making imitations that trout love.

Wayne Moore produced a small book called *Fly-Tying Notes,* a little gem unknown to many anglers. Wayne spent his first forty years in Wisconsin, and his book is full of ideas he developed while living and working in the Badger State. George Close, from Kiel, near Sheboygan, has been an ardent teacher of fly-tying and is the developer of many practical patterns making innovative use of rug fibers (Antron-like materials). Arling Erickson was a fly-tier well known to anglers fishing northeastern Wisconsin, particularly the Wolf River. Arling operated a fly shop, and the flies he tied and sold have become prized possessions for many. Finally, we must mention our close friend, the artist Dick Berge, who occasionally sells his flies. Dick tied and taught fly-tying in Madison for many years before moving to his Iron River retreat in northern Wisconsin. Dick is a high school art teacher by trade, and all of his ties reflect his artistic talents (which are also evident in much of this book's artwork).

Among the other trout-fishing crafts, Wisconsin can also claim some fame in rod-building. The St. Croix Rod Company, one of the largest graphite rod manufacturers in the United States, is located in the northern Wisconsin community of Park Falls. St. Croix produces some beautiful, reasonably priced fly rods. We own several and have been very pleased with them. Should you fish the North Country, a trip to the St. Croix factory store can result in some real bargains.

Many individual craftsmen have won kudos over the years for their rod-making, including bamboo specialist Don Schroeder of Janesville, Dennis Franke of Cross Plains, and Bill Sherer of Boulder Junction.

CONCLUSION

Finally, no discussion of Wisconsin's trout-fishing heritage would be complete without mentioning some of the presidents who have trout-fished Wisconsin before, during, or after their presidencies. "Silent Cal" Coolidge made the Bois Brule River country his summer White House in the 1920s. Other presidents that have visited the Bois Brule at some point in their fishing lives include Grant, Cleveland, Hoover, and Eisenhower.

Wisconsin has a trout-fishing heritage as interesting, varied, and important as any state. This heritage, and the tradition that evolves from it, is more than just anecdotal. For those of us who find that trout fishing has special meaning in our lives—much more than just catching fish—this heritage evokes a feeling. A sense of place. A sense of past and present. A bond with fishers of the past. A baseline from which we expand our knowledge and ex-

Trout Unlimited leader Duke Welter with one of the "rewards" of his conservation work in Wisconsin's Driftless region. Photo courtesy of Duke Welter

perience. Fishing the Bois Brule or little Lawrence Creek becomes more than just fishing—it becomes an act of homage to those before us, from presidents to fishing bums, who have loved, nourished, and venerated our sport in the Badger State, and beyond.

2

Wisconsin's Environmental Management Legacy

OPINIONS of high courts are rarely exciting reading, and, even more rarely, sources of angling wisdom. But in 1995, two avid trout anglers who served on the Wisconsin Supreme Court issued an opinion that nicely sums up the emotions of Wisconsin trout fishers. The case involved an arcane zoning issue—whether or not commercial fee fishing in an artificially constructed pond is legal in a shoreland conservancy district. We won't bore you with the details, but we want you to read the opinion written by Justice Bill Bablitch, and concurred in by former Chief Justice Nat Heffernan, both long-time acquaintances. They speak for us all.

At times, the syllogisms of legal analysis must bend to the spirit that emanates from within. This is one of those times. Simply put, this is not fishing.

Fishing is many things, the least of which to many who indulge is the catching of fish.

It is, in the winter doldrums, the casual browsing through the fishing catalogs, the fisherperson's equivalent of the gardener's seed catalogs, contemplating the coming renewal;

It is the snap of a twig across the water on a dew-filled morning signaling the approach of a deer taking the first sip of dawn;

. . . It is the screech of the owl ten feet above the river bend warning the invader of its displeasure as we approach at dusk to witness the fleetingly hypnotic hatch of the mayfly, ironically renewing itself at the moment of its demise;

It is the swish swish swish of the giant wings of the heron as it rises reluctantly from its shallow water preserve, glaringly reminding us that this is its home, not ours.

It is all of this, and more, that brings us back again and again. This
is fishing; the catching of a fish is merely ancillary . . .

Thinking about our sport in this way will enrich your entire angling experience. Beyond fishing philosophy, you'll appreciate your days astream even
more when you're aware of the many conservation efforts that went into protecting the future of Wisconsin trout: habitat management improvements, dam
removals, stream restorations, pollution control programs, public land acquisition programs, and fishery management innovations. In some ways, every
stream is both a unique angling experience and a conservation laboratory. Paying attention to conservation will not only make you a better trout angler, but
a better steward of this vulnerable resource. In that vein, we present you with
a brief sketch of our state's resource management and conservation efforts.

Wisconsin, long a national leader in environmental management and protection, has made a big commitment to nurturing wild trout fisheries throughout
the state. But threats to the well-being of cold-water resources and wild trout
are everywhere—mining, logging, urbanization, road-building, losses of fish
and wildlife habitat, pollution, stream diversions, and dams. Some core natural
resource and environmental protection programs are

there to assure high-quality water, fish-friendly flows,
and watershed land uses compatible with cold-water
resource conservation. But the best in-stream fishery
management practices are doomed if watersheds and
stream corridors aren't protected. Long-term protection of these fragile resources depends on far-sighted
pollution control, water quantity management, stream
corridor management, and, ultimately, watershed-wide land-use planning and
management. Only by caring for the entire watershed will we be able to protect
and manage the trout resources we care so deeply about. The success of these
efforts won't occur, however, without citizen demands for strong enforcement of
environmental laws and active conservation work by government.

WATER QUALITY MANAGEMENT

Wisconsin has been a pacesetter in protecting surface water quality since the
early part of this century, when laws were passed providing state-level supervision and control of sewage. With the enactment of the 1972 federal Clean
Water Act, Wisconsin aggressively encouraged industrial and municipal wastewater treatment. Twenty-five years later, more than $3 billion in public and pri-
vate funds has been devoted to cleaning up our state's waters, and Wisconsin's

rates of municipal and industrial compliance with water quality regulations are among the highest in the nation. Cleaning up these end-of-the-pipe sources of pollution has led to successful new fisheries, such as those in numerous Great Lakes tributaries, and to the restoration of several trout streams, such as Spring Brook below Antigo. Serious threats to water quality remain because of various toxic chemicals found in pipe discharges and buried in sediments, but it's safe to say the state's water quality management programs have dealt quite successfully with pollution from so-called point sources.

To continue the clean-up of our waters, the state is now tackling a more insidious and less obvious pollution source—contaminated runoff from farms, fields, and urban areas, usually referred to as non-point-source pollution. The state's efforts to address these problems center on the Nonpoint Source Pollution Abatement Program, a watershed-based program providing grants to farmers and communities in selected watersheds. Initiated in 1978, this program was one of the first in the nation to comprehensively address the non-point-source pollution problem. Over the years, this largely voluntary program has been continuously reviewed and modified, selectively adding regulatory components in an effort to increase its effectiveness. Having spent tens of millions of dollars by the mid-1990s, the program is helping to protect and rehabilitate many trout streams around the state by implementing better controls for manure and farmland, as well as for urban construction and stormwater runoff.

The program has been controversial, in part because it directly affects individual landowners and farmers, rather than faceless corporations and municipalities. It raises questions about landowner rights and responsibilities, and who should pay for taking care of public waters. Through cost-sharing and technical assistance, the program helps landowners undertake measures to protect and improve water quality in our rivers and streams. While the results of controlling polluted runoff are difficult to measure, protection of much trout stream water quality and habitat will depend on the success of these programs. Cooperation among anglers, conservation organizations, state and local government agencies, and landowners—as demonstrated in places like the Black Earth Creek watershed in south-central Wisconsin—will become increasingly essential. Anglers fishing in the Timber Coulee Creek area and other southern Wisconsin locales may note innovations in livestock-grazing practices, like rotational grazing, intended to keep cows from breaking down stream banks.

A variety of other state and federal programs over the years have targeted agricultural pollution and soil conservation. The contoured hilly farmlands of parts of southwestern Wisconsin are a legacy of New Deal soil conservation programs. Contemporary agricultural conservation programs, such as the Conservation Reserve Program, protect wetlands and limit farming on highly erodible areas. These programs have been enormously positive not only for trout, but also for wildlife, waterfowl, and farmers.

These programs raise our interest in research done by scientists with the U.S. Geological Survey, who examined long-term trends in stream flow in the Driftless Area of southwestern Wisconsin. They found that annual low flows in streams have increased significantly over the decades since the early 1900s, while annual flood peaks have decreased—a result generally of less surface runoff and more infiltration. The same trends were not found in forested areas in the northern part of the state. Although the reasons for these trends—which should have positive effects on fish populations— are not well understood, other researchers have attributed changes such as significantly decreased erosion rates to improved agricultural and land-use practices in southwestern Wisconsin. Years of conservation work, along with changes in farming, seem to be making a difference.

Another important water quality protection program involves designation by the Wisconsin Department of Natural Resources of certain lakes, streams, and rivers as "outstanding" or "exceptional" resources. These designations grew out of the federal requirement for each state to draft antidegradation policies, recognizing that the federal Clean Water Act only set minimum clean-water standards, and didn't adequately protect unpolluted waters. The resulting policy, approved in 1989, is intended to prevent pollution from reaching waters already meeting state standards. Our wild-and-scenic rivers and trout streams with self-sustaining natural populations enjoy added protection as a result of such designations. Concerns about the possible adverse economic impacts of this program led to a 1995 study in northeastern Wisconsin's Marinette County, which has the highest number of trout streams classified as outstanding or exceptional resource waters. The results of this research reaffirmed both the economic benefits and the public support for this surface water protection program.

Finally, given the importance of groundwater to trout, as noted in subsequent parts of this book, we must mention Wisconsin's pioneering 1984 groundwater protection legislation. This law, and companion federal enactments, involves not only protective regulations, but a variety of monitoring programs aimed at tracking pollution from agrichemicals, landfills, and other sources. As a result of these programs, certain pesticides and herbicides have been restricted or prohibited. While these actions were driven by public health concerns, many cold-water fisheries are beneficiaries as well.

Water quality and water quantity management are closely linked. Reductions in flow can affect water chemistry, and surface water runoff can add sediment, nutrients, and oxygen-demanding organic materials to streams. The federal Clean Water Act encourages the maintenance of in-stream flows because

Stabilization of stream banks and habitat improvements on middle reach of Black Earth Creek. Photo by Lowell Gennrich.

The same Black Earth Creek section, one year later, after vegetation has "healed" the streamside environment. Photo by Steve Born.

treatment requirements for pollutors are designed based on specific flows. Wisconsin's Public Trust doctrine and the state Environmental Policy Act provide reasonably strong assurance that actions significantly altering flows and affecting the aquatic environment will be carefully considered in state decision-making processes. Reporting and permitting requirements for diversions or withdrawals from streams and rivers—and for installation of high-capacity wells—try to ensure that the effects of such activities on surface water quality and stream life will be considered in making the decision whether to approve them. Additionally, the state requires that water releases from dams be regulated to protect aquatic life downstream. Parties maintaining dams on navigable streams must pass at least twenty-five percent of the natural low-water flow at all times. Nevertheless, in prolonged droughts such as Wisconsin experienced in the late 1980s and early 1990s, trout streams like the Prairie River have incurred severe losses of trout populations as a result of diminished flows and related water quality degradation.

PROTECTING HABITAT, STREAM CORRIDORS, AND WATERSHEDS

Most of our watershed and habitat protection programs benefit water quality and flow. Regulatory programs that control or influence land uses streamside and within watersheds play an important role in protecting stream resources. Perhaps foremost among these programs is the state's shoreland-floodplain management program. Enacted in 1965, this first-in-the-nation program requires all counties, cities, and villages to adopt zoning regulations that meet state standards within 1,000 feet of lakes and flowages, and within at least 300 feet of rivers and streams. Zoning provisions include shoreline building setback requirements, vegetation removal limitations, and other resource-protective controls. This pioneering program, modified in recent years to give more flexibility to property owners, still furnishes stream corridors a fair degree of protection from development.

In a 1972 national-landmark decision, the Wisconsin Supreme Court upheld the state's shoreland zoning program, in the case of *Just v. Marinette County.* The lead opinion began by recognizing that the basic purpose of the ordinance was to protect navigable waters and public rights from uncontrolled use and development of shorelands. The opinion went on to characterize the case as "a conflict between the public interest in stopping despoilation of natural resources, which our citizens until recently have taken as inevitable and for granted, and an owner's asserted right to use his property as he wishes." In this oft-cited case, the court further held that "changing of wetlands and swamps to the damage of the general public by upsetting the natural environment and the natural relationship is not a reasonable use of that land which is protected from police power regulation." This inspiring decision, the bane of developers and strict private property rights advocates, has underpinned the protection of riparian corridors and wetlands in Wisconsin ever since.

The state has lost to development and agriculture almost half of an estimated ten million acres of wetlands that existed before European settlement. Streamside and floodplain wetlands are critical to the ecologic and hydrologic health of rivers and streams. State wetland protection legislation now requires that local units of government regulate development and other activities that threaten wetlands as part of their shoreland-floodplain zoning programs. The U.S. Army Corps of Engineers, along with the U.S. Environmental Protection Agency, has primary regulatory authority over dredge-and-fill activities in wetlands. Provisions of the federal Clean Water Act allow the states to use water quality standards to protect these vulnerable ecosystems, and Wisconsin has pursued this authority aggressively. However, this approach has proven more effective in state decision-making—for example, in granting or refusing permits to alter waterways by damming, dredging, and grading—than in ensuring federal compliance with Wisconsin's strong wetland protection policies.

Because land-use laws can be changed, or weakly administered and enforced, the surest way to protect trout streams and rivers is through public land acquisition. This can involve fee-simple acquisition, or purchase of development rights or conservation easements. Acquisition of critical watershed sections can keep land in a natural or near-natural state, which, given the intimate relationship between land and water, will invariably be good for trout. In addition to state agencies and local units of government, lands can be acquired by nongovernmental conservation organizations and local land trusts.

Wisconsin was one of the first states in the country to establish a program for large-scale public acquisition of prime environmental and recreational lands. Initiated by Governor Gaylord Nelson in 1961, the Outdoor Recreation Act Program (ORAP) raised $50 million from a tax on cigarettes. The program was expanded in 1966 and 1969 under Governor Warren Knowles, and over the ensuing years thousands of acres of important recreational and ecologic treasures have been acquired and preserved. New parks have been opened and developed, wildlife habitat has been preserved, and scenic and fishery easements have been acquired.

In 1990, a successor program, called Stewardship, was begun to protect environmentally sensitive areas and to increase quality recreational opportunities across the state. The ten-year Stewardship program represents the largest program of its type in state history. It provided authority for $250 million of land acquisitions and recreation enhancements that will help protect our heritage for the enjoyment of future generations. The program has also greatly aided local conservation efforts. Nonprofit local groups have been awarded millions of dollars in grants for the acquisition of conservation lands and easements, and for habitat restoration projects. Under these and other funding programs, lands have been acquired by the Wisconsin Department of Natural Resources (WDNR) within designated "fishery management areas" and "state wildlife areas."

In 1965, Wisconsin was the first state to establish a system of wild rivers in order to preserve them in a natural, free-flowing condition. Three trout streams were named at that time—the Pike, the Pine, and the Popple—all in the northeastern part of the state. These streams were "to receive special management to assure their preservation, protection and enhancement of their natural beauty, unique recreational and other inherent values." Although there were provisions for other rivers to be added to the system later by the legislature, the state wild-and-scenic-river program has never been expanded. But water quality management review, as part of the "outstanding" and "exceptional resource waters" classification scheme, has the potential—with proper enforcement—to provide tremendous protection from land uses incompatible with high-quality trout waters. The only federally designated wild-and-scenic rivers in Wisconsin are the St. Croix and the Namekagon; these near-legendary trout and smallmouth bass streams are now protected in perpetuity. The Wolf River was also named in the federal law, but the state didn't take the necessary actions to include this famous river in the federal system, preferring to protect it with state programs.

Other public land–related efforts can achieve comparable results—the special protections within state forests, along the Bois Brule River, for example, and incorporation within county park systems, as in Marinette County's spectacular parklands along the Peshtigo River. In addition, the Wolf River, not named in the state wild-rivers law, has been the subject of special legislation prohibiting dams and navigation improvements. Coupled with an aggressive WDNR land acquisition and easement purchase effort, this special river's future is more secure. Some corporations and utilities also have been excellent natural resources stewards by protecting their lands and waters and providing access to sportsmen.

Of special interest to anglers, this vast array of government acquisition and preservation programs not only protects irreplaceable ecologic assets like trout streams, but provides widespread public access points. This is unlike the situation in many states, where resources have been protected but often can't be reached by anglers of modest means. Wisconsin's bountiful trout resources are available to everyone.

The Big Green River—one of numerous challenging spring creeks with extensive public access in southern Wisconsin. Photo by Jim Bartelt.

DAM REMOVAL

Dam removal is another significant trend, especially in Wisconsin. Since passage of the Mill Dam Act in 1840, thousands of dams have been built on our rivers and streams to provide mechanical and hydroelectric energy, and they played a significant role in the economic development of our state. Today, approximately 3,600 dams exist in the state, with more than 1,000 on trout streams. Dams caused an immediate loss of cold-water fisheries, but we are just beginning to understand the profound long-term ecologic effects of dams on river systems. Many of these older dams have deteriorated and are now unsafe, and impoundments behind many dams are afflicted with water quality problems. For the past few decades, a relatively small dam-safety program administered by the WDNR has aggressively pursued dam removal and river restoration, helping to remove more than thirty dams. Trout anglers owe a debt to now-deceased WDNR state dam safety engineer Dick Knitter—"the dambuster"—for his leadership in seeking opportunities for river restoration while addressing public safety concerns. Dam removals are highly emotional community decisions, and river conservation advocates like Trout Unlimited chapters are at their strongest when the prospects loom for re-creating a cold-water fishery. Important dam removals have created significant reaches of new free-flowing inland trout waters on the Prairie and Tomorrow-Waupaca rivers, and on Black Earth Creek. The removal of dams on Great Lakes tributaries, such as those at Clarks Mills on the Manitowoc River and the North Avenue Dam on the Milwaukee River, has also opened up miles of river to migratory trout and salmon, dramatically expanding fishing opportunities. In some cases, however, removing a dam can be a mixed blessing, because the migratory species may hurt inland trout populations. But on the whole, dam removal is a management option that is gaining momentum in river restoration. We believe it has enormous implications for renewing trout streams in Wisconsin.

FISHERY MANAGEMENT

Sid Gordon, one of the state's early stream-improvement advocates, relished approaching run-down waters and visualizing what could be done to attract trout. "You build a trout nursery, hotel and grocery store for the fish. This you do within a few hours with the help of other fishermen in the construction of a V Deflector, one of various types of stream improvement devices," Gordon wrote in his 1955 book, *How to Fish from Top to Bottom*. "That deflector, in-stalled at the beginning of [a] sandy 150-foot stretch of the stream, provides a good spawning bed by creating a current that sweeps the sand off the bottom and deposits it behind the structure. Spawning trout can henceforth fan off the newly exposed gravel, deposit their eggs, cover them and retreat to the hotel the new current has built for them in the quieter side waters 100 feet downstream. The fast current you have created over the gravel aerates the water every moment, summer and winter. No silt, sand or debris will cover that gravel and smother the eggs because the speed of the water will now carry it all away." The essence of fisheries management philosophy hasn't changed much in the years since Gordon supervised this kind of stream work and made Wisconsin a leader in habitat improvement and management.

To provide the most favorable living conditions for trout, Wisconsin fish managers and research biologists have developed and tested numerous im-provement measures, grounding their work in sound science. Many of the stream improvements described in this book—bank covers, wing-deflectors, LUNKER structures, rock dams, submerged shelters—and innovative methods for their installation were pioneered and described by Ray White and Oscar Brynildson in their benchmark 1967 publication, *Guidelines for Management of Trout Stream Habitat in Wisconsin*. Bob Hunt and his colleagues—with strong leadership from WDNR's Robert Heding—continued the good work of design-

A LUNKER structure in place providing cover for trout

ing and installing fish-friendly cover. Hunt's informative and beautifully il-lustrated book, *Trout Stream Therapy,* summarizes decades of habitat research and management in Wisconsin. Spring pond restoration by dredging has also been an important part of the management toolkit, particularly in the north-ern part of the state. And many a northern fish manager has spent countless hours dealing with the harmful effects of beaver dam-building.

Funding, however, had always been a limiting factor in carrying out hab-itat improvement programs. In 1933, Wisconsin residents eighteen or older were required to obtain a "rod and reel license" for an annual fee of $1.00. In 1977, with strong support from Wisconsin Trout Unlimited, the legislature approved a special Inland Trout Stamp, required of all anglers who intend to fish for trout. The extra revenues generated by this stamp were exclusively for habitat improvement and maintenance on inland trout streams. While this mechanism didn't finance protective work in the watershed away from the stream, it has been a critical ingredient in the enhancement of many miles of trout streams. Anglers should never fail to connect that slight surcharge and the picturesque stamp on the back of their license with a program that in its first two decades spent over $11 million improving more than 530 miles of trout stream on almost 400 different waters.

There is a long history in Wisconsin of hatchery-supported sport fishing. Put-and-grow stocking and planting of catchable trout in waters lacking sus-tainable naturally reproducing populations has been a mainstay of fish man-agement, with a dozen trout-salmon-steelhead hatcheries around the state. Great Lakes salmonid fisheries simply couldn't be sustained without regular-ized stocking. In 1995 alone, nearly $2 million was spent to stock inland and Great Lakes trout fisheries, with more than $1.3 million earmarked for the Great Lakes. But in recent years, the efficacy of hatcheries and stocking programs has been challenged by wild trout advocates, like Wisconsin-trained fisheries expert Ray White. White argues that hatchery-bred trout are genetically inferior and poorly adapted to natural environments, and that they compete with wild fish for available habitat and live shorter lives. White has led a frontal assault on hatcheries. He certainly makes a good point when he argues that fish factories manufacturing trout undermine the necessity of protecting wild trout stocks and ecosystems.

In spite of the heated current debates over wild vs. planted trout, we suspect that many casual anglers care little about the difference. But progressive fishery biologists and committed trout fishers are increasingly coming down on the side of wild fish. Stocking is seen as a supplement to enhance sport-fishing opportunities in marginal waters, and not a panacea for trout stream management.

There are about 5,000 miles of prime trout stream water in Wisconsin—waters that have sustainable, naturally reproducing trout populations. For several years, some fish managers have been experimenting with transferring wild trout from their home waters to other, similar streams in their area. Fish managers in western and southwestern Wisconsin have succeeded in establishing self-sustaining populations of wild trout in such streams as the Big Green River partly through this transfer method. Innovative fish managers like La Crosse-based Dave Vetrano transferred fish from productive streams like Timber Coulee to other area streams. This infuses wild stock into streams that need it and lowers fish numbers in Timber Coulee, improving growth rates in that spring creek. Cold-water fisheries programs are now moving rapidly in the direction of wild trout management.

Lee Kernen, retired director of fisheries for the WDNR, says "our trout stocking program is beginning to go wild . . . after years of evaluation, we have seen better survival of trout from 'wild' [naturally reproduced] parents over 'domestic' [hatchery] parents." An increasing percentage of the total number of trout stocked in the state will be wild fish derived from Timber Coulee Creek trout eggs and milt. Paradoxically, hatcheries—such as the Nevin Fish Hatchery south of Madison—are playing a key role, growing fingerlings for stocking from wild trout roe. Ultimately, state budgetary factors, more than fishery science and ecology, may accelerate the shift from hatchery to wild trout populations in our streams. Former WNDR inland trout specialist Larry Claggett observed that "stocking of inland trout is an expensive operation and revenues from license and stamp sales have not kept pace with increases in the cost of running hatchery programs." Whatever the forces causing it, we welcome the increased emphasis on wild trout. The real message in all this is that if we're not to depend on "cookie-cutter trout" from hatcheries, we need to rededicate ourselves to the protection of streams and watersheds where wild trout thrive.

Few things trigger debate among trout anglers as much as the subject of fishing regulations. Across the nation, bag limits are being reduced, to zero on some waters. Just as we are recognizing the limitations of supply-side stocking solutions to better fishing, we are also recognizing the need for demand-side management—limitations on harvest and angling methods. With growing numbers of anglers and increased pressure on trout streams, such progressive regulations are essential.

Having a high-quality recreational experience is beginning to take precedence over harvesting a commodity called trout, at least for many anglers. We aren't opposed to taking a few trout for the pan from waters that can safely yield those delicious meals. We simply recognize that there must be limits to the harvest of wild trout—through reduced bag limits, slot sizes, and the like—and that catch-and-release fishing in many waters is necessary to preserve self-sustaining populations of trout. This is not a new line of reasoning. In 1496 Dame Juliana Berners in *A treatyse of fysshynge wyth an angle* warned her readers "not to be too greedy in catching your said game, as in taking too much at one time . . . that could easily be the occasion of destroying your own sport and other men's also."

Regulatory change in Wisconsin parallels national trends. One of the state's first "fish for fun" (no-harvest) regulations was applied to southwestern Wisconsin's Castle Rock Creek, and the response from anglers has been wildly enthusiastic. The Peshtigo and Wolf rivers had the first fly-fishing-only regulations in the state, helping to promote fishing methods that make it easier to catch and release trout without killing them. Early season regulations call for catch and release with artificial lures only. With supporting research by WDNR fishery professionals, regulations have been put in place to reduce limits, establish higher minimum sizes or slot limits, and require artificial-lures-only angling.

In 1990, a dramatic overhaul of Wisconsin trout-fishing regulations took place. A category-based system was installed based on stream type and biology, potential of the fishery, and a desire to provide a diversity of angling experiences. That system, which established five classes of streams, has been fine-tuned over time, especially with regard to expansion of Category 5 Special Regulation waters. Agency fish managers and anglers alike are generally pleased with the changes, although we have occasionally heard disgruntled anglers complain about the complexity of the regulations, and have even heard a WDNR warden disparagingly describe the *Trout Fishing Regulations and Guide* as "that trout coloring-book." We have little sympathy with those viewpoints. Fitting varying human desires to the diverse character of a natural resource is a complex undertaking. Our trout-fishing regulations, and the valuable publication and maps that describe the regulations, are the envy of many states. While we're sympathetic to the notion that rules should be as simple as possible, simple regulations work only in simple situations. Reconciling stream ecology, trout biology, and angler demands on the resource doesn't fit well with simplicity.

Throughout this book we frequently mention state fish managers, research biologists, and others who have committed their professional lives to improving trout fisheries and fishery management in the state. They have been an innovative and hard-working collection of people, and we have drawn upon their knowledge extensively while writing this book. Without these committed public servants, we wouldn't have the splendid Wisconsin trout fisheries we sometimes take for granted.

3

Getting Started

IN THE PAST, about the only way to enter the trout-fishing world was through private lessons from your grandfather, dad, or other mentor. Nowadays, beginners have many choices. In fact, there has never been a time in the history of trout angling when more help and information existed for the angler, especially the beginner. Fishing schools, YouTube videos, books, audio files, Internet sites, and a growing network of fishing and conservation organizations offer the interested angler an incredible variety of advice and assistance. Hundreds of books related to trout fishing have appeared in just the past few years.

But sometimes it seems as though there's too much information. The novice angler perusing any of the myriad fishing magazines, guidebooks, or newsletters would rightly be intimidated by the complexity, degree of specialization, arcane vocabulary, and generally cryptic subject matter. Witness these headings from various tables of contents we've seen: "Shooting Taper Systems," "Nymphing the Film," "Coping with Caddis." Entire books are devoted to what appears to be the narrowest of subjects: a single group of insects (*Caddisflies*), a particular stage of insect life (*Emergers*), tiny flies (*Micropatterns, Fishing the Midge*), a particular style of fly (*The Soft-Hackled Fly*), trout behaviour (*What the Trout Said, The Ways of Trout*), tying specific types of flies or building specialized tackle (*Tying and Fishing Terrestrials, The Master Fly Weaver, Building a Bamboo Fly Rod*), and innumerable entomological treatises and uncountable numbers of books devoted to specific geographies or salmonid species. Yet these are all part of the literature, learning tools, and culture of the committed angler. To the beginner, however, this wealth of information must make the prospects of ever becoming a competent trout angler seem hopeless.

So our job, as we see it, is to make things a little simpler. It wouldn't make sense to try to summarize all these resources. Instead, we want to outline a few basic techniques and tactics for fishing in Wisconsin, so that the novice can

A successful Dr. Mark Ratner with a soon-to-be-released brown trout. Photo by Steve Born.

make contact with some trout and take the first steps in the lifelong learning that characterizes trout fishing. More advanced concepts and techniques are addressed in a later chapter describing Wisconsin's "Don't Miss" fishing opportunities. But let the first lesson be this: no fishing educational resource is more important than spending time on the water.

One final suggestion: after learning some basic casting skills, you might consider hiring a guide. A good guide can help you gain a wealth of knowledge in a single day—from casting to streamcraft.

GETTING THERE

With 13,000 miles of trout streams in the state, every place in Wisconsin is within an hour's drive or so of a trout-fishing locale. The single most essential guide to our trout waters is *Wisconsin Trout Fishing Regulations and Guide*, available *free* from the Wisconsin Department of Natural Resources. Don't forget to pick one up when you buy your license and trout stamp. The first-rate set of maps included in this brochure identify the trout streams, set out the regulations, and give you some idea about the type of angling experiences available.

This booklet should be accompanied by either the *Wisconsin Atlas and Gazetteer* or the set of four regional maps produced by Milwaukee Map Service. Both of these map sets are widely available in tackle stores, fly shops, and many good bookstores. They are invaluable for locating town and minor roads not found on other maps, and they provide the detailed geographic information lacking in the WDNR trout guide. Some anglers may wish to procure U.S. Geological Survey topographic maps for areas they fish (these can be purchased from the Wisconsin Geological and Natural History Survey, 3817 Mineral Point Rd., Madison, WI 53705). Maps also have been prepared by area tourism groups and businesses for some regions and rivers in the state, and these can provide added details about access points, lodging, canoe rentals, restaurants, and other recreational activities. And don't be shy about asking local sporting goods dealers and fly shops for advice on where to go; most are willing and able to help you. Finally, the state Department of Tourism (1-800-432-TRIP) distributes a wide range of informative materials, such as a directory of historic inns and bed and breakfast establishments, that will allow you to tailor a fishing trip for yourself as well as guarantee a wonderful Wisconsin vacation for nonfishing companions and family members.

Anglers who have encountered problems gaining access to rivers and streams in many other states will find Wisconsin's stream access laws almost too good to be true. Wisconsin adheres to one of the strongest Public Trust doctrines in the nation. The doctrine means that the waters of the state are held in trust for the public. Navigability determines whether a waterway is public or private, and the courts have consistently applied a very liberal test of what is meant by navigability. In short, if a watercourse can float a recreational canoe at some time of the year it is deemed navigable, and thus accessible to the public. So if you can enter a stream at a bridge crossing or other public access point, you can fish or boat your way up or downstream as long as you stay in the stream—that is, keep your feet wet. You can't, however, walk across private lands to get to a stream without permission of the landowner. A good rule of thumb is, when in doubt—*ask*. Violating Wisconsin's trespass laws can lead to a hefty fine, and our laws have been revised recently to relieve landowners from the task of posting their land. Still, Wisconsin anglers enjoy extensive access to the state's waters via public lands, easements, and access points. To keep this privilege, be responsible and respect landowners' property rights. In our neck of the woods, most farmers and other landowners, if asked politely, will

A young angler (helped a little by guide Jim Bartelt) shows off his catch. Photo courtesy of Jim Bartelt.

Steve Born with a fine Driftless Area brown trout that ate a leech imitation. Photo by Mike Grimes.

give anglers permission to cross their property. If you are granted such privileges, be sure to close gates behind you, and treat the land as if it were your own. And it's always a good idea to let the landowners know that you appreciate the opportunity to fish on or through their property; the next angler to seek permission will be thankful for your good manners afield.

TACKLE SELECTION

Technological advances over the past few decades have changed the face of trout angling and given the fisher an amazing array of choices in rods, lines, reels, leader materials, waders, and clothing. There is so much to choose from that selecting equipment can become a bewildering exercise. Moreover, the selection of one's fishing gear is highly personal, and there is no single answer to questions about the "best outfit" for trout fishing. Experienced anglers invariably wind up with an ever-growing collection of rods, reels, and related equipment, much of it specialized for particular angling situations.

For Wisconsin, we recommend 4- to 6-weight rods ranging from 8 to 9 feet in length. The lighter-weight rods will serve the spring creek and small-stream fisher well; heavier rods with more firepower are generally necessary on larger waters, or for casting bigger flies. Shorter rods can be effective fishing tools in hemmed-in or brushy locations, while longer rods allow better line handling and fight fish more efficiently. We often use 2- and 3-weight rods in delicate fishing situations, but the beginning angler should start with an all-around, medium-fast-action graphite trout rod. Between $100 and $200 will buy a rod that will serve you well for years, and some excellent brands, such as St. Croix rods, are manufactured right here in Wisconsin. An acceptable single-action reel costs about $30, although you will also find finely machined fly reels for hundreds of dollars, if you're so inclined. Either a double-taper or weight-forward floating line will meet most of Wisconsin fishing demands. Bright-colored fly lines help the beginning angler see and correct casting errors and aid line control on the water, but your next line should be a natural, dull color so as not to scare wary trout.

While experienced trout-angling friends can help, as can tackle dealers, the best way to get a balanced outfit is to buy one of the packaged combinations offered by manufacturers like Sage, Loomis, Cortland, and Scientific Anglers. These packages are also available through major mail-order distributors such as Orvis, L.L. Bean, Cabela's, and others. Typically they will include line, backing, and leaders, along with a good-quality rod, a reel, and rod case—often at a significant financial saving from the cost of buying them separately. You can purchase everything you need to get started for about $400, which compares well to the start-up costs of golf or downhill skiing. Of course, the neophyte angler might do well to borrow equipment initially, or get used equipment at local fishing club swap nights. We know some terrific anglers who started with borrowed equipment, K-Mart waders, and tennis shoes.

For the spin-fisher, a 5–5 ½ foot ultralight graphite rod with a matching ultralight reel will fill the bill. Load the reel up with 4–6 pound test monofilament and you'll be ready to go.

Of course, there's a variety of other equipment you will want or need. We always use polarized sunglasses, a vest, rain jacket, waders, a net, flyboxes, tippet material, snippers, forceps, fly floatant, microshot, insect repellent, sunscreen, and a small flashlight. You may want to add other items, such as a stream thermometer, fish stomach pump, compass, insect-collecting net, and functional adornments, like hats and neckerchiefs. A look at any sales catalog featuring trout-fishing equipment will convince you that the list is endless!

Equipment

There's an amazing array of equipment available to the fly-fisher. Here's a sample "starter package" that should be more than adequate for the beginner.

- Resident fishing license, trout stamp and Great Lakes salmon stamp
- Rod, reel, backing, and line package available through many catalogs (we recommend 4–6 weight rod measuring about 8 feet)
- Tapered leader and tippet materials
- Olive- or tan-colored vest to carry flyboxes and other gear
- Two flyboxes (to organize flies)
- Metal forceps (to remove hooks from fish and to apply split shot)
- Nail clippers (to snip line and leader)
- Net (to land fish)
- Split shot assortment (to get nymphs and wet flies into strike zone)
- Fly floatant (to keep dry flies afloat)
- An assortment of 50 flies
- Polarized sunglasses (to help you see trout before they see you)
- Maps
- Hat
- Insecticide and sunscreen
- Flashlight
- Compass

WHERE ARE THE TROUT?

The ability to "read" the water is one of the most valuable skills a trout angler can possess. Learning to read a stream will allow you to anticipate likely areas where fish will be, even on your first visit to a new stream. Reading the water will also suggest the best way to approach the fish, where to wade—and where not to. Like most other topics related to trout fishing, reading the water is the subject of informative books (see Tom Rosenbauer's *Reading Trout Streams*) and splendid videos (like Rick Hafele's *Anatomy of a Trout Stream*). Here we simply want to introduce you to enough of a stream's character so that you can begin your fishing in the places where trout are likely to be.

Above all else, trout require cold water. Thus they inhabit the upper reaches of river systems where water temperatures rarely exceed 75 degrees or so. Wisconsin is blessed with an abundance of these ecologically critical and sensitive headwaters. During the "dog days" of summer, trout move from warming waters and can be found concentrated around springs and cooler inflowing tributaries (which is why a thermometer can be a handy tool for the angler). Brook trout are the least tolerant of warmer water, and brown trout are the most tolerant. So our native brookies tend to be in headwaters, while the imported browns often inhabit the lower reaches of streams. Additionally, trout require unpolluted, well-aerated, oxygen-rich water (a minimum of 5 parts per million of oxygen is the accepted lower limit).

A pool-riffle section of a stream

Trout also need shelter from the currents, and protection from overhead and in-stream predators. The fish find cover by lying near logjams, deadfalls, and other obstructions; under overhanging vegetation, undercut banks, and ledges; behind boulders and rocks, and in deep pools and runs. Of course, the fish must have ready access to food. A prime lie, where a fish can safely hold *and* feed, exists where both these requirements are met. Learning to recognize and fish prime lies correctly is the mark of a first-rate angler. The old maxim that 10 percent of the water holds 90 percent of the fish underscores the need for successful anglers to concentrate their efforts in these places; you must be willing to risk losing flies and lures to fish the spots where trout live. One added requirement for sustaining naturally reproducing trout: suitable spawning habitat. In short, an amazing combination of factors are required to make a trout stream. Gary Borger estimates that trout waters make up less than one millionth of a percent of the earth's water flowing in streams at any one moment, a statistic that highlights the special circumstances, scarcity, and fragility of the trout's environment.

Rick Hafele divides trout streams into four different water types—riffles, runs, pools, and flats. These types are typically repeated with some regularity over the length of the stream. Riffles are shallow (usually less than a few feet) high-gradient parts of streams with gravel, cobble, and pebble stream bottoms. The rough substrate causes the surface to be choppy. Riffles are the most biologically productive parts of streams—veritable insect factories—so any obstruction or seam in a riffle is a potential prime lie.

Runs are slower, less energetic, and deeper than riffles. Their surfaces are smoother, with flow irregularities, such as an upwelling, reflecting deeper structure. The heads of runs, where riffles enter and furnish a continuous menu of drowned insects, and the seams along the edges of runs, deserve the fisher's careful attention: trout can hold and feed in the slower waters while watching their next meal move by in the faster currents.

Pools are the deepest and slowest-moving parts of a stream. They provide habitat for crayfish, leeches, and baitfish, all of great interest to bigger trout. The head of a pool, where faster water enters and forms a tongue of agitated water protruding into the calm of the pool, represents a conveyor belt of trout food. The current is slower on either side of the tongue, giving rise to seams often identified by concentrated trails of bubbles and debris. In some stream configurations, the slower waters will form a back-eddy or whirlpool, where currents next to the bank are running the wrong way—upstream. A smorgasbord of fish food can be concentrated along these seams and in back-eddies, and the angler should focus on such areas.

Flats, the fourth stream category, are broad stretches where velocity decreases and the stream spreads out. These areas offer little protection from kingfishers, herons, and other predators, and trout feeding in such places are extremely wary. We might add another category, rapids, to Hafele's classification. Rapids are fast-flowing whitewaters loved by kayakers and rafters. The stream bed can be strewn with larger boulders and rocks, which provide some holding water for trout. Wading in rapids can be quite a challenge, however, and is often dangerous.

Whatever the type of stream reach, you should fish carefully when you spot current seams, where waters moving at different speeds come together; obstructions and other cover which may provide prime lies; and undercut banks. Meander pools, with undercut outside bends, are "A-number-one" trout habitat, don't ever pass them up, for they often hold large trout. In Wisconsin, the Department of Natural Resources has done extensive habitat improvement work to deepen streams, provide bank cover, and increase in-stream holding areas. The manmade structures that WDNR has put in place are an attempt to emulate nature, and after a few years the artificial habitat will be discernible only by observant anglers. Fish population surveys show that fish gravitate to these habitat improvements, often with huge increases in numbers. Artificial undercut banks and other manmade habitat improvements should get at least the same level of fishing attention as nature's work. Given our bounty of meandering meadow streams and spring creeks, anglers should also be alert for fish holding in midstream weedbeds and channels cutting through vegetation, especially during the luxuriant growth periods of summer.

Of course, streams change during the course of the year, and the fish adjust accordingly. Spring creeks, fed by an influx of 50–55 degree groundwater, have relatively constant temperatures and flows, and are generally less affected by early season runoff and summer rainstorms than streams strongly reliant on surface water inflows. The latter tend to be "flashy," flooding after rains, and suffering from low levels and flows during times of drought. The most pronounced changes in alkaline-rich spring creeks may be associated with peak periods of underwater plant growth, which creates new structure and holding lies for trout. When streams are running high and off-color, the trout relocate to backwaters, undercut banks, and other areas where they can escape the pounding of the current and still have access to food. As the season progresses, the wild rapids of early spring become summer's sparkling riffles, often alive with insect hatches and feeding trout. Successful anglers must continuously adjust to changing water conditions and flows, rethinking where and how they fish.

Trout Foods

In fertile spring creeks, microscopic plants called phytoplankton and other vegetation are produced within the stream. Freestone streams, where flows are determined by surface water runoff, depend more on leaves, streamside plants, and other vegetation that falls or is washed into the stream. The animals that feed on phytoplankton and detritus range from microscopic invertebrates to small crustaceans, like crayfish. These in turn can be important foods for trout and forage fish. The lure of fly-fishing for trout is associated with the thrill of figuring out what the fish are eating—or are likely to be eating—and fooling them with an imitation.

Common aquatic insects in Wisconsin streams include mayflies, caddisflies, stoneflies, dragonflies, damselflies, and midges. They live their early lives amid rocks and vegetation and are eaten in their immature nymphal, larval, and pupal stages. With polarized glasses the angler can often see trout "flash-

Trout rising to a mayfly hatch

ing" and opening their mouths as they forage on these underwater insects. Later in their life cycles, these bugs swim or crawl to the surface and emerge as adult winged insects. Trout feed heavily on these emergers, and the angler who can match the hatch may experience memorable fishing. Surface feeding is also prevalent when the winged insects mate and return to the stream to lay their eggs and die—the fabled mayfly "spinner falls" being one example. The diet of trout is not restricted to aquatic insects. Land-borne insects—called terrestrials—are an important trout food. Ants, beetles, crickets, and grasshoppers fall or get blown into the stream. After many of the larger aquatic insects have hatched, these terrestrials form a substantial part of the trout menu. Trout lie in sheltered places, looking up for these aliens, often taking them from the water's surface with a savage rise. Is it any wonder that many anglers look ahead to summer "hopportunities"?

Crustaceans—scuds, cressbugs (often called sowbugs), and crayfish—along with leeches and worms are also staples in a trout's diet. Large trout prefer bigger meals and feed aggressively on these larger food forms, as well as on forage fish, like chubs and dace, and on smaller trout. Mice, frogs, and other visitors are welcome additions to the diet of large predatory trout. A trout's feeding decisions are a balancing act between energy consumed and energy expended in the task of finding food. While a large food item may seem the obvious choice to us, efficiency-minded trout may feed on an abundant stage of an emerging mayfly or caddisfly, meeting their caloric needs with the least expenditure of energy. This behavior, the ultimate challenge to the fly-fisher, is called selectivity For a guide to deciding what fly to use, review Chapter Four and its insect chart.

Presentation—Thinking like a Predator

Trout are extremely skittish creatures, and as the fishing season unfolds they get even more wary. If they sense or see anything unusual or out of the ordinary in the window through which they view the world, they disappear for cover instantly. Those who don't are soon removed from the population, either by wild predators or humans. Many books go into great detail about this aspect of fishing. Here, we'll emphasize the importance of exercising care so you don't undermine the potential for success before you've even begun to fish. Wear dull-colored clothing that blends with streamside vegetation or the sky. Don't just go wading into the stream; stay back from the stream bank and move with stealth. Stay low, using streamside brush and other vegetation to conceal your presence. Crawl on your belly if you must, but do everything you can think of to stay out of the fish's view. When you do wade, don't charge noisily upstream. Stay low and move slowly, taking care not to move ripples or waves into pools and runs, announcing your arrival to all the trout in the area. The most successful trout fishers are always vigilant, stealthy, and predatory in their thinking and action, knowing that their quarry will tolerate nothing less.

Selected Techniques and Tactics—A Beginning Menu of Strategies

We're making the assumption that you have learned the rudiments of assembling your fly-fishing outfit, casting, line handling and mending, essential knots, and the like. Introductory books and videos—which can be borrowed from club or community libraries, rented from dealers, or purchased—provide excellent instruction on these basic skills. And chapters of Trout Unlimited, Federation of Fly Fishers clubs, schools, sporting goods dealers, and fly shops offer clinics and seminars to introduce beginners to the basics. Take advantage of these learning opportunities. We'll trust you have acquired the skills to make a 15–40-foot cast with reasonable accuracy, a distance you'll rarely have to exceed on our rivers and streams. As in any other sport, acquiring proficiency means practicing, and we'll assume you've done your homework so that time on the stream is spent learning to fish, not learning to cast. In fact, trying to learn to cast and to fish at the same time can be counterproductive.

As we've noted repeatedly, there are volumes written on every aspect of trout fishing, and the subject of tactics and strategies is no exception. As you grow into the sport, you will probably want to read Joe Humphreys' *Trout Tactics,* Gary Borger's *Presentation,* and later in your learning cycle, Swisher and Richards' sophisticated opus, *Fly Fishing Strategies.* Here, in very abbreviated form and without all the theoretical underpinnings, we want to give you a selection of tactics and strategies to take to the stream with you now. While nothing in trout fishing is guaranteed, the angler who employs these tactics in Wisconsin streams will soon be connecting with the often-elusive brook, brown, and rainbow trout of the Badger State.

Technique #1—Upstream, Dead-Drift Nymphing

Although trout anglers will talk ad nauseam about great hatches and dry fly fishing they've experienced, the bulk of a trout's feeding is done underwater. It is no surprise, therefore, that nymph fishing is such a deadly technique. There are diverse nymphing techniques (see Gary Borger's *Nymphing* for a first-rate education). But we're going to focus on only one—the highly effective upstream dead-drift approach.

The general approach is to cast upstream or quartering upstream to either fish you have spotted or promising-looking water. The angler casts upstream of the target, stopping the cast abruptly, causing the fly to tuck back and sink naturally in the stream. The critical factor in success is rigging appropriately for the circumstances, and casting far enough ahead of the target area so that your nymph is rolling along just above the bottom when it enters the fish's zone. How far above your target should you cast? That depends upon the water depth, the speed of the current, and the weight of your fly. It will take some experimentation on your part, but the point is to cast several feet above where you know or expect trout to be, and allow the fly to sink so that it drifts past the fish's nose, or at least near it. As the nymph drifts down towards you, raise your rod and strip in line so as to stay in gentle contact with your lure. Try to minimize drag and movement on the fly; it should be tumbling along in a dead-drift near the bottom, like the natural. Lower your rod as the fly passes downstream, trying to prolong the drift for as long as possible. At the end of the drift, hold your rod pointing downstream until your line straightens out, and then gently cast or pitch your fly back upstream as you continue to explore prospective water. Carefully fish the heads of pools, cut banks, current seams, and areas around obstructions. It will often take several drifts before things look just right to the trout. In warmer months, trout will move into shallow lies and riffles and the angler should carefully and methodically prospect the entire riffle, as the trout may be anywhere.

Rigging for this technique involves our general-purpose fly rod, and floating line attached to a sufficiently long leader tapered to 4X or 5X. We like longer leaders, at least 9 feet or so, because they aid significantly in getting flies quickly to the bottom. A weighted fly, with supplemental split shot clamped on a foot or so up the leader from the fly, will get the nymph in the trout's feeding zone. Anglers should be prepared to keep adjusting the weight by adding and subtracting split shot so that the fly stays in the strike zone but doesn't snag continuously on the stream bottom. Believe us when we say that all the fooling around with rigging is worth the effort. The most proficient caster won't catch fish if the lure isn't in the fish's feeding zone.

Because all the action is underwater and a trout's take of a nymph is amazingly subtle, the addition of a strike indicator helps focus the angler's attention and adds a strong visual dimension to this kind of fishing. The indicator can be many things: a simple piece of poly yarn tied in an overhand knot, tightened, trimmed with a scissors, and greased with floatant; a hollowed-out piece of fluorescent fly line threaded on the leader; or any of a number of commercially available strike indicators, ranging from press-on or roll-on foam to small buoyant Styrofoam or wood "bobbers." The angler should use the smallest visible indicator for the task at hand, because fish can be scared by them. The indicator should be attached to the leader 4 or 5 feet above the fly; a good rule of thumb is to attach the indicator above the fly one and a half times the depth of the water you're fishing.

We've had great success dead-drift nymphing a two-fly rig, and strongly encourage you to try this modification. The use of two flies can be a big advantage, sinking your imitations more quickly and allowing you to offer a varied menu to the trout. Casting the rig is not much of a problem, provided that there is not too much weight on the leader and your cast is gentle, with an open

loop. There are many ways to rig two flies. We prefer an "in-line" arrangement, in which a foot or so of tippet material is tied onto the hook bend of
the upper fly using a clinch knot. The trailing nymph is then clinch-knotted
or loop-knotted to the end of this short tippet. While this rig also makes it

Two-nymph tandem rig

possible to snag and lose two flies at a time, we believe it greatly increases the
chance of success. The risk of snagging the entire rig can be minimized by
leaving a tag end of tippet extending from either fly, and pinching split shot
directly on the tag end. We use a larger (#10–14) weighted upper fly (Scud,
Hare's Ear, Stone-fly Nymph, Caddis Larva, the new beadheads, Zug Bugs,
Prince Nymphs, or small Woolly Buggers), trailed by a smaller (#16–20)
nymph (Pheasant Tail, Serendipity, or Brassie, for example). There are an
infinite number of variations on this technique, so feel free to experiment. If
you take the time to learn it well, catching trout is in your future.

Technique #2—The Down-and-Across Wet Fly

The down-and-across wet fly method is a traditional technique that has
fallen into neglect in recent years, but it can be an enormously effective method
during a hatch, when the fish are feeding just under the surface. It also can be a
great way to search the water. The cast is made across stream, or slightly down
and across, and the fly is allowed to swing through the potential holding water.
You should cover the water methodically, first fishing the water near you, then
extending the cast to cover more distant areas. After you have thoroughly fished
the area, move quietly downstream a few steps and repeat the sequence. If your
line starts dragging the fly and moving it faster than the current, lift the belly of
your line gently off the water and flip, or mend, it upstream. Follow the drift of
the fly with your rod and be prepared for a strike at the end of the drift, when
the line straightens and the imitation rises in the water column, mimicking an

emerging insect. Hold your line in the water at the end of the drift, actively
retrieving your fly a few inches at a time; this will sometimes trigger a strike
from a trout that has been following it across stream. Remember to carefully
probe every possible lie, keeping your imitation in the water and working.

For a general pattern, a small
(#14–20) Soft Hackle is hard to
beat. A Hare's Ear or olive-bodied
Soft Hackle can resemble a lot
of different food sources. Flies
can be slightly weighted or unweighted and fished just below
the surface. This method can be
especially deadly fished through
riffles when trout are chasing
emerging caddis or mayflies. For
more information on this tech-
nique, find a copy of Sylvester Nemes' classic book, *The Soft-Hackled Fly
Addict.* We should note that the same approach can be used to fish streamers
like a Muddler Minnow or Woolly Bugger. Fished down and across through
the tails of pools during summer's early mornings, a #6–10 streamer always
offers the prospect of your fly being consumed by an actively feeding lunker
venturing out for an early breakfast.

Soft-hackled wet fly

Technique #3—Fishing the Attractor Dry Fly

Hatches—those magic events when insects, fish, and the angler meet—
may be what most fly-fishers live for, but most of a long fishing day will be spent
astream between hatches, with sporadic surface feeding at best. While underwater methods are good options at these times, dry fly fishing is still an alter-
native. In fact, many anglers will opt to fish the dry fly out of pure enjoyment
for the method, even if it means catching fewer fish. The classic up-and-across
dry fly presentation to prime lies can produce good fishing. In some situations,
down-and-across slack-line presentations are called for. Our all-around rod,
floating line, and 9–12-foot leader tapered to 4–5X (and occasionally finer) is
the right equipment. The challenge is to learn to make effective dry fly presentations through casting techniques (serpentine or wiggle casts, parachute casts,
puddle casts, reach casts) and effective handling once the line is on the water.
The goal is to present a drag-free imitation over potential trout lies in spite of
the complex currents grabbing the line. Don't forget to act like a predator and
keep a low, inconspicuous profile. Watch your shadow—to the trout, your
shadow on the water might as well be the arrival of King Kong. Read the water

and plan your casting strategy. Fish efficiently, but keep moving and cover the water. As some old-timers say, "When the fishing's slow, move fast."

There are a wide variety of dry fly attractor patterns—flies which give the impression of being edible and alive, but that are not designed to imitate specific insects. We'd recommend a #14 or #16 Adams, Pass Lake, Royal

Adams

Coachman Trude, and Elk Hair Caddis as your basic arsenal for this kind of fishing. During the summer, a #16 Beetle or Ant and #10–12 Grasshoppers are good bets to fool trout awaiting misguided terrestrial insects. Dress your fly with a good floatant, and keep it on the water. Too many beginners spend far too much time false casting, their line waving in the air out of reach of

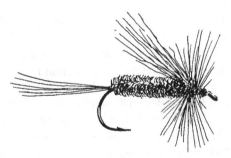

Pass Lake

hungry trout. Tippet size and length may need to be adjusted, depending on the air resistance of the fly; you want your leader to fall on the water in serpentine coils that improve the chances for drag-free drifts.

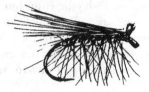

Elk Hair Caddis

If you happen upon a hatch, capture a natural and try to match the size, shape, and color from something in your flybox. You don't have to know the Latin name to do that. Watch the rises of the trout to make sure they're taking insects from the surface, and not from just under or in the surface film. If you see the trout's mouth open, a drifting fly disappear, and a bubble appear on the surface in its place, a dry fly is the ticket. Matching the hatch can be a complex game, with fish apparently feeding on the surface but actually tak-

ing emerging nymphs, partly hatched adults, crippled insects, and stillborns. Experienced fishers will study the rise forms and draw upon a variety of fly patterns to cope with these difficult fishing situations.

Technique #4—An Introduction to the Griffith's Gnat and Fishing Small Flies

For some anglers, the champagne of fly-fishing is deceiving trout with tiny dry flies. Sooner or later you'll encounter trout feeding across an entire flat or pool or in a large back-eddy, their subtle dimpling rises looking almost like raindrops. These fish are delicately sipping minute flies called midges by fishers and Chironomids by entomologists. These ultra-tiny flies, ranging in size from #20–22 to nearly invisible no-see-ums, intimidate many anglers even as they intoxicate others. Again, entire books have been devoted to this genre of fishing (like Ed Koch's *Fishing the Midge* or Darrel Martin's *Micropatterns*), and you will have lots of time to decide if midge fishing is your cup of tea. Here we just want to introduce you briefly to fishing one pattern, the Griffith's Gnat, as a way of exposing you to this kind of angling. There are times when this method and this fly will catch the most and the largest trout—times when most of the rest of your fly inventory will prove futile.

The Griffith's Gnat is nothing more than a wisp of peacock herl wrapped around the hook and overwrapped with a grizzly hackle. Named after one of the Michigan founding fathers of Trout Unlimited, George Griffith, the fly simulates individual midges as well as mating clusters or clumps of midges—a common phenomenon with these tiny insects. The fly has good general appeal, and should be tried whenever trout appear to be feeding on tiny bugs on the water's surface or in the surface film. Fished in sizes #16–22, it is both visible and effective. The key to fishing such tiny flies is using a long, limp, fine tippet. Three or four feet of 6X tippet material tied onto a 9–12-foot leader tapered to 4X will allow you to delicately present this little dry fly, with curves and coils in the leader aiding a drag-free presentation. Because the fly may be hard to see, strike at any hint of a rise in the general vicinity of your fly. Set the hook gently so as not to break the fine tippet. Simply raise your rod until you begin to feel the fish, which will hook itself with its initial move. If the fish are picky and refuse the Gnat, try trimming the hackle off the bottom of the fly so it sits farther down in the film. Or let it swing underwater at the end of the drift—a trick that often saves the day for us. Midge hatches can last for hours, and they occur throughout the season, even in winter. Don't head out to the stream without a few Griffith's Gnats in your flybox.

A MINIMALIST FLY ASSORTMENT

How many different flies do you really need to carry to be consistently successful fishing Wisconsin trout streams? Since there are hundreds of mayfly, caddisfly, stonefly, and other insect species in Wisconsin, and numerous imitations possible for each, how does the angler avoid carrying hundreds of different flies afield?

Actually, some fly-fishers do, although we've never seen a fly-fishing article on the "essential one thousand"! As you gain experience, you'll probably discover that you want more than a single dry fly to use during a Sulphur mayfly hatch. You may want several different patterns of dry flies—a traditional or Catskill-style imitation; a parachute type; a No-Hackle; a dun with a trailing shuck to suggest an emerger; and so on. Moreover, the same pattern can be tied (fly-tiers would say dressed) sparsely or more heavily, that is, thinner or fatter. Colors can be modified in many subtle ways. In addition, the thinking angler may want his pattern choice in several hook sizes. For example, the classic Adams—almost everybody's favorite generalist dry fly—might be carried in sizes #12–20.

Have we confused you yet? Don't worry, we've sometimes been confused, too. To help lessen the confusion, we're going to suggest a short list of flies that have proven effective on Wisconsin waters. They're generic and impressionistic patterns that often don't closely match the insect or fish they're intended to resemble, but trout take them. When you begin fishing specific insect hatches, check with local fly shops or knowledgeable fishers from the local Trout Unlimited chapter or Federation of Fly Fishers club; there are always patterns proven effective by resident experts, and most anglers are willing to offer suggestions to help you improve your fishing skills and success.

Fly selection is a daunting task. A look into a friend's flybox is a look into his angling soul, his fish-catching secrets, his strategies and philosophies—and you thought it was just a flybox! With all these qualifications, let us recommend a basic set of flies that will catch trout in Wisconsin. They work for us, and they'll work for you.

Dry Flies

Our dry fly selection begins with the Adams (#12–20), an all-purpose mayfly imitation. To deal with light-colored mayfly hatches, add some Light Cahills (#14–18). If you're feeling adventuresome, get a few Adams tied parachute-style, and a few Cahills tied Comparadun-style, without hackles. Attractor patterns we would not be without include the Pass Lake (#14–16), Royal Coachman Trude (#16), and a Brown and White Bivisible (#10–14). Our choice of a caddisfly imitator is the venerable Elk Hair Caddis (#14–18) in both olive and tan colors; and as noted above, don't be without a few Griffith's Gnats (#18–22).

If you'll be fishing southern Wisconsin in the summer, carry some Grasshoppers (#10–16). Any of the standard patterns will work, although we'd be sure to have some in green, yellow, and brown. During the course of the season, the dominant hoppers along Wisconsin streams shift from greenish to brownish. Incidentally, don't worry if your Hopper gets soaked and sinks; trout love drowned hoppers, and some old-timers have made this a mainstay of their summer fishing. We'd also make sure to have a few Crickets (#16), Beetles (#16), and Ants (#16–18) to fill out our basic terrestrial inventory.

Wet Flies and Nymphs

While there are hundreds of historic wet fly patterns, our essential flybox includes only soft-hackled wet flies ("flymphs"). In sizes #12–18 and colors olive, tan, and yellow, they'll fill a variety of needs, from a general underwater searching pattern to an all-purpose emerger for those periods when fish are locked in on emerging caddis or mayflies. The all-star of nymph flies, the Hare's Ear, must be in your nymph portfolio (#10–16). The classic Pheasant

Pheasant Tail Nymph

Tail Nymph in sizes #14–18 will simulate most smaller mayfly nymphs. We wouldn't be astream without a nymph made with peacock herl, a material that ranks high in fooling trout. Choose either a Prince Nymph (#10–16), one of our favorite nymphs, or a Zug Bug. You'll need a good stonefly replica; a Montana Nymph (#6–10) is a good choice. And while we're unsure what fish envision when they see a #6–14 black, rubber-legged Girdle Bug drift by, it's a killer that works well everywhere. Scud imitations (#12–14) in pink or peach, gray, and tan are a necessity on Wisconsin spring creeks. For a caddis larva imitation, we'd choose a Peeking Caddis (#10–16). We've become huge

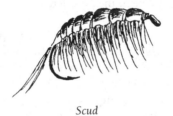

Scud

fans of Serendipities (#14–20) in olive, brown, and black, especially as the trailing nymph in a two-fly setup. Many nymph patterns are now available as beadheads, an innovation that gets the fly down in the strike zone quickly; you might want to have a few beadhead Hare's Ears or Caddis in your flybox.

Streamers

Streamers are intended to imitate baitfish. The renowned Muddler Minnow (#6–10) is our top choice, partly for its versatility. Our other streamer would be a selection of Woolly Buggers (#6–12) in olive-black, black, and white; a bit of flashy material adds to their allure. Woolly Buggers suggest a number of food items to trout, from leeches and crayfish to baitfish. There seems to be no way to fish them wrong.

That's it! Not a magic flybox, but a representative and reasonable selection of tried-and-true flies for Wisconsin. We hope it gives you a good start in building your ultimate arsenal of trout flies. One word of advice: be attentive and examine the life in the stream you're fishing. Turn over rocks, look at aquatic

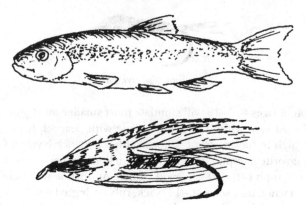

The natural minnow, and a good imitation—the Grey Ghost streamer

vegetation, and look at submerged sticks and logs. Try to match your imitations in size, color, and shape to the prevalent aquatic life in the assortment of critters you observe.

Like any encounter with Mother Nature, be prepared for some tough times. There'll be days when you arrive at your stream of choice to find it running high and off-color. Give it a go anyway, using nymphs and streamers worked deep and near protective cover. On a hot, low-water summer day, don't be afraid to seek out a spring creek and try some of the techniques covered here and in our spring creek chapter. Remember, we all learn from our failures, and every day astream should be a learning experience.

A BASIC SPIN-FISHING APPROACH

Spin-fishing is a devastating method for catching trout, and we've spent many years fishing this way. The spin angler should adhere to all the lessons of reading the water and approaching streams like a predator, staying low, and kneeling where necessary. Cast above visible fish or prime lies. Shoot low trajectory casts under overhanging cover. Retrieve your lure slightly faster than the current, keeping it moving along in lifelike fashion; or try a dead-drift retrieve, allowing your lure to move with the current. In deeper pools, allow time for your lure to sink down to the level of the fish; trout will hit a spinner fluttering downwards, probably because it looks like an injured baitfish. Try a variety of casts—upstream, across, and downstream. We've seen them all take fish. Good lures include small spinners (#00–2) like Mepps, Rooster Tails, and Panther Martins. A small black or olive jig, like those used for panfishing, worked very slowly in deep runs and pools, can fool a lunker trout. Small spoons are also effective, especially in faster water. And few lures can top the minnow-imitating qualities of Rapalas, which are among the deadliest trout lures ever created.

TOWARDS BECOMING A RESPONSIBLE TROUT ANGLER

As we've indicated, conservation and fishing clubs welcome your involvement, and usually have a variety of clinics, seminars, and other events to help you become a better fisher. Nothing, however, beats spending time on the stream with an experienced friend who can help you develop the knowledge to cope with the unending array of challenges that arise every day of trout fishing. A mentor, or a good guide, can accelerate your learning dramatically by sharing a lifetime of experience with you.

Trout fishing is a privilege, and with this marvelous privilege come some responsibilities. The ranks of trout fishers have grown rapidly, putting ever-increasing pressure on our fisheries. At the same time, development, construction, pollution, and other human activities have trashed some of our vulnerable trout streams. In spite of extensive stream rehabilitation work by the WDNR and groups like Trout Unlimited, the resource base is getting smaller, and the battle to protect what we have goes on every day. More anglers and diminishing habitat: the conclusion seems clear to us. Beyond assuming the role of environmental stewards, we can no longer harvest trout as if the populations were infinite. Reduced harvest regulations—no-harvest, "fish for fun" rules—are becoming widespread. Limiting our kill is a critical means for improving everybody's recreational fishing. It needs to be more than a regulation. It must be part of our angling credo.

We're not being preachy here. There's nothing wrong with taking an occasional brace of moderately sized trout for the pan. But instead of bringing home that trophy fish to mount on the wall, why not think of a great photo, or a fiberglass replica? Then you get the added pleasure of watching a great trout swim back into the stream depths, knowing it will help pass its good genetic stock to the next generation. You'll inevitably wind up releasing fish, either as a matter of personal ethics or to comply with fishing regulations, so spend a little time learning to do it right. According to the Trout Unlimited video and the companion brochure "CPR—Consider Proper Release," more than two million Wisconsin trout are released by anglers each year. If anglers would properly play and carefully release every trout they hook, mortality could be substantially reduced. Consider using barbless hooks so that fish can be released quickly and with a minimum of handling. TU estimates that, properly done, catch-and-release fishing could recycle more than 250,000 trout each season—fish that now die after being improperly released. The WDNR fishing regulations pamphlet also includes instructions on how to release fish safely. Out of respect for this special animal and out of our own self-interest in better fishing, isn't this your duty?

Finally, a few basic guidelines about angling ethics and etiquette are worth mentioning. Trout fishing is not a confrontational or competitive sport, and many of the rules of the game are unwritten and are learned over time. Common sense and respect for this quiet sport should shape your behavior astream. If someone else has arrived at your secret spot first, honor that and don't crowd or intrude. Don't encroach on anglers fishing upstream or downstream from you; extend them the same courtesy of a few hundred yards of fishing room that you would like extended to you. Watch where you wade, and how you travel around other anglers. Don't be afraid to ask fellow fishers whether or not your planned approach or wading might interfere with their fishing; they might even give you some tips for success.

Success is a relative concept. There are few stories written about the glories and challenges of catching 9-inch trout, but on most Wisconsin streams, the average size of the fish you'll catch is likely to be less than a foot. We hope you catch your share of trophies, but have realistic expectations. Enjoy the experience. You'll, come to love the places where trout live, and will want to help keep them clean and healthy. This is a noble sport, with an unsurpassed heritage. As author Ted Leeson (whose first trout-fishing experience was in the limestone coulees of southwestern Wisconsin) notes in his fine book *The Habit of Rivers,* "I don't think I'm stretching the matter at all to say that given half a chance, a trout stream can make you a better person." We agree! As you gain skill and understanding about the joys of trout fishing, perhaps you'll want to give something back to this sport that gives us so much. Look to the future by joining the fight to conserve cold-water resources. And take some time to introduce kids or help beginners get started in our sport—we think teaching others is part of a long-range investment in trout angling and conservation.

Safe and Comfortable Fishing

We don't consider trout fishing a hazardous sport, but it can present problems if you don't take some precautions. In Wisconsin, you don't have to worry about grizzly bears or mountain lions, but you should be aware of the following when you go fishing.

- **Wading:** Always wade carefully, but be especially careful in tumbling, whitewater streams such as the Wolf and Peshtigo rivers. In addition, parts of the Peshtigo are regulated by power dams, so the water level can change rapidly no matter what the weather. And watch out for electrified fences—the voltage isn't dangerous, but it can give you an unfriendly jolt.

- **Thunderstorms and tornadoes:** Wisconsin has plenty of both in the summer. When you see a thunderstorm approaching, it's not a good idea to be waving around a highly conductive lightning rod made of graphite, so please take precautions. Ditto for tornadoes. If you can't find a basement, lie down in a depression away from trees and power lines.

- **Ticks:** They have become a problem because of the debilitating effects of Lyme Disease. The best way to protect yourself is to wear a hat and long-sleeved shirt and long pants when outdoors, tucking in your pant legs if necessary. Use insect repellent. And at the end of the day, do a tick check, pulling off any ticks before they have a chance to burrow. If you notice an embedded tick or a bite, watch for flu-like symptoms and see a doctor if necessary. Again, serious cases are very rare. We've fished thousands of hours in tick-infested territory and have never experienced a problem.

- **Mosquitoes:** The unofficial Wisconsin state bird is everywhere, so you'd better learn to live with it. These buggers have been blamed recently for the appearance in suburbia of mosquito-

(continued)

borne diseases like encephalitis, but the occurrence of serious diseases spread by mosquitoes is rare. Disease-carrying or not, though, mosquitoes do have bites that are irritating and leave nasty welts. Insect repellent is a must. The most effective contain a chemical with the nickname "deet"; try to use a repellent with deet in the single percentile range, because too much of it over time can be toxic. We find a low-level deet-based repellent combined with cigar or pipe smoke most effective at keeping the bugs away from your exposed parts. But then again, there's that danger of tobacco smoke. We think it is a calculated risk, worth taking as long as fish are feeding.

- **Cows:** They are a generally sedate part of the Wisconsin landscape, but they are big animals that shouldn't be underestimated. Be especially wary of the bulls. Don't hook one on your backcast. Walk around, not through, the herd. Cows are naturally curious animals, so don't be overly concerned if you see them wandering your way.

- **Bears:** As we've said already, there aren't any grizzlies in Wisconsin, but there is a healthy population of black bears in the northern part of the state. Killings of humans by black bears are extremely rare, but never get in the way of a mama and her cubs. Campers especially should take precautions with their food. We've had black bears rip apart a cooler to get the delicious brats that we thought were safe inside.

- **Rattlesnakes:** Rattlers are present in Wisconsin, primarily in the southwest. We've rarely seen them, but you should be cautious when getting to your fishing spot. Watch where you stick your hand, especially in rocky areas with a sunny southern exposure.

- **Exposure:** Wisconsin weather is, well, very changeable. Temperatures can drop rapidly, especially near the Great Lakes and other large bodies of water. DO NOT overestimate your body's ability to stay warm if you get wet; hypothermia

(continued)

is serious. Carry good rain gear, wear fast-wicking clothing, and always have some waterproof matches or a good lighter in your vest, along with an extra flashlight.

When it's hot, make sure you have sunscreen, a good pair of polarized sunglasses, a billed hat, and even a kerchief to protect yourself against the sun—when it shines!

- **Eating fish:** Yes, unfortunately, this is a hazard for those who fish the Great Lakes and their tributaries. The state of Wisconsin has a very detailed guide for people who eat sports fish from Wisconsin waters; it's available from both the WDNR and the Division of Health Services. Pending the outcome of ongoing studies, the major dangers appear to be from PCBs in migrating fish and those inhabiting major Great Lakes tributaries, and mercury in inland, warm-water fish. These pollutants have been in Wisconsin and other waters for decades because of careless industrial practices. Those practices have now largely been eliminated but the pollutants remain, and they work their way up the food chain to big fish, like migrating trout, that feed on other, smaller fish. The danger is mostly from eating big, lake-run fish from Lake Michigan. Women and children should be especially wary. The state guide tells how to trim the pollutant-tainted fat from the PCB-contaminated fish. Bottom line: remove the skin, and cut away the dark fat along the backbone and other fat along the belly before cooking the fish.

4

Insects and Crustaceans of Wisconsin Trout Streams: A Quick Survey

DARKNESS is winning the slow tug of war with sunlight as dusk approaches. The northern Wisconsin river tumbles serenely on; it is a balmy June evening—that magical time of the day that causes every Wisconsin trout angler's heart to beat a notch faster. You catch a glimpse of a rapidly flying insect, and then another comes into view over a wide riffle. You guessed right! Female Gray Drakes are beginning to deposit their eggs on the surface. Soon, male and female Gray Drakes begin falling, spent, onto the water. The river erupts as trout slash at the flies struggling on the surface. The fly imitation you've selected fills the bill, and the fish you cast to eagerly accepts your imitation. A few more fish are landed, and much too quickly it is dark. The event is over, and the river is again calm. You missed several fish, but hooked and landed enough to give you that smug sense of satisfaction that comes after you have matched the hatch.

Trying to imitate the food of trout with artificial flies or lures is an old tradition, going back several centuries, pre-dating the days of Izaak Walton and his English chalk streams. For many Wisconsin trout anglers, matching the hatch is the ultimate pursuit. Fishing trips are geared to the time of year when certain species of insects emerge. Special flies are designed to imitate the insect and sometimes even constructed for the conditions of a particular stream. Even when you're armed with foolproof imitations, though, catching trout is rarely easy. Stream conditions vary from year to year, so emergence periods of insects can vary. Even if you are on the stream at the right time of day, the expected hatch is occurring, and the fish are feeding, you can still get skunked. Other insects may be on the water at the same time, and the fish may be feeding on them while ignoring the ones you're trying to imitate. During intense hatches so many insects may be on the water that the odds of a fish rising to your imitation, even when perfectly presented, may be next to nothing. Insects may hatch one day and not the next, even though the weather and water con-

60

ditions seem exactly the same. We recall a visit to Timber Coulee Creek in late July, with hopes of fishing the Trico spinner fall in the early morning. We could see the tiny, black-bodied mayflies glinting in the sun as they hovered over the stream, but the insects never fell onto the water and the expected rise never happened! All the tiny Trico imitations we had tied, and all the special presentations we had planned to try, would have to wait to be used another time. But it's this uncertainty that makes trying to meet and match the hatch so engaging and challenging. If it were easy and precisely predictable, it wouldn't be nearly as captivating. When everything clicks, however, the sense of satisfaction is all the greater.

In our "Getting Started" chapter, we've already introduced you to mayflies, caddisflies, midges, stoneflies, dragonflies, and damselflies, as well as crustaceans and terrestrial insects. Here we'll provide some additional information on the Wisconsin insects and crustaceans that are important components of a trout's diet. This general information, and the accompanying insect emergence chart, will help you fish the hatches common to Wisconsin trout streams. Wisconsin's most famous mayfly, the Hex, is so special that we've treated the Hex hatch in a separate chapter. You'll find further stream-specific information on hatches in our individual stream profiles.

But first a cautionary note: this quick survey of trout foods isn't intended to be a treatise on the subject. Many writers have come before us on the subject of aquatic trout foods and their imitations. Entire books have been written on fishing and imitating a single stage in the life cycle of a particular group of insects. As your expertise and passion for trout fishing grow, you'll come to appreciate the detail and complexity of the lives of aquatic organisms. For now, here are a few of the books we recommend to the angler interested in further exploration: Dave Whitlock's marvelously illustrated *Dave Whitloch's Guide to Aquatic Trout Foods*, Gary Borger's *Naturals*, Bill Willers' *Trout Biology*, Dick Pobst's pocket-sized *Trout Stream Insects*, Ross Mueller's *Upper Midwest Flies that Catch Trout and How to Fish for Them*, and UW–Madison Professor William Hilsenhoff's *Aquatic Insects of Wisconsin*.

If you haven't paid much attention to the insects and crustaceans you encounter astream, we urge you to do so. Knowing a little about the habits of these creatures will pay off in your fishing success, even if you aren't a fly-fisher. There's no sense flinging a spinning lure to fish keyed in on small midges. More important, this knowledge will greatly increase your general understanding of the aquatic environment that trout inhabit. For example, southwestern Wisconsin's spring creeks, because of their inherent productivity, generally support higher numbers of aquatic insects and crustaceans than the less-productive freestone streams located in the central and northern parts of the state.

MAYFLIES (ORDER: EPHEMEROPTERA)

Probably no other aquatic insect typifies the thrill of fly-fishing for trout as much as the mayfly. Mayflies have four main life stages: egg, nymph, dun,

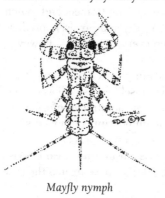

and spinner. Most species complete their life cycle in a year, but species in the genus *Hexagenia* generally live a couple of years as nymphs before hatching into duns. During its larval or nymph stage, a mayfly lives underwater. As it comes out of its nymphal shuck at the surface of the water and struggles to fly, it's referred to as an emerger. Trout feed readily on mayflies in this vulnerable state; imitations have sparse hackle and wing materials designed to suspend the fly in the surface film, simulating the behavior of natu-

Mayfly nymph

Hexagenia *nymph emerging from nymphal shuck* . . .

ral insects. The next stage is the subadult or subimago; these flies are referred to by anglers as duns. They are weak fliers, especially susceptible to fish as they struggle to get off the surface of the water. Duns of various mayfly species will

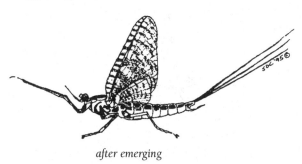

after emerging

rest on streamside vegetation anywhere from several hours to several days before they molt a second time and are transformed into the adult spinner stage. Spinners usually have clear, glassy wings and long tails. Generally good fliers, the spinners form mating swarms, often over riffle areas where they lay their eggs. After mating, the insects quickly collapse; the dying spinners can blanket the water. Spinner falls are distinctive for prompting rises of super-selective, sipping fish, difficult to catch because they have plenty of time to inspect the dying flies and any imitations you cast over them.

Blue-Winged Olives (Genus: Baetis)

Blue-Winged Olive is a common name applied to several mayfly species—a name used because the many species of *Baetis* are difficult to tell apart without a microscope. Olives are abundant on most Wisconsin rivers and streams, with hatches occurring as early as March and as late as October; they are multi-brooded and can hatch more than once during a year, which explains the presence of *Baetis* mayflies on our waters throughout the season. These insects are particularly abundant on spring creeks and the groundwater-dominated creeks in the Central Sands area, and are most commonly found in riffle areas or at the heads of pools, especially where beds of aquatic vegetation are present.

The Blue-Winged Olive is a particularly handsome mayfly. After emerging, it can float for substantial distances on the surface before flying off to begin the transformation to the spinner form—the final stage of its life cycle. The duns are a little over a quarter of an inch to less than an eighth in length, with bluish-gray wings and olive-to-gray bodies. The silvery wings of the duns are very erect, and when a good hatch is on, these flies look like a fleet of tiny sailboats traversing the currents. They are often blown about by the wind, which can drive trout crazy. Some of the best hatches occur on overcast, chilly days. We have observed hatches during snow squalls, and to see these proud little mayflies floating down the creek, their wings held high in defiance of the weather, is a bit of an inspiration.

A favorite imitation of the nymph stage is the well-known Pheasant Tail Nymph. Emerger patterns include the RS-2 and floating nymphs such as the CDC Blue-Winged Olive Nymph (#16–20). One of the most effective

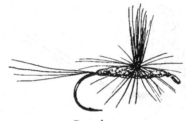

Parachute

techniques when fishing a hatch is to use a nymph or emerger pattern fished downstream and across to rising fish. When duns are on the water, in addition to traditional Blue-Winged Olive patterns, your flybox should also be stocked with fly styles designed for slow-water applications, such as Parachutes and No-Hackles.

A small species of the Blue-Winged Olives is one of the most significant *Baetis* hatches in southern and central Wisconsin. It may also be found on rivers with abundant aquatic vegetation in the northern part of the state. Many of these tiny "Baetis" mayflies may actually belong to the genus *Pseudocloeon*. The distinction matters little to the practical angler, who should use a #22–24 fly to imitate these tiny greenish-bodied mayflies. The duns begin to emerge around the first of June, and continue to hatch well into September. Duns generally hatch during the late afternoon, a prelude to spinner falls in the evening. Streams can be extremely clear and low when this fly is hatching, so presentations must be delicate. Dun and spinner imitations should be very sparsely dressed; a tiny Parachute Adams sometimes works well.

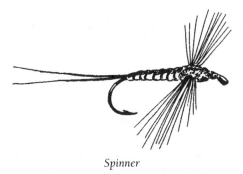

Spinner

Hendrickson (Ephemerella subvaria)

The Hendrickson is the first major spring hatch of medium-sized mayflies (#12–14) that anglers are likely to encounter. In most years Hendricksons appear during the first two weeks of May, at the start of Wisconsin's regular fishing season. For a nymph imitation an appropriately sized Pheasant Tail Nymph works well. The male dun of this species has a reddish-brown abdomen and bluish-gray wings; the female has a creamish-gray body with a light pink cast, and bluish-gray wings. Some fly-fishing veterans carry flies of slightly different colors for the male and female Hendricksons. A famous old fly recipe called for urine-stained fur from the belly of a vixen red fox for the body of a female Hendrickson pattern (thankfully, synthetic material that provides the right color is now available). Frankly, we aren't convinced that such subtle color differences matter much to the trout, but we usually carry some imitations of both male and female Hendricksons in case the trout are more particular than we give them credit for.

Sulphurs (Genus: Ephemerella)

Three species of *Ephemerella* that are commonly called Sulphurs are found in Wisconsin streams: *Ephemerella invaria*, *Ephemerella rotunda,* and *Ephemerella dorothea*. This dependable hatch can be found on most Wisconsin trout

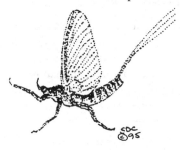

streams and often consists of all three insects. Most anglers cannot, and should not bother to, distinguish among them. They range in size from #14 to #18; *dorothea* is the smallest of the three. Sulphurs usually hatch in late May or early June, following the Hendricksons, although we have observed both types hatching at the same time. Hatches occur at different times on different rivers, from early to late afternoon. The duns have pale light-gray wings and yellowish-cream bodies. Spinners are bright rusty brown with transparent wings. When fishing the hatch, we prefer the fully hackled Light Cahills, Comparaduns (sometimes tied with a shuck/tail of Zelon fibers), or No-Hackles in sizes #14–18.

Brown Drake (Ephemera simulans)

The Brown Drake is the first large fly of the season on many rivers. It favors silty-bottomed, slow-moving sections of the larger rivers in the northern part of the state. The duns are brownish-yellow on the abdomen with dark blotches in the wings, and are quite large—they measure over half an inch in length. Duns usually start hatching around 7 P.M. and continue until dark. The spinner fall usually occurs at dusk, with clouds of spinners forming mating swarms several feet over the water. For the dun pattern, Brown Drake Paraduns (#10) are excellent imitations. Many anglers also use the indispensable Cap's Hairwing. We also use soft-hackle emerger-type patterns, which we fish throughout the hatch. For the spinner, we like a large Spent-Winged Adams (#10) with the bottom hackle clipped off so the fly will float flush in the surface film.

Gray Drakes (Genus: Siphlonurus)

Gray Drakes are found on several of the larger rivers of northern Wisconsin. The peak emergence period for these species is generally the first two weeks of June. Gray Drake duns don't constitute a major hatch, since they swim to the shallows to emerge and therefore aren't available to the trout. However, the spinners provide good fishing as they fall en masse to the surface of riffle areas, and the trout relish them. For this reason, the angler should get positioned in a riffle section where the spinners will mate, and be ready for some fast fishing when they fall to the water. A Spent-Winged Adams (#12) is the fly most frequently used to imitate the Gray Drake.

Hexagenia (Hexagenia limbata and Other Species)

The monarch of all the aquatic insects in Wisconsin is undoubtedly the Hex (H. limbata), the biggest of the midwestern mayflies. The imitations conceived by the fly-tier at the bench must be as numerous as the grains of sand in the Wisconsin River. Virtually every imaginable material, natural and manmade, has been used to try to create a better Hex imitation. For the Hex nymph you can't beat the Strip Nymph popularized by Gary Borger (#6–8). The Hex Paradun (#6) is an excellent dun imitation. For a spinner pattern, the Swisher-

Richards Spent-Winged Spinner (#6) is one of many good choices. The emergence of these insects is so important we've devoted an entire chapter to fishing the mystical Hex hatch.

Light Cahills (*Genus:* Stenacron)

The name "Light Cahill" is applied to a host of species in the *Stenacron* genus of mayflies (formerly known as *Stenonema*); the duns are pale or creamy white, and measure approximately one-half inch in length. The flies hatch most often at dusk in riffles or areas with moderate current. They rarely appear in large enough numbers to constitute a major hatch, but when they do emerge, trout definitely key in on them. The traditional Light Cahill imitation (#12–16) should be carried in every angler's flybox.

White Mayflies (Ephoron leukon *and* Ephoron album)

The White Mayflies are found on several of our larger rivers in the slower, siltier sections, especially in the central and northern regions of Wisconsin. Both the dun and the spinner are pale white. These mayflies, which often hatch with such intensity that we think we're in a summer blizzard, are over half an inch in length. The White Mayflies can almost be said to be hot-water mayflies, since the best hatches occur when the water temperature is between 65 and 70 degrees, usually from middle to late August. Because the nymphs leave their burrows, swim to the surface, and hatch very quickly, the fish key in on the more vulnerable spinner stage. The transformation from dun to spinner occurs almost immediately after hatching. Although many anglers believe that this transformation occurs in mid-air, Gary Borger informs us that this is a misconception passed on from each generation of anglers to the next. The duns must land to molt their wings, but often take flight before the skin is fully shed. Thus the loose shuck falls off as the insect flies, making it look as though it were molting in mid-air. A good *Epheron* imitation to use is a White Wulff (#12–14); a trailing shuck can often make the imitation more enticing.

Tricos (*Genus:* Tricorythodes)

Tricos are tiny mayflies; several species hatch on a number of our larger rivers, as well as on some spring creeks, but seldom in numbers sufficient to excite trout. Look for reaches of stream with abundant aquatic vegetation. The emergence of duns, formation of mating swarms, and return of egg-laying spinners happen over a short period of time; spinners and duns are often on the water simultaneously. The trout often key in on the spent insects, which are easier prey. We prefer spinner imitations in sizes #20–22 that use clipped hackle wings or hackle-tip wings. Wings constructed of Antron, Zelon, or similar synthetic materials will work fine if they are tied very sparsely. In this hatch, which occurs early in the morning in the late summer, it's best to cast to specific fish and use a very careful approach. Often the fish will be feeding on the Trico spinners in the flat water or the tail of a pool, so presentation will be the critical factor in determining success. We often cast from an upstream position so that we can guide the fly right into the fish's feeding lane without the trout's ever seeing the leader. Get as many drifts over the fish as possible.

CADDISFLIES (ORDER: TRICHOPTERA)

The main caddisflies for the Wisconsin angler include the Little Black Caddis (*Chimarra*), the Grannom (*Brachycentrus*), the various Sedge species (*Hydropsyche*), and the Green-Bodied Caddis (*Cheumatopsyche*).

Other caddisflies occur—such as the White Miller (*Nectopsyche*)—and they can be important on some waters, but they usually aren't common enough to trigger intense trout-feeding activity all on their own. Caddisflies have four life stages: egg, larva, pupa, and adult. During the larval stage most species build the familiar cases we find attached to the undersides of rocks. During their pupal stage, caddisflies live in a cocoon. After hatching, the flying adults mate and return to the water to lay eggs. Caddisflies don't hatch with the same punctuality as mayflies, and they tend to hatch over longer periods of time. Flies are tied to imitate the larval, pupal, and adult stages; the latter two are the most significant to the angler. Imitations are tied to mimic the pupa as it breaks out of its case and ascends to the surface. These flies include patterns such as the popular Soft Hackles, which have fur or floss bodies of various colors and soft wet-fly hackle collars of grouse or partridge. The caddis pupa and emerger imitations designed by Gary LaFontaine, which incorporate a synthetic fiber such as Antron in the fly recipe, are especially effective. Cast the pupa imitations quartering downstream and let the current swing the fly. Adults are imitated by the ubiquitous Elk Hair Caddis (#12–18), and the Adams (#12–18) in tan, olive, and gray; use heavily hackled patterns in fast water. The fly can be fished dead-drift, or you can manipulate the Elk Hair Caddis by fishing it across and downstream and letting it pull under the surface of the water. Let the fly pop back to the surface of the water and then skitter it across the surface; this will often produce explosive strikes.

Why does this technique work so well? Because most caddis adults go underwater to lay eggs. When done, they release their hold on the bottom and float to the top in the air bubbles they carry. At the surface film they pop out, just like a hatching insect. If caddis adults are "popping out" and there are few or no pupal husks floating in the film, then it's egg laying, not hatching, that's going on.

The Little Black Caddis and the Grannom are usually found in the headwaters of creeks; as the stream warms and becomes more enriched by nutrients, other caddis, like the *Hydropsyche*, will predominate. The *Brachycentrus* larvae are easily recognized by their beautifully constructed and tapered four-sided cases. In contrast, the *Hydropsyche* are net builders, with houses of pebbles and detritus attached to the undersides of larger, cobble-sized rocks. To ascertain the presence of caddis and to find out what type of caddis you are likely to encounter, always check the rocks on the stream bottom.

Little Black Caddis *(Genus:* Chimarra*)*

The species of the Little Black Caddis are dark blackish-gray and small, averaging approximately a third of an inch in length. They are found in great numbers in the headwaters of many rivers and streams, especially in spring creeks. They usually hatch in late April or early May, but this insect has been observed to have small but steady hatches well into summer. Non-point-source pollution is probably the culprit responsible for the low numbers of Little Black Caddis on streams that should otherwise harbor large populations.

Grannom *(Genus:* Brachycentrus*)*

The various species of *Brachycentrus*—the well-known Grannom—can be counted on to be among the earliest caddisflies to hatch, usually in April in southwestern Wisconsin. The larvae build the rectangular, chimney-like cases familiar to anyone who has examined insects inhabiting trout streams. For the larval stage, a Hare's Ear Nymph is a good general imitation. Pupa imitations are numerous—we favor a LaFontaine Emergent Sparkle Pupa. Grannom adults are a little less than half an inch in length and are a mottled cinnamon brown with a yellowish-brown abdomen. When adults are on the water, a tan Elk Hair Caddis (#14) will usually do the trick; however, a lower-floating fly like the Delta-Wing Caddis will mimic the spent egg-laying caddis better in many situations. Try both.

Sedges *(Genus:* Hydropsyche*)*

The net-spinning members of the *Hydropsyche* genus of caddisflies are represented by various species making their initial appearance in April, but also hatching at other times of the year. The adults are a bit larger than the

Little Black Caddis, just under half an inch in length, and range in color from gray to tan. These insects are more tolerant of warmer water temperatures and pollution, so they are usually the prevalent caddis in the lower reaches of many of our streams and rivers.

Green-Bodied Caddis (Genus: Cheumatopsyche)

The Green-Bodied Caddis could be referred to as the summer caddis because they usually make their appearance in the middle of the fishing season, around the first of June. Adults of these species can be recognized by their bright green bodies, and are rather small, so an Elk Hair Caddis in sizes #18–20 tied with a green body will usually work in the riffle sections. Don't forget to try pupa imitations when the trout are bulging to caddis pupae as the insects rise from the bottom of the stream to the surface.

MIDGES (ORDER: DIPTERA)

Most trout streams and rivers will have good hatches of midges at one time or another. Some anglers hate to see midges hatching because the fishing can be very difficult. But if you have a reasonably good imitation and present the fly carefully, you can enjoy some excellent fishing. Spring creeks, especially, are ideal midge habitat. Their lush aquatic vegetation and biologic productivity mean that unbelievable midge hatches can occur, producing conditions for some very technical fishing. Watch for midge hatches almost every day during the season at the heads of pools, where mating swarms gather. These are the times to try very small imitations, like a Griffith's Gnat or an Adams (#18–22). We can't strongly recommend any particular color because there are so many color variations among all the species from stream to stream. However, we've found cream or bright olive-green to be recurring colors. We usually carry several pupa imitations in these colors, plus Griffith's Gnats with olive-green or cream bodies. In addition, we use larva imitations of midges, including small versions of the Brassie and red or olive Serendipities (#18–22).

STONEFLIES (ORDER: PLECOPTERA)

Stoneflies are easily recognized by their set of two wing cases and flattened bodies. Like other aquatic insects, stoneflies live most of their lives as larvae on the bottom, feeding on detritus or—in some species—other aquatic insects.

They are found underneath the rocks, stones, and wood debris in the faster currents and riffles of the river. Stoneflies aren't readily noticed by most anglers for several reasons. They usually don't hatch all at once like mayflies (although some, such as the Yellow Sally, appear in good numbers on some streams with better water quality), and the egg-laying flights of the females generally occur at night.

Stonefly nymphs are another matter; they tend to crawl to the shallows, where they often molt on rocks and emergent vegetation. If they're not on your streamside agenda now, get to know them. The larger Black, Brown, and Golden stoneflies (including such well-known genera as *Pteronarcys* and *Acroneuria*) are well worth the angler's attention. For these large dark nymphs, a heavily weighted Brooks Stonefly (#4–8) is an excellent choice. Montana Nymphs and March Brown Nymphs are also popular and effective patterns. This isn't dainty fishing with a small fly, microshot, and a tiny strike indicator—when you use these big nymphs, you're going after the largest fish in the river. Fish the lure as close to the bottom as possible through the rips, runs, and deepest parts of pools. And equip yourself with a suitable line, a 5–7-weight rod, a stout leader and tippet (9 feet long and a 1–3X tippet), and a hat. Yes, a hat! To paraphrase the late Charles Brooks: fishing stonefly nymphs is like playing Russian roulette with your ears and eyes as stakes. You don't want to hook yourself while flinging these heavily weighted flies.

SCUDS (GENERA: GAMMARUS AND HYALELLA)

Scuds, with their preference for alkaline water, live in every spring creek. Often called "freshwater shrimp" by anglers (though only distantly related to the true shrimp), scuds are found in almost all habitats, but they seem to be most abundant in bottom detritus and beds of aquatic vegetation. Because these crustaceans are a primary food item for trout in our spring creeks, they're of great importance to the angler. Scuds may be found in association with cressbugs; they may be gray, tan, or yellow, and of various sizes (#12–16), so the angler should have a variety of imitations on hand. We've found shades of tan to be effective most of the time. Weight the fly, and use a dead-drift presentation with a strike indicator. There are many effective scud patterns available; one of the most widely used imitations in southwestern Wisconsin is a pattern developed by spring creek authority Tom Wendelburg of Middleton. It consists of an all-fur dubbed body (usually cream-colored, from a hare's mask), trimmed close on top with no shellback and tied with a yellow head.

CRESSBUGS (GENUS: ASELLUS)

Cressbugs (anglers often use the name "sowbug" interchangeably), like scuds, prefer alkaline water, but they can tolerate poorer water quality. Because many Wisconsin spring creeks exhibit some degree of organic pollution, cressbugs are extremely abundant. In fact, biologists regard the lowly cressbug as one of the most pollution-tolerant of all the aquatic organisms. Look for them on the bottom or on the undersides of rocks and dead wood in streams. In fishing, what goes for the scud also applies to the cressbug. Most imitations are tied in sizes #12–16. Ed Schenk's all-fur Cressbug is a traditional pattern. We've also had consistently good fishing with a cream-colored soft-hackled imitation.

TERRESTRIALS

These land-based insects that happen to fall or get blown into the water are also significant food items for trout. In the doldrums of midsummer, after the blackberries have ripened, it's time to use imitations of beetles, ants, grasshoppers, and crickets. Trout will sometimes look for these land bugs dropping into the water on windy days. We've also seen mating swarms of flying ants

Flying ant

that take on the dimensions of a hatch. Meadow stretches of our spring creeks are exceptionally good places to fish terrestrial imitations. The trout will hold beneath the undercut banks and boldly slash at either a hapless grasshopper or your fly, if the current brings the bug tight against the bank. An adequate selection of terrestrials would include Dave's Hopper (#10–16), Dave's Cricket (#10–16), Black and Red Ants (#14–18), and Black Beetles (#14–18).

EMERGENCE SCHEDULE

The emergence schedule in Figure 4.1 is for the main fly hatches found in Wisconsin. Many other aquatic insects are found in Wisconsin streams, but the chart depicts only those that are typically most important to the fly-fisher. Insect abundances vary from stream to stream. Remember that weather and location on the streams (colder headwaters or warmer waters downstream) can affect the timing of the hatches.

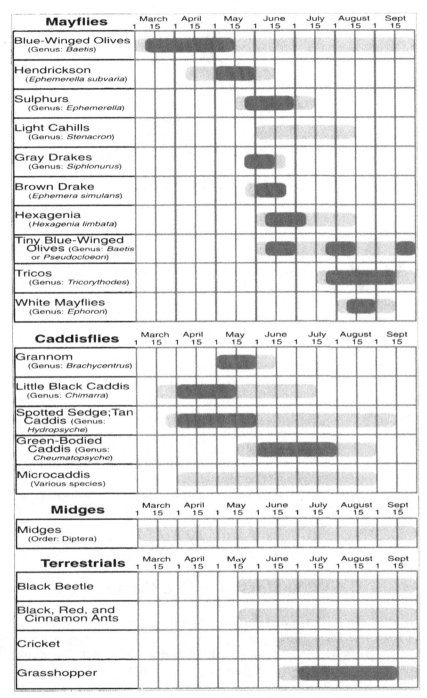

Figure 4.1. Aquatic and terrestrial insect emergence schedules. Note: The more heavily shaded areas indicate the time when the most intense hatches are likely to occur

5

"Don't Miss" Wisconsin Fishing Opportunities

W ISCONSIN, like any trout-fishing locale, has its list of "Don't Miss" fishing opportunities. We've compiled three of the major "Don't Miss" trips here—three special opportunities that should be experienced by any trout angler who lives in or visits the Badger State. We've entitled them 1,000 Miles of Spring Creeks, Magic in the Dark: Fishing the Hex Hatch, and Battling Big Salmonids in the Great Lakes Tributaries.

The first section takes you to the southwestern part of the state, known as the Driftless Area, where top-notch spring creeks abound. We'll tell you how these spring creeks were formed, why they're unique, and what spring creek angling methods catch trout. Next we'll fish the magical Hex hatch. That's when the largest of the mayflies hatch, delighting anglers who are there to see the biggest trout in a feeding frenzy. Finally, we'll visit Wisconsin's coastlines and their rivers. Every fall and spring, big salmon and steelhead rush up Lake Michigan and Lake Superior tributaries to spawn, creating spectacular fishing opportunities. We'll tell you how Pacific salmon and steelhead came to the Great Lakes, and outline some techniques for hooking these monster salmonids.

Come along with us on a Wisconsin "Don't Miss" fishing expedition.

1,000 MILES OF SPRING CREEKS

The term "spring creek" evokes an image of gentle currents, rich insect life, and big trout. The trout inhabiting spring creeks are picky eaters and spook easily in clear, glassy water. Luxuriant growths of aquatic plants, harboring many insects and other fish food, undulate rhythmically in the cool waters. These images depict classic trout waters that excite and challenge even the most experienced angler. Fortunately, Wisconsin is blessed with an abundance of these premium waters—we have one of the highest concentrations of spring creeks in the world.

To fish a Wisconsin spring creek is to explore a wondrous, flowing piece of nature's handiwork. The gin-clear creek often meanders through an emerald-green valley laced with picturesque dairy farms and fields of purple cone-flowers, black-eyed Susans, and Queen Anne's lace in full bloom. In the hillsides above the creek, varieties of cactus can sometimes be found on the sandy southern exposures. The fresh, pungent scent of mint and other streamside plants fills your nostrils as you ease into the stream's chilly waters—waters that will cool your body on sweltering summer days, and refresh your soul any time of year. You may not even notice the cry of a red-tailed hawk as it soars overhead, scanning the nearby pasture, but you will hear the sound of rising trout. And if you make that perfect cast with the right fly and manage to hook and land a wild trout, you'll be astounded by its sheer beauty.

A trout-filled spring creek, in short, is very special. But what distinguishes a spring creek from other trout streams? First of all, spring creeks are fed by a nearly constant supply of groundwater, providing a stable environment for their inhabitants. The abundant groundwater flow also keeps the temperature relatively stable, so in the winter the water stays well above freezing and in the summer the water remains cool. This stability creates ideal growing conditions for aquatic plants and animals. Flooding doesn't occur often, and so the aquatic plant community (made up of rooted aquatic plants like watercress) is undisturbed and supports an abundance of trout food in the form of scuds, sowbugs, and various aquatic insects. Moreover, trout grow all year long because of the relatively constant temperature.

Groundwater enters a spring creek in several ways—via large gushing springs, small rivulets that bubble out of a tiny side channel, seepages, or most common of all, through the stream bed itself, where the stream channel intersects the water table. Where groundwater enters the stream in gravel-rich areas, trout spawning conditions are ideal. This is one reason why spring creeks with abundant areas of groundwater recharge through the stream bottom typically have healthy populations of wild trout: the groundwater inflow keeps the eggs from freezing in the winter, and also tends to keep the redds (trout "nests") free from sediment.

True spring creeks also have a less obvious characteristic—a water chemistry that, combined with the other factors, produces high biological productivity. The special chemical content is due to the dissolution of minerals as the groundwater flows through carbonate rocks, like limestone and dolomite. The water tends to be hard because of high concentrations of dissolved calcium

Bill Engber with a beautiful brown trout fooled by a Baetis nymph imitation on a south-western Wisconsin spring creek. Photo by Jim Bartelt.

and magnesium, and to have high alkalinity or high acid-neutralizing capacity due to dissolved carbonates.

Why does dissolved limestone and dolomite rock make spring creek water so special for trout? There are several reasons. First, the high concentration of carbonates provides plenty of the carbon that plants need to grow. These plants form the base of the stream's food chain, and also provide shelter for aquatic insects and crustaceans. Second, the carbonates help buffer the water against photosynthesis-created acidity that can limit fish growth. Third, the water contains plenty of calcium and magnesium, minerals needed to form the calcareous shells and exoskeletons of many aquatic insects. When these minerals are present, enormous populations of certain fish food organisms, such as the shrimp-like scud, can occur. We often encounter trout rooting among dense growths of aquatic plants in Wisconsin spring creeks. The fish are dislodging scuds and then dining on them as they drift in the current. In short, spring creeks have a special chemical quality that makes them very fertile and capable of supporting lots of trout.

Wisconsin spring creeks rarely exceed 15 miles. As the distance downstream from the headwaters increases, the stream will warm if it receives no more groundwater, a factor that often limits the section of stream that can support trout. Most of Wisconsin's spring creeks are not more than 25 feet wide, and you can jump over many of them. Despite their relatively small size, their high trout-carrying capacity sets them apart from other trout streams.

While springs and seepages occur throughout Wisconsin, the underlying geologic materials through which groundwater moves vary from region to region. Groundwater in much of the western part of the state, particularly the southwestern part, comes from dolomitic aquifers, and tends to have the special mix of dissolved minerals that results in productive trout streams. However, in other parts of the state the bedrock geology is shale, sandstone, and other rock types that don't produce the same fertile water chemistry as in the southwest. So while there are groundwater-fed streams throughout the state, the spring creeks with the highest productivity waters are mostly found in southwestern Wisconsin.

Freestone streams are different. They rely on external sources of productivity, such as leaf litter and other plant material (often called detritus) that fall into the stream. They don't have the productivity that spring creeks have, so they can't support as much aquatic life. One study of a spring creek in Pennsylvania showed that true spring creeks are twenty times more productive than freestoners in terms of aquatic insect biomass.

A comparison of the water chemistry of the twenty Wisconsin streams profiled in this book is shown in Figure 5.1. The hardness and alkalinity are shown for each stream. Streams with the highest hardness and alkalinity—Black Earth Creek, Mt. Vernon Creek, Castle Rock Creek, the Blue River, Timber Coulee Creek, the Big Green River, Willow Creek, and the Kinnickinnic River—are all found in the western and southern parts of the state where dolomitic rocks are common. We classify all these streams as spring creeks. Streams of the far north, like the Pike and Namekagon rivers, don't have nearly as much alkalinity and hardness. Other streams, like the Mecan and the Tomorrow in the central part of state, have many characteristics of spring creeks, but don't have quite the same rich chemistry as the spring creeks. We simply call these waters "groundwater-dominated" streams to differentiate them from our true spring creeks. Figure 5.1 contrasts Wisconsin's true spring creeks with other top Wisconsin trout streams.

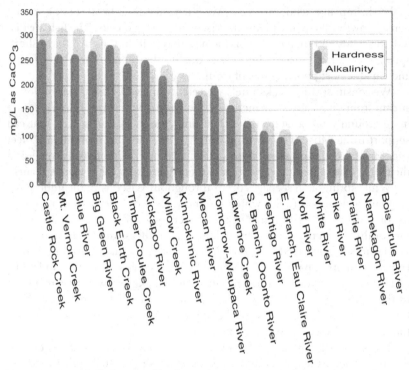

Figure 5.1. Typical alkalinity and hardness of Wisconsin trout waters, indicating the most fertile streams. The streams with the highest alkalinity and hardness are true spring creeks.

All the streams we write about are good trout streams, but not all the spring creeks in Wisconsin are super trout streams; channelization, pollution, stream bank erosion, siltation, and other factors can ruin any stream. As Wisconsin fishing sage Sid Gordon once observed: "To me, all waters are good if they have fish in them." But true spring creeks are an exceptional and increasingly rare resource, and few places have the concentration of spring creeks found in Wisconsin. The storied chalk streams of England, where the traditions of trout fishing and fly-fishing had their origin, are similar to our spring creeks. These streams are often referred to as chalk streams because the groundwater that feeds them flows through chalk rock, a type of limestone. Wisconsin's spring creeks also resemble central Pennsylvania's famed spring creeks, so often chronicled in the trout-fishing literature. These spring creeks are called "limestoners" by the locals because of the limestone geology of the groundwater system that feeds them. Wisconsin's spring creeks haven't received the attention in the literature some of these other waters have, but aesthetically, biologically, and chemically they are on a par with the world's most acclaimed trout waters.

Like many other spring creeks of the world, Wisconsin's spring creeks flow through fertile farmland. While this provides a pastoral setting, pollution from farming operations is a major problem. Runoff from barnyards can be especially devastating, overfertilizing the stream and robbing it of life-giving oxygen. Cattle grazing near the stream also cause stream bank erosion that can destroy trout habitat and bring about siltation of the stream bottom. Some of Wisconsin's spring creeks, like Black Earth Creek, are close to population centers and are being threatened by urban encroachment. Fortunately, the spring creeks lie in an unglaciated part of the state that has many hills and valleys. Not all of the land is farmed. Forested slopes provide areas where water can infiltrate and replenish the groundwater reserves. In addition, improved conservation practices by farmers have reduced cropland runoff in some places. The flow of some streams has actually increased since the sixties, so there is hope these streams will be available for future generations to enjoy. But we can never take them for granted.

The Trout of Wisconsin's Spring Creeks

What about the trout found in Wisconsin's spring creeks? Brookies are the native trout of Wisconsin, and once flourished in our spring creek systems. There are still some small populations of the true native brook trout in the headwaters of our most pristine spring creeks, but the genetics of most native fisheries has probably been altered through years of stocking. In general, few spring creeks today have fisheries dominated by brook trout. However, there is interest in restoring brook trout fisheries in some of our spring creeks, especially those with recent water quality improvements and increased groundwater contributions to stream flow.

Rainbow trout have been stocked throughout Wisconsin since 1872, when 20,000 were let go in Lake Geneva and the Madison lakes. Today rainbows are stocked in many spring creeks, but they aren't known to reproduce readily. Fisheries personnel may decide to stock rainbows instead of brown trout in the marginal or lower reaches of the stream to increase the catchable numbers of trout. There is some evidence to suggest that rainbows don't compete with brown trout directly because they use slightly different habitat.

Browns, though a non-native species, are the dominant trout in most Wisconsin spring creeks. They have adapted particularly well since 1887, when Wisconsin imported about a thousand European brown trout eggs, which were hatched at the Bayfield Fish Hatchery in northern Wisconsin. In creeks with

 good water quality, some gravel areas for spawning, and sufficient groundwater inflow, browns reproduce naturally and no supplemental stocking is required. Almost all spring creeks have some degree of natural reproduction of brown trout. In the late sixties and early seventies, fisheries managers discovered that the stocking of hatchery brown trout in streams with populations of wild browns tended to suppress the growth of the wild population. For this reason, many of our spring creeks that were dependent on stocking now are managed as wild trout fisheries. Some biologists suspect the wild fish are genetically disposed through natural selection to survive better and to have better reproductive success. Brown trout can also tolerate warmer temperatures than brookies and rainbows, and so can survive farther downstream from groundwater sources.

Tackle

In spring creeks, standard light fly rods and the appropriately matched line and reel are the norm, suggesting an 8–9-foot, 3–5-weight rod with a progressive action that allows delicate presentation. The powerful, fast-action graphite rods that have been popular lately are definitely out of place on the small spring creeks of Wisconsin. The trend towards lighter line weights has been taken up by many of the spring creek regulars, especially by anglers who are confident they won't often be casting a big Woolly Bugger. Wisconsin spring creeks are tailor-made for the exacting, technical fishing that one associates with fly tackle in the lighter line weights.

Because of the small size and often lush streamside vegetation of Wisconsin spring creeks, some experienced anglers have opted for shorter rods. This has spurred a revived interest in rods of 7 feet—or even less—made of fiberglass or other materials, allowing anglers to negotiate small waters. Fishing these streams can be a claustrophobic experience as the angler crouches underneath a canopy of brush and overhanging trees, and shorter rods in these situations can be useful. Still, there's enough relatively open water so that most anglers prefer a longer rod (over 8 feet) to help keep the backcast over surrounding meadow vegetation. Another advantage to the longer rod is the better roll casting it can provide, for when fishing small nymphs, a well-executed roll cast is often essential. The obvious answer to this dilemma is for you to own rods in both the long and the short lengths—so you can enjoy the advantages of both!

There have been volumes written about leaders and their various designs, lengths, and materials. The basic formula for compound leaders developed by George Harvey, an innovative angler, author, and teacher from Pennsylvania's spring creek region, has served our purposes well in Wisconsin. At the butt end, it starts with a segment of monofilament keyed to the line's thickness, followed by a long section of tapered mono, and at the business end, a long, supple tippet (there are many variations, but look at Harvey's own book, *Techniques of Trout Fishing and Fly Tying,* for more information). The length for most leaders (including tippet) is 9 feet, although some conditions such as low and very clear water may require a longer length—even exceeding 12 feet. You must pay special attention to the tippet, the very end of the leader. A long, fine tippet is the rule when making delicate presentations in clear water with small flies. The starting point for most fishing is a 5X tippet at least 18 inches long, and we often go to 3 or more feet of fine tippet to cope with drag complicated by the unseen spring creek currents. Come equipped to use an even finer tippet when you are in a situation requiring small flies (#18 and up). You can also buy a prepackaged leader and tippet from a fly shop. When your tippet gets too short (from snipping off bits of leader as you tie on new flies) you can just add some new tippet material. We use the easy-to-tie double surgeon's knot to attach the tippet to the leader.

Tactics for Spring Creeks

Although the basic techniques we discussed in the "Getting Started" chapter are the foundation for fishing any Wisconsin stream, we want to highlight some tactics that are particularly useful for fishing in the conditions usually encountered on spring creeks—clear water, flat surfaces, tiny flies, and very selective trout.

Our first bit of advice is to approach the stream cautiously, thinking and acting like the predators that stalk trout when we're not around. Spring creek trout haven't grown large by being heedless to the threats of kingfishers, herons, and otters. Since the creeks are not very wide, the fish are never far from an animal looking for dinner. Keep a low profile, walk far away from the bank if possible, and creep into your casting position. Careless wading or a sloppy cast will send trout bolting for the protection of a submerged log or an undercut bank.

When you don't need to wade, don't. You can't afford to disturb the water unnecessarily, and gentle spring creek flows and pools are very easily disturbed. If at all possible, stay on the bank when casting to the fish. Keeping out of the stream also allows you to spot rises and potential lies. You may also find that casting from the bank instead of entering the water is the most effective way to fish a particular area. When using this approach, we try to hide ourselves in the vegetation. You can get quite close to the fish using this technique, and the closer you are to the fish the more control you have over the line. Take your time, savor the environment, and fish in a relaxed manner. Such an approach usually pays off for both your state of mind and your fishing success.

If wading is necessary to present your fly effectively, move with great care. Avoid wading into the deeper part of the pool, or any part of the pool that is likely to hold fish. Small fish holding in the fringe of this deeper water will sometimes dart away and spook the other fish in the pool, so disturb as little water as possible. In a spring creek with dense mats of aquatic vegetation, use the mats to block the waves created by your movement. Often you can wade up a parallel channel in the aquatic vegetation and get quite close to the fish. In these channels the bottom has usually been scoured free of sediment, and the wading can be quite easy. When wading upstream, mimic a heron. Lift each leg completely out of the water, if the water is not too deep, and slip it straight into the water toe first. Creep upstream, just like a heron, and you won't create any waves. If you have large fish steadily sipping in midges it will be worth it to approach your fish as stealthily as possible. Wading downstream requires a different technique from upstream wading. Try not to wade directly above feeding fish. You can ease into position above a fish by moving very slowly and letting your feet drift downstream with the current. Move your feet one by one and you'll be able to get into position without kicking up silt, sand, and gravel. We use this wading technique when fish are feeding in the middle or tail of a long pool.

Even though our spring creeks look small, we recommend that you use chest waders instead of hip boots. Although these creeks are rarely over your head, at least once in a fishing trip you will need the extra freeboard of chest waders. You generally don't need felt soles, because the rocky areas are usually restricted to the easily wadable riffle sections. For late spring and summer wading, light stocking-foot waders work well. We sometimes enjoy wet-wading, wearing lightweight pants and wading boots instead of the entire ensemble, but an experience with leeches taught us that even in very warm weather, tennis shoes and shorts may not be the most functional fishing outfit.

Fishing with Wet Flies and Nymphs

The most common fly-fishing tactic employed on Wisconsin spring creeks is the upstream dead-drift nymphing technique. Our spring creeks typically have many riffle-pool sequences, with gentle riffles giving way to a pool that has its deepest point on the outside of the bend. Position yourself so that you can methodically fish your nymph with a natural dead-drift through the trough along the outside bend. Approach the pool carefully from below and fish progressively upstream to the head of the pool. Trout frequently will hold at the point where the current from the riffle slides into the pool. Sometimes you will glimpse the flash of nymphing trout, revealing their positions. When you reach the upper part of the pool, cast upstream into the riffle and let your fly drift into the pool. You may need to add a small split shot (preferably non-toxic) to sink your fly to the proper depth. If your fly occasionally touches bottom you know you're doing things right. Leaders should be at least 9 feet long and should have a light tippet (5X minimum) for normal, clear-water conditions. A tippet at least 2 feet long will allow the fly to drift naturally. Some spring creek specialists advocate much longer tippets to get an even more natural drift out of their fly. Strike indicators are a big help in detecting takes; a good rule of thumb is to place your strike indicator up the leader by a distance equal to one and a half times the depth of the water you're fishing.

Our minimalist's fly list (from "Getting Started") is a good place to start in discussing spring creek wet fly patterns. Of the flies listed, Scuds (#12–16), the Pheasant Tail Nymph (#14–18), and the Girdle Bug (#12–16) are usually good bets. Some old-time anglers tie a Girdle Bug-like fly called a Bomber, similar to the Girdle Bug but with stubbier legs. Like the Girdle Bug, the body is usually black chenille, but it can be olive or brown, too. Any avid spring creek angler would also add these patterns: the Cressbug (#12–16), fished like the Scud; the Muskrat's Regret (#14–16), a simple tie composed of a dubbed muskrat body with a palmered ginger hackle; a Grasshopper tied to fish wet; the Muddler Minnow and other squirrel-tail streamers; and nymphs tied in the beadhead style (using a fly with a golden or silver bead at the head of the fly helps get the lure down without the use of split shot). These are by no means recent innovations in spring creek wet fly fishing. We knew some old spring creek veterans—Madison postal workers Lowell Gennrich and Del Richardson come to mind—who successfully fished the streams in southwestern Wisconsin with a handful of these tried-and-true patterns.

Perhaps the most unusual aspect of spring creek nymph fishing is the use of very small nymph patterns. We have used nymphs as small as #22 or #24 to catch trout, although we generally use #18 or #20. Pheasant Tails in these small sizes work well. Almost any small, dark-fur nymph pattern will work when the fish are feeding on small nymphs, which is frequently. The pattern doesn't have to be elaborate. For example: a short tail, some sparse dark fur for an abdomen, and the same fur tied a little heavier for a thorax. The Serendipity, part of our minimalist assortment, is another good small-fly pattern, especially when the fish are feeding on midges. While these flies can be fished alone with a strike indicator, we normally use them as part of a two-fly system. You can use two wet flies or you can tie a nymph as a "trailer" about 10 inches behind a dry fly. The dry fly serves as a strike indicator. This is delicate fishing, to be sure.

Fishing the Hatch—Dry and Wet

What do you do when a hatch is underway? If you see fish snatching duns cleanly from the surface and you recognize the fly, the answer is simple: you tie on a matching dry fly. But what if the rise forms indicate subsurface feeding activity on hard-to-identify hatching insects? Wet flies can be especially effective when a hatch is in progress or just beginning. For spring creeks we sometimes like to use very small (#18–22) sizes; as the current swings the fly past the line, the tension will cause the fly to rise naturally and simulate a tiny emerging insect rising to the surface. These small flies can be just what the trout are looking for, since fish will sometimes be selective towards the ascending insect rather than the floating dun. Here's another situation. What if all appearances point to use of a dry fly, but none of your patterns work? One trick we have found useful: try floating nymphs. One time when we were on a late May spring creek trip, fish started rising. They seemed to be feeding on a small mayfly, perhaps a Sulphur mayfly (#16) or a Hendrickson (#14). We tried a dozen or so different dry fly patterns, but none produced. Finally, we noticed an unweighted Hare's Ear nymph in the corner of the fly box. Dressing it with a little fly floatant, we cast upstream to a rising fish and allowed the nymph to float back drag free. For the next hour of the hatch, we took nearly every feeding fish. A slight variation of this technique is to use floatant on the leader, not on the nymph, which will allow the fly to sink a few inches below the surface. A lightly weighted nymph will help break the surface tension of the water. Fish probably take the pattern as an emerging mayfly.

When fishing a floating nymph or a dry fly, a conventional upstream presentation is often a problem. The leader, or worse yet the fly line, may fall over the trout and spook them, or it may be impossible to get a drag-free float over the fish. As we said, spring creek trout are very spooky. Consequently, a technique that is often a savior on spring creeks is the downstream dead-drift. Make a short cast upstream of the fish but across its feeding lane. Pull the rod tip and fly line back to position the floating fly in the fish's feeding lane, and then slowly lower the rod, allowing the current to carry the fly directly to the fish. If the fish doesn't take, tilt the rod away from the fish so you can repeat the cast. There are many variations on this approach, and we recommend Gary Borger's *Presentation* for detailed instructions on them. The downstream dead-drift tactic is especially effective for fishing small dry flies like the Griffith's Gnat or a Tiny Blue-Winged Olive pattern. Small mayflies can be numerous, so the fish don't have to move much to feed. If your fly is outside the fish's narrow feeding lane, it won't have a chance to draw a strike. The downstream dead-drift tactic allows you to be very precise in the placement of your fly, but no tactic is foolproof. Hooking the fish can be difficult when using the technique, because the hook point will likely be facing away from the fish's mouth. Be very patient. Let the fish take the fly and turn its head before you set the hook. And strike gently, as you will probably have a light tippet. Usually all it takes is gently lifting the tip of the rod.

Fishing Terrestrials

Aquatic insects aren't the only trout food in spring creeks. The lush countryside harbors a multitude of insects, and many of them find their way into the creeks. Terrestrials become very important from June until the end of the season in September. Land insects such as grasshoppers, beetles, and ants are mobile—by their own accord, or by the wind. Fishing terrestrials is most effective during the early morning hours when the water temperature is at its coolest. But watch for specific fish locked in on terrestrials at any time, including the middle of the day, and especially during windy afternoons. Patterns of choice include the Black Beetle (#16–18), Black Ant (#16–18), Cricket (#14–16), and Grasshopper (#12–16). Most of these are part of our basic fly selection.

The meadow stretches of our spring creeks seem to be tailor-made for Grasshopper and Cricket fishing. Using smaller sizes (#16), fish your imitation to specific lies, including undercut banks and deadfalls. Fish them very deliberately and cautiously, with a minimum of wading or false casting. You will rarely see fish in these situations, although keen observation will increase your sightings of opportunistic feeding trout. Big fish are often caught during terrestrial time because they occupy the prime locations for intercepting insects that fall into the water. Smaller fish aren't able to defend these lies.

When you encounter a section of the stream with overhanging willows— and especially when a slight breeze is blowing—always keep your eyes peeled for fish sipping ants, beetles, or other insects falling off the trees. A Black Beetle (#18) has proven to be especially productive for us in these situations. Before you even tie on the fly, though, assess the situation and decide on a strategy of presentation. The fish will likely be skittish, since they are usually feeding in flat water under the trees instead of tucked in an undercut bank. Although you may be able to present your fly casting from a position downstream, consider whether a presentation from above the fish might be more effective. One way to effectively present the Beetle to the fish in this manner is to get out of the stream and position yourself on the bank above and out of sight. Cast down and across with plenty of S curves in the leader for a drag-free drift. Long leaders are the rule, with a tippet no heavier than 6X.

Fishing Attractor Flies during Nonhatch Situations

What if all these spring creek tactics fail you? We try attractors. This may be surprising to some, because tiny, delicate flies are usually considered to be the spring creek lures of choice. Unlike the big gaudy flies used on the brawling rivers of the West, the attractor flies we use are the smaller sizes (#14–18). We like attractors such as a fluorescent green-bodied Adams, a Royal Coachman Trude, or a rubber-legged, yellow-bodied pattern called the Madam X. In other words, try something different that gets the trout's attention. We're not recommending that you fish blind, or try to cover vast reaches of water. Fish to specific holding areas, such as downed logs or undercut banks. More than a few trout can't resist the attraction of that appealing conglomeration of feather, thread, and steel. We'll never forget one 25-inch brown with a taste for attractors. We caught that southwestern Wisconsin trophy three times in one season—every time on a Madam X.

Another tactic not generally associated with delicate spring creek fishing is to use large flies such as Leeches, Sculpins, and Woolly Buggers (#4–8). Leeches, sculpins, and crayfish are abundant in all our spring creeks, so imitations of them should be logical choices. Trout are predators, and these patterns seem to bring out the trout's instinct to attack viciously. Cast to specific locations—the deeper parts of the stream, or snags in the water. Hold on! The strikes can be quite explosive. But the strikes also can be subtle, so be alert. Nobody is better at teasing up big, finicky fish than spring creek expert Tom Wendelburg. We've seen Wendelburg cast a big Strip Leech into a deep pool, pause to light a cigarette, and then start twitching the big lure to the surface, slowly and deliberately. While he talks, he teases the fish up and into his net. Similarly, we use something nicknamed the "trash" technique. Leeches and Woolly Buggers are fished to upstream trash—deadfalls, snags, and the like. We view this as playing the odds. If you cast your fly to enough of this good fish-holding cover, a certain percentage of the fish residing there will strike. We usually fish upstream, and black seems to be the most productive fly color. You should also use a heavier tippet—3X or 4X.

Night Fishing

Are you a trophy hunter? Then we recommend night fishing. Brown trout, the predominant trout in Wisconsin's spring creeks, are known for their propensity to feed under cover of darkness. That usually means there will be a few lunkers prowling about at night on the middle and lower portions of our spring creeks.

In selecting your place to fish, pick a reach you've fished during the day so you're well acquainted with it. Remember that big fish will usually take up residence near an undercut bank, log jam, or snag with a good feeding area nearby—a pool or riffle, for example. It pays to have a specific strategy for each area or pool you plan to fish. Pinpoint specific holding cover and cast with well-planned presentations to avoid disturbing the fish. A cautionary note about wading. There aren't many treacherous riffles and rapids to deal with on our Wisconsin spring creeks, but there are pools that will be over your head. Silty or clay bottoms require extra caution. A moonless night can cause confusion, even in a well-known stretch of water. Knowing the area you're fishing will ensure that the mysterious excitement of night fishing does not turn into a dangerous dunking.

For choice of flies, keep one thing in mind: move water with your fly. Generally, these flies should be large (#4–8). Large streamers such as Muddler Minnows are frequently used. Big-bodied surface flies work well; we like a mouse pattern made out of deer hair. One of our fishing friends even uses big bass poppers at night with a fair degree of success. We recommend casting to known sheltering lies and the larger pools, but don't forget the shallows. At night big fish leave their daytime shelters and cruise the shallows in search of minnows and other midnight snacks.

During night-time expeditions, use heavier tackle than you would during the day. A 6-weight rod 8 to 9 feet in length would be excellent for most spring creeks. The leader can be relatively short; approximately 6 feet long with a 2X or 3X tippet. You also want to use a net to make sure of landing your trophy.

Wisconsin's spring creeks offer endless variety. Enjoy the challenge these little gems offer; you won't always be successful, but that's part of the fun. We've outlined some of the tactics that we've found work on Wisconsin spring creeks, but there are many more, the real skill in angling is to adapt these techniques to meet the individual challenge each spring creek presents. Above all, treat these streams with respect. They are a rare and threatened breed of trout stream, and in order to survive, they'll need the care and love of anglers who appreciate their relatively rare and special nature.

MAGIC IN THE DARK: FISHING THE HEX HATCH

Your introduction to fishing the fabled Hex hatch can be quite rude. Imagine being dropped off in the early evening next to a bridge over a central Wisconsin stream. You slog through the swamps and slash through the tag alder to get to the appointed spot. You wait and wait while the mosquitoes prick your now sweaty skin. Then you fish awkwardly to sounds of fish feeding in the eerie night, and eventually return to the bridge, sweating, cussing, and embarrassed, to disclose that you caught only one 6-inch trout. You vow this will be the first and last attempt at fishing the Hex hatch.

Now imagine that it's a dozen years later. You're again waist-deep in another central Wisconsin stream. You and patient red-winged blackbirds are awaiting the mystical moment. Whip-poor-wills are singing in the distance, and the sun is sinking magically over the horizon. This time your wait is filled with excitement and anticipation. Finally a few Hex duns emerge, but an hour later it looks as though there will be no hatch tonight. While you're pondering whether to leave, something whizzes by your head. And then another. Hex spinners! Within minutes the air is filled with these giant insects winging their way upstream, seeking out that destined reach of stream for their final act of egg-laying. The hummmmm of this mayfly airforce increases to a loud drone, reminding you of the electric buzz one sometimes hears under power lines. Soon Hex spinners are struggling, twitching, or floating motionless on every square foot of stream—perhaps ten to the square foot. And fish are responding to this conveyor-belt buffet, gorging along countless feeding lanes. Explosive fishing ensues. Euphoria!

Yes, we're addicted. We average some thirty nights a year chasing the Hex hatch as it moves north across Wisconsin. And now we understand the lore, the stories, the lies, and the near-insanity that characterize this cult-like quest. But be forewarned: fishing the *Hexagenia* hatch is not for everybody—unless you enjoy being assaulted by mosquitoes, barraged by bats and muskrats, mired in what must surely be quicksand, getting snagged in brush, and being alone in the pitch black night of the wilds. It's definitely an acquired taste. But we believe that no trout angler in Wisconsin should miss trying this special kind of angling. While Michigan and other Great Lakes and midwestern states are well known for their Hex fishing, Wisconsin takes a back seat to none.

The Insect

In North America, the *Hexagenia* genus is the largest insect of the mayflies. While the scientific community recognizes several species of *Hexagenia,* for our purposes the distinctions are largely academic, and we'll deal with the insect as a single group. In angling lore and literature, the insect goes by many names, the worst and most widespread misnomer being the Michigan Caddis. But just mention the Giant Yellow Mayfly or the Hex, and veteran trout anglers will tune in. The most striking characteristic of the Hex is its size, with bodies more than 1.5 inches long and wingspreads exceeding 2 inches.

Like other mayflies, the Hex has a life cycle without a pupal stage, maturing from egg to nymph to winged adult. *Hexagenia* is one of a group of burrowing mayflies, adapted to living in soft, silty, muddy, detritus-laden, and often marly stream bottoms. The three-tailed nymphs live in U-shaped burrows dug up to 6 inches into the bottom mud. They live and grow in their burrows, going through multiple molts of their outer skeletons over what generally is a

A magnificent Hexagenia *spinner headed for egg-laying. Photo by Steve Born.*

two-year period. The nymphs have prominent gills along the sides of their abdomens, and swim by undulating their bodies. We often observe the numerous small holes made in streamside banks by these nymphs, and look forward to their coming out party.

When they hatch, the Hex nymphs wiggle to the surface film, struggling to emerge from their shucks. This process can take several minutes and can be watched by the observant angler, either by capturing an emerging nymph or by watching the transformation take place on partially exposed mud banks. The duns are glorious insects, with prominently veined wings and thick bodies painted in colors ranging from pale cream to yellow to almost chartreuse. The two-tailed duns are intent on drying their wings, getting off the water (often after a clumsy, fluttering set of trial take-offs), and out of the air into the safety of nearby vegetation. The trout, birds, and bats, of course, have another fate in mind for these giant mayflies, and the predator-prey contest is a spectacle to watch, often distracting the angler from fishing.

After one to three days in streamside trees and bushes—or on buildings, bridges, and roofs—the Hex dun (technically the subimago stage) crawls out of its skin one last time, turning into a glassy-winged beauty (the spinner or imago stage) with a bright-colored body and long tails. Now that it is sexually mature the only thing left on the Hex agenda is procreation, and it closes off its life cycle by mating and then returning to the water for its amazing, egg-laying spinner falls.

The number of Hex nymphs in a stream, river, or lake can be staggering. Biologists say that up to a million nymphs per acre are possible in very favorable habitats, such as certain reaches of the Mississippi River. That's why highway crews in river towns like La Crosse and Prairie du Chien report having to plow slippery layers of *Hexagenia* off bridges, so don't be surprised by the scale of emergences and blanketing spinner falls. On the other hand, either event can be quite spotty, and the geographic distribution can be incredibly irregular. On both the Mecan River and Black Earth Creek, we've enjoyed spectacular Hex fishing in one spot, while 100 yards up- or downstream there were no Hexes at all. Hatches typically begin at dusk and last from several minutes to one or two hours. On occasion, there will be pulses of insects, one hatch following another, and the angler has to decide how late a night is worthwhile. The emergence may be followed by a spinner fall, but simultaneous hatches and spinner falls are common, and present a real challenge to the angler. Although Hex fishing is normally associated with hot, muggy evenings, we've also fished hatches on cool, windy nights, after major storms, and, although infrequently, during overcast afternoons. In short, there simply is no formula for assuring that the Hex will happen. You just have to be there to know.

Hexagenia emergences typically start in very early June in southern and central Wisconsin, and from middle and late June to mid July in the North Country rivers. But nature determines the ultimate timing, and climatic factors can significantly alter hatch periods. The guessing game of when the Hex will start to emerge on any given stream is sort of a parlor game for trout anglers. We've discovered no sure-fire indicator, but old-timers report that the Hex starts hatching when the peonies are blooming in their backyards. Another often-repeated bit of folk wisdom: the Hex hatch doesn't really get going until the June bugs have run their course. We've seen decent Hex hatches on the lakes of Sylvania in Michigan's Upper Peninsula during August, with small-mouth bass gorging themselves. We've encountered spotty and remnant Hex hatches on streams where the emergence presumably was long over. And of course, there are good and bad Hex years, reflecting the variability of nature.

Fishing the Hatch

Fishing the legendary Hex hatch can only be compared to fishing the salmonfly hatches in the West, or the fabled Green Drake hatches in the East. All three have in common giant flies, massive hatches and spinner falls, and the added dimension of fishing after the sun has set. These factors set the stage for memorable trout angling. Wisconsin is blessed with many classic Hex waters—slowly meandering silt-bottomed rivers and streams with undercut banks, copious deadfalls, overhanging vegetation, and other cover. Often they flow through extensive wetlands, with banks of black silt and mud that are ideal habitat for the Hex nymphs. Among the many rivers and streams you might want to consider adding to your June–July angling calendar are Mt. Vernon Creek, Black Earth Creek, the Mecan, Willow, Pine, White (West Branch), Plover, Prairie, and Tomorrow-Waupaca rivers in the southern and central parts of the state, and farther north, the Namekagon, White (Ashland-Bayfield counties), Bois Brule, Iron, and Clam rivers. In addition, many of the small impoundments on trout streams, such as the Wild Rose millpond on the Pine River, can offer some marvelous still-water fishing during the Hex hatch.

Once the hatch is under way, it generally moves upstream. This is an irregular progression at best, however, and the distribution of hatches and spinner falls is highly variable. Some anglers find the earlier days of the hatch to be the best fishing—less selective, less cautious, and more voracious feeding on the part of the trout. We've noted that it sometimes takes a few days after the beginning of the hatch season for the fish to really focus on the Hex. What is more mystifying to us are those evenings when the Hex hatch out in good numbers for up to an hour, and then drift downstream without a single rising trout. What could possibly explain such fickle behavior? Even more inexplicable are those nights when the trout continue to actively feed on tiny mayflies and midges, ignoring the *Hexagenia* emergers and duns. One Hex insect must have the caloric content of hundreds of the tiny flies; under these conditions, we simply can't understand the trout's choice.

Sound preparation is essential to the enjoyment and successful pursuit of this unique angling experience. Besides your usual fishing gear, make sure you've got two working flashlights of the type that you can attach to your hat or vest, or hold in your mouth while changing flies. We recommend two because one will surely get lost or go dead at a critical moment. Other items on our Hex hatch check list are insect repellent, magnifying glasses such as the Flip-focal to aid you in changing flies, and a compass. We've come to value this latter item, having spent a night or two lost in places like the White River's Bibon Marsh in northern Wisconsin. With Hex fishing, the adventure doesn't end when the fishing is over, but when you get safely back to your car.

Before you go fishing, you need to decide what flies to carry. There are hundreds of patterns that have been concocted by innovative fly-tiers to imitate the Hex, and you can get tried-and-true local patterns at your area fly shops. Traditional patterns like a #6 or #8 White Wulff or Humpy, or long-time reliables like the Hart Washer and deer-hair-body Mayfly, are still effective flies. A variety of hairwing flies such as the Comparadun, Deer Hair Bulletheads, and parachute-style flies have joined traditionally hackled Hex imitations. Tiers have been substituting closed-cell foam for traditional dubbing to enhance the floatability of dry flies. Foam, deer hair, and other materials have been used to construct extended bodies to better imitate the *Hexagenia*. These flies present realistic silhouettes in the water, but we've observed that overly stiff, extended bodies seem to impair hooking efficiency.

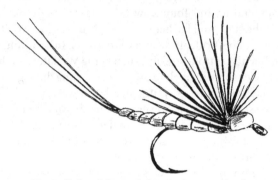

Hex Bullethead (Extended Body Comparadum)

There are numerous specific Hex nymph patterns, although our choice would be an impressionistic fly such as Gary Borger's Strip Nymph, or a weighted Woolly Bugger. Because the Hex nymphs often go through a lengthy struggle to shed their nymphal shuck, emerger patterns can be particularly effective early in the hatch. These patterns range from standard emergers with pared-down wings, to flies with imitative shucks of poly yarn, feathers, or Zelon. We've had great success with an emerger patterned after Quigley's Cripple. It relies on a foam thorax and collar hackle to float buoyantly, while the abdomen and shuck of ostrich herl or marabou hang vertically in the water. Some anglers have a single favorite fly, and use only variations of it. Our late Hex fishing friend Larry Meicher from Cottage Grove, known as the Pass Lake Kid because of his devotion to that fly, fashioned his own version of the Hex emerger in black and white. Its success causes us to ponder the importance of fly color, at least for this hatch. These emergers are fished in the film, and when given small twitches, mimic a dun escaping its nymphal case. Whether emergers or duns, or for that matter spinner imitations, we agree with Wisconsin expert Tom Wendelburg, who is constantly modifying his assortment of patterns in an effort to show the fish something a little different. In heavily fished waters the fish see a lot of imitations, and seemingly minor adjustments in pattern color or body profile can help distinguish your fly.

Now let's go fishing. We arrive at the stream before dusk, and need to figure out our beat for the evening. If we're not familiar with the water we intend to fish, we'll scout the stretch while it's still light; better to find out where the deep holes and submerged branches are in advance. Check the streamside vegetation and brush, and figure out casting distances and important landmarks before darkness closes in. For the most part, Hex fishing does not involve long casts—30–40 feet at a maximum, and in some cases we'll be dapping our fly next to snags and bank cover, with little casting at all. The critical step is to plan your evening strategy, mapping out casting lanes and taking every precaution to avoid spending the evening tangled in streamside trees and brush.

Before the onset of the hoped-for hatch, we've got some other fishing options. We could pursue rising trout that might be feeding on Light Cahills, Tiny Blue-Winged Olives, or other mayflies and caddisflies. We've also had some very good pre-Hex fishing using a Hex dry fly, often in a slightly smaller size (#8). Another strategy is to fish a Hex nymph imitation under the water before the hatch. Cast these heavily weighted nymphs up and across the stream, letting the fly drift through the prime lies near undercut banks and deadfalls. An occasional twitch to simulate the undulations of the swimming Hex nymph will often do the trick. A final choice, and the one we see followed by some of our most experienced Hex fishing compatriots, is to select your stream location and find a good spot on the bank to await the hatch. We did mention mosquito repellent, didn't we?

Now we're on the stream, waiting expectantly with the birds. As the sun drops out of sight, the first Hex appears, followed soon by others. The hatch is under way, and if wading is necessary, we slip quietly into the water. Small fish are feeding early on, but we keep our eyes peeled and our ears open for signs of bigger fish. We've attached a dun imitation to our leader, and are carefully moving into position to make our cast to a rising trout. Feeding intensity has increased now, and it's important to pick a specific feeding fish to pursue, rather than flailing away at every feeding trout we see. Even in the middle of a Hex feeding frenzy, trout generally stay in their feeding lanes or protected lies, feeding rhythmically, and they will rarely succumb to a poorly presented fly. So we work on our target fish, putting several drag-free drifts over its feeding location. A twitch or two to emulate the struggling mayfly should be tried just as the fly enters the trout's vision. By now we're either fast to a fighting trout or we're ready to change flies, moving to a smaller size or a different pattern.

We're hearing occasional "slurps" from big fish, back under some tag alder snags. If we can shoot our cast under the overhanging vegetation and get even a short drift, our chances for a really memorable fish increase dramatically. Another approach is to reach out with our fly rod towards the rising fish and drop the fly on the water. Either technique can bring explosive rises from good fish, but of course, hooking, fighting, and landing them in such cramped quarters is a low percentage undertaking.

It's difficult to see anything, but the sound and tempo of rising fish seems to have changed. We shine our flashlight on the water, off to the side so as not to scare the trout, and see a parade of Hex spinners flush in the film. Some are writhing and the movement brings forth the occasional savage sounds of feeding fish, but most of the spinners are lying immobile with their glassy wings extended. It's not always apparent when fish are taking spinners, and the Hex angler must watch closely. To capitalize on this final phase of the Hex's life cycle, we must immediately change to a spinner imitation. A spent-wing pattern of deer or elk hair, poly yarn, or feathers is now the key to success. Again, there are innumerable Hex spinner patterns to choose from. We like Parachute Spinners and other extended-body imitations with Zelon, deer hair, and hackle wings. Accurate, drag-free presentations are essential; downstream casts, where we can position the fly in the fish's feeding lane, are effective if circumstances allow. Frequently, the spinner fall is so dense that our imitation stands little chance of being singled out by the trout. One successful tactic we've used on such occasions is to tie on a large spun-deer-hair fly or an oversized (#4) Madam X, to differentiate the prey we're offering from the thousands of naturals floating past the trout's eyes.

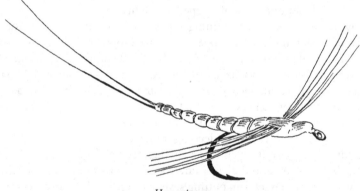

Hex spinner

By now we've landed a few, missed some others, and broken off one lunker who took our spinner and immediately wrapped the line around a submerged log. The hatch and spinner fall appear to be over. Rather than sit in the swamp for a few hours and see if there might be any later activity, good judgment prevails and we climb out of the stream and head towards the car and a cold drink.

Before ending this section we want to reflect briefly on tackle for Hex fishing. A 5- to 7-weight rod is ideal, although in recent years we've found ourselves using lighter-weight rods. They allow us to fish some of the smaller fly hatches early in the evening, and with the faster action of today's graphite rods, they still have sufficient strength to punch out the big Hex flies. Local fishing conditions will influence your desired rod length, but rods in the 7–9-foot range are the norm. We use a knotless 7.5- or 9-foot leader tapered to 3X. Tippets in 2X to 4X sizes can be added as the leader gets cut back with use, or to fit particular fishing conditions. Leaders must be heavy enough to turn over the big flies, to insure a drag-free drift, and to move big trout from heavy cover. A net makes it easier to handle your fish, making sure the trophy trout of the season is more than just another fish story. You'll find lots of clues in succeeding chapters about where to try your hand at this spectacular hatch. Don't miss the opportunity—this is one hatch where anglers' expectations and reality can become one.

BATTLING BIG SALMONIDS IN THE GREAT LAKES TRIBUTARIES

First, there were the native lake trout. Then came the commercial anglers and sea lampreys that killed the lake trout. Then came an explosion in the number of alewives because they were no longer preyed on by lake trout. And finally, there came massive populations of Pacific salmon, stocked in part to keep small-but-troublesome forage fish, like the alewife, in check. The Great Lakes haven't been the same since.

Many midwestern anglers have heard stories of fishing success on the big lakes, but the thrill of fishing the tributaries for lake-run salmonids is less well-known. While the focus of such fishing is usually the Pacific Northwest, Wisconsin is also a place where wading stream anglers can tie into these tackle-testing monsters. We've caught our share of them, but few can match the experience of Reedsburg musician and Great Lakes fly-fishing pioneer John Beth. Beth, also a freelance writer, captures the essence of this fishing in his short story, *Indian Summer Salmon*. Beth has just caught a 40-inch king salmon and is preparing to return the beautiful male fish to an unidentified Great Lakes tributary: "Stooping to lay the salmon in a shallow run, I saw his eye instinctively roll toward the water as the dry leaves of autumn eddied around him. This great fish would soon spawn and die, predestined, mysteriously, as would all of the river's salmon. Somewhere downstream his bones would bleach on a shallow riffle in December, other animals having feasted on his flesh, drawing life from the king salmon's death . . . The big male swam away, slowly, regaining power necessary for the run through the rapids and to once again join his mate. He was gone, but the best part of him remained in my heart and memory. I contemplated his final, sad expression before he returned to his river, his home, his grave. He knew."

With John Beth's help we've also discovered the mysteries and joys of this brand of midwestern fishing, which is readily available most of the year along Wisconsin's 620-mile coastline. One memory that stays with us is a trip to a little tributary of the Pigeon River, near Sheboygan. We spent most of a cold winter day hooking salmon and then running up- and downstream, over dead-falls and through brush, trying to land the big fish. It was fun, but our landing ratio left a lot to be desired. On the Manitowoc River, we have waded after silvery salmon in a gorge shrouded by red-tinged maples. Catching fish somehow became secondary to taking snapshots. Sometimes we've found ourselves backed up against a dam in less aesthetically pleasing locations, but at such a place on the West Twin River at Shoto, we've adjourned for refreshment at a lovely supper club to watch other anglers trying their luck in the dark, turbulent pool below the spillway. We've even ended up on golf courses in pursuit of these giant salmonids. While golfers squeezed in their final rounds of the year at places like Blackwolf Run on the Sheboygan River or the Racine Country Club on the Root River, we were casting to sweeping bends in the rivers, hoping for fish instead of birdies. So far, golfers and anglers have co-existed without major incident. No matter the location, the angler can always find a certain elemental escape. As veteran Great Lakes guide Bob Nasby told an interviewer: "The rivers talk to you."

Although many people quit trout fishing from the September 30 close until the early March opening of the catch-and-release season, thousands of anglers head to Wisconsin's coastal waters and Great Lakes tributaries. Some waters are open all year. Check the Wisconsin fishing regulations to make sure of the rules governing the place you plan to fish and the fish you plan to catch, and to find out what trout and salmon stamps may be required in addition to your license. Timing is everything, so if you miss a major run you have to hunt for and cast persistently to strays.

Even for those who live away from the coastal waters such excursions are worth the trip—especially during those months when cabin fever takes hold and inland stream fishing is closed. Many angling tourists, if boatless, sign up for a charter boat and troll the bays where migrating fish congregate before spectacular runs up the tributaries. More than 200 charter operators ply the Great Lakes, helping more than 40,000 anglers take some 80,000 fish a year. One of the state's largest charter fleets sails out of Algoma, on the northern Lake Michigan coast. Many other anglers use their own boats to troll for big fish, and records continue to be set.

It's fun and productive to fish the big lakes from boats, but we, along with many other anglers, wait for the runs and try to catch the fish as they head

Bill Engber holding a trophy steelhead from southeast Wisconsin's Pigeon River. Photo by Hunter Dorn.

A fine April Brule River steelhead that ate a pheasant tail nymph. Photo by Mark Maffitt.

97

toward their tributary spawning grounds in the spring and fall. Most of the spawning runs are in the fall and it takes a hardy and dedicated stream angler to wade the cold waters of our Great Lakes tributaries in search of giant salmonids. Some fish partial to summer and spring runs have been planted also. Wisconsin Department of Natural Resources records indicate that some fifty Michigan and Superior tributaries and bays in Wisconsin harbor migrating salmon or trout sometime during the year. We stream anglers, armed with heavy-duty equipment, are after fish that dwarf their inland cousins. Steelhead, the fighting, leaping rainbow trout that have been stocked in the Great Lakes since the late 1800s, weigh up to 16 pounds, and chinook salmon, nicknamed the "king," can weigh over 40 pounds. Other stream migrators are coho salmon, or silvers, and lake-run brook and brown trout. The native lake trout—on its way back in Lake Superior after decades of intensive management efforts—spawns in deep water or near-shore waters of the lakes, so it's not usually a quarry of the stream fisher, but the restoration of these native trout is one of the great fisheries successes. Lake trout are now self-sustaining off the Bayfield Peninsula's Apostle Islands, and stocking has been halted in most of the lake.

The timing of the migrating trout runs is triggered by favorable water temperatures and water levels; such conditions usually follow rains. The optimum temperatures appear to be between 40 and 55 degrees. Pacific salmon are fall runners, as are lake-run brown and brook trout. Wild steelhead, such as the Bois Brule River strain, are spring spawners, but the three main strains of steelhead rainbows stocked in Wisconsin—Skamania, Chambers Creek, and Ganaraska River—have varying schedules. The Skamania steelhead migrate from June through late fall and spawn from mid-December through mid-March; the Chambers Creek from late October through mid-March with peak spawning in March; and the Ganaraska River migrate and spawn in April.

A lot of fishing methods, using either spin-casting or fly-fishing tackle, will work. If you hook up—watch out! These lake-run fish are big and strong; they'll hit the lure with a jolt and peel off your line in a minute. It's the closest thing to saltwater fishing in middle America, and it's available in some rather nontraditional places—like inside the city limits of Milwaukee. In fact, fish run up the Milwaukee River all the way into Ozaukee County now that they can get past the old North Avenue Dam.

Since Pacific salmon die during spawning, we occasionally eat our catch with no guilt feelings. We must tell you, though, that toxic chemicals that have found their way into the lake work their way up the food chain and into the fat of these big migrating salmon, steelhead, and other trout. The state issues health advisories that you should read before eating a lot of this tasty fish.

The story of how these fish came to the Great Lakes is a fascinating one. The commercial fishery crashed in the forties and fifties because of a combination of overfishing, deterioration of spawning habitat, and invasions of exotic species, including the sea lamprey, alewife, and rainbow smelt. During the sixties, when alewife populations were peaking, periodic die-offs turned beaches into squishy, smelly messes. When they weren't polluting beaches, the alewives drove out other species and clogged industrial and municipal water pipes. Scientists, looking for a natural predator, focused on salmon and steelhead— migrating fish that swim part of their lives in saltwater seas and part of their lives in freshwater tributaries. In 1963, the Wisconsin Department of Natural Resources stocked 9,000 rainbow steelhead in several Door County tributaries to control alewives and to boost a sagging sports fishery. The initial stocking was successful, and the experiment expanded. Michigan began massive stockings of coho salmon in 1966; Wisconsin and the other Great Lakes states followed, setting off what Great Lakes historians call "coho fever." By 1995, tens of millions of salmonids had been stocked in Lakes Superior and Michigan. In 1995 alone, Wisconsin stocked more than 4.7 million Great Lakes trout and salmon in the two big lakes; hundreds of thousands of these stocked fish are caught each year.

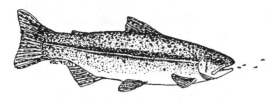

Keeping the fish population balanced is a big effort that requires the use of modern egg-collection facilities and hatcheries. Usually, young fish are planted in the streams or in the mouths of streams that feed into the lakes, imprinting them with the scent of their home river (as shown in the pioneering research done by UW–Madison's Arthur Hasler). The fish go into the big lakes and often feed on the alewife, a silvery-blue sardine-like fish that swept into the Great Lakes via the St. Lawrence Seaway in the forties and fifties. The alewife population is now in check, thanks to the voracious appetite of these migrating salmonids. After several years of feeding and growing in the big lakes (how many years depends on the species), the big salmonids that have survived go back to the tributaries they knew as youths to spawn. This is when they stage spectacular runs, hurdling rocky riffles and low falls until they reach their spawning grounds—unless they are stopped by a dam. If they can't reach their spawning grounds and are not stripped of their eggs at a weir, they die still carrying their eggs. Pacific salmon die after spawning in any case, but steelhead survive and may spawn two or three times during a lifetime. Brown and brook trout can also spawn more than once, but resource managers doubt that many of the multiple spawners make it back out into the lakes, because of fishing pressure.

The migrating salmonids have adapted amazingly well to all-freshwater conditions, but natural reproduction is still the exception, not the rule. Natural reproduction sometimes occurs in the Lake Superior tributaries, but stocking is needed to augment the population. In Lake Michigan streams, few if any of these naturally laid eggs survive because of warm water, and because silt buries the gravel spawning beds, or redds, that are so important to the process.

Along the way upstream, fish are stripped of eggs and milt at several Wisconsin locations. You can watch migrating fish at these spots, which include the Root River in southeastern Racine County, and the Kewaunee River on the lower Door Peninsula. The eggs are then taken to Wisconsin hatcheries that keep the fishery going. In addition to federal stocking efforts, most of the state's seventeen hatcheries produce Great Lakes stockers. Eggs are fertilized under controlled conditions and grown into young salmonids. Chinook stocking strategy established in late 2013 shows the myriad of factors at work for fish biologists. Research showed that where the highly mobile Chinook are stocked has a greater effect on fishing in the fall than in the spring or summer. Research suggested that more than half of the chinook salmon in Lake Michigan are wild and that chinook swim all over Lake Michigan during the spring and summer. That means stocking plays a much more important role in determining where fish are caught in Wisconsin in the fall, with the bulk of fish returning on their spawning runs to streams where they were stocked. "We focused our strategy on striking a balance between providing opportunities along the coast in the fall and responding to public concerns to provide more fish where the angler pressure, harvest and economic impact are the greatest in fall," said Mike Staggs, Wisconsin's fisheries director.

Tributaries are assigned priorities for stocking depending upon depth, flow, mouth opening, and pollution levels. These young fish are released either in the stream or at the mouth of the stream, allowing them to get a taste of their home water before venturing out into the big lake for years of feeding and growth. They'll travel tens of miles away from their place of stocking, and sometimes further—WDNR biologists say some fish have been recorded traveling up to 600 miles. Coho return the fastest, after about two years in the lake; chinook take two or three years to mature; and the steelhead's return varies depending upon the strain but is usually between two and four years. The average steelhead spawner in Wisconsin varies from three years of age to six.

While stocking keeps the sports fishery going, other researchers are trying to revive the original migrating Lake Superior brook trout, the native coaster brookie that helped make Bois Brule River country a legendary fishing destination. These cousins to the speckled trout that inhabit many inland streams live part of their lives in Lake Superior, and make fall spawning runs up the Superior tributaries. Until the late 1800s they were the dominant near-shore indigenous fish of Lake Superior; now they are close to extinction. But imaginative stocking efforts are underway to augment remnant stocks believed to remain in the wild Apostle Islands off Wisconsin's Bayfield Peninsula, and in selected spots along Michigan's Upper Peninsula. Federal, state, and tribal officials have been cooperating to plant eggs, fry, and fingerlings drawn from the Nipigon River (Ontario) strain of coaster brookies. It's a big challenge, however. As the U.S. Fish and Wildlife Service's Lee Newman said, referring to man's effect since the coaster's prosperous days: "It's not the same lake."

Lakes Superior and Michigan represent some of the nation's most vexing natural resources management challenges. They are big (Lake Superior is the largest freshwater lake in the world, with a maximum depth of 1,399 feet; and Lake Michigan is the sixth-largest, with a maximum depth of 923 feet); they are complicated ecosystems filled with exotic species that have exploited niches in the system; they are plagued by continuing toxic pollution and leftover sediment pollution; and they harbor diseases that periodically undermine man's best fish-management efforts. And there's always the specter of another biological-ecological surprise looming down the road; some even worry that an old nemesis, the lamprey, could return in great numbers. In a Great Lakes—wide program, lamprey populations have been controlled for decades through the use of barriers (such as on northwestern Wisconsin's Bois Brule) and a chemical that kills lamprey larvae in streams where they spawn. But lampreys are still present in deep, open water, and their populations could spiral again if a resistant strain develops, or if government budget constraints cause cutbacks in the use of the lampricide. "The only thing that's predictable," says Sea Grant Institute fisheries specialist Cliff Kraft, "is probably that something strange and bizarre is going to hit the system one more time." But Kraft and others who watch the effects of alien species (the zebra mussel is one example) say the ongoing experiment of stocking Pacific salmon, steelhead, and other nonnative trout species in Lakes Michigan and Superior has been a success. The population of alewives is under control, and a great sports fishery is thriving.

Yes, there have been setbacks. The sports fishery still is largely "put-grow-and-take" because of stream siltation, water temperature, and other factors, and Lake Michigan, which lost its native lake trout populations by the mid-fifties, has seen no evidence of lake trout reproduction. But the stocking effort is paying for itself, and making a profit when spin-off economic development is taken into account. In a system that has a long history of unpleasant consequences from accidentally and intentionally introduced exotics, it's nice to know that introducing Pacific sports fish has had few negative effects on the environment. "All in all it has been good for the native fish," Kraft says.

And good for guides, charter boat captains, restaurateurs, hotel-motel operators, and tourist outlets, too. The recovery of the Great Lakes sports fishery has been a linchpin for some handsome redevelopment efforts, especially in factory towns along the Lake Michigan coastline. The manufacturing city of Kenosha, once called Southport, has a new marina from which charter boats sail. A little farther north, along Racine's redeveloped waterfront, a giant fishing contest called Salmon-a-Rama has been held each July. Between Racine and the rugged Door Peninsula is the revitalized maritime community of Two Rivers, where the ice cream sundae was born in 1881; now the cherry on top is fine fishing. This commercial port and sports fishing center also boasts Rogers Street Fishing Village, which features historical displays such as a fishing tug and a restored lighthouse. Nearby Manitowoc has several attractions, including a fine maritime museum where you can see a World War II submarine built at the local shipyards. You can also board a car ferry for Ludington, Michigan; it's said to be the only steam car ferry sailing the Great Lakes. While maritime history has been preserved, there's also been attention given to saving the vital wetlands that filter water going to the big lakes, which are a source of drinking water for many communities. One of the government programs helping to educate people about these wetlands is the state Coastal Management Program, begun in 1978.

The biggest beneficiaries of the Great Lakes' recovery, of course, are we anglers. We can find genuine salmon and steelhead fishing without boarding an airplane. Try it! We think you'll like it. But if you haven't fished the coasts, you need to be aware that fishing this way requires heavy equipment and a willingness to try different methods. There are many ways to angle for Great Lakes fish. Trolling from a boat designed to handle the capricious weather encountered on the big lakes is the most popular way to catch salmon and trout. You can also fish from a pier, from a breakwater, from shore, or even from a float tube (but you'd better know what you're doing). Finally, there's our preferred method, fishing the streams that flow into the big lakes.

Great Lakes fishing isn't the focus of our book, but we can pass along some basics. John Beth, expert Great Lakes angler, often uses what he calls the "spot and plot" strategy. When using this stalking method, you spot fish without letting them see you first, then plot a strategy to drift a fly to them without being seen. "'Spot and plot' is a little like hunting, and 90 percent of the fish you catch will be ones you see and fish to," Beth writes. "Of course, in the large rivers water becomes very turbid during peak spring runoff while the steelhead run is on. Then it's either fish blind until clarity improves or stick with the small, clear streams." Beth prowls the water in the early morning, trying to spot fish holding still in the current. "The main talent," he says, "is to remain unnoticed."

Here are some basics that have helped us catch Great Lakes fish:

- **Work on getting good information. Establish contacts that will tell you when the rivers are ready for prime runs, so you maximize your outings. The Internet is becoming a great way to get such information.**

- Where to fish? Remember, aside from the Bois Brule and some other Lake Superior tributaries, Lake Michigan runs are wholly dependent upon stocking, so look to those streams that get the most fish. The Root and Kewaunee rivers are designated brood streams with weirs, so they are obvious choices. The Root is an urban fishery, packed with anglers and migrating fish in the 6 miles from its mouth to Horlick Dam. The Kewaunee, a primary brood river for steelhead, coho salmon, and Seeforellen strain brown trout, also has higher stocking quotas to assure adequate returns. The less-crowded Kewaunee, unique among top-priority tributaries because it has no dam and some limited natural reproduction, has 22 miles of fishable habitat, including its tributaries. Other top Lake Michigan rivers are the Oconto, the Ahnapee, the East and West Twin rivers, the Manitowoc, the Pigeon, and the Sheboygan.

- Look for sections of the river where migrating avenues are narrow, like riffles. Fish will pool below this section in moderate to slow water before getting on with their journey.

- Also look for redds, or scooped-out gravel spawning beds. In areas with natural reproduction, we don't fish for females on the redds because we don't want to interfere with the egg-laying process. Instead, look for the males positioning themselves downstream.

- Don't forget to explore the feeder streams to lake tributaries, but be aware that the tight quarters make it hard to cast and land fish.

- Don't ignore cover. Migrating fish, like all trout, seem to prefer dark holes, undercuts, back-of-the-boulder scoops, and logside lairs. Avoid fishing extremely rapid water; they'll only move into that when making their next energy-draining run upstream. Look for resting fish in channels of moderately flowing water, or in the slicks right above a stretch of rapids.

- Wear a brimmed hat and polarized sunglasses to help you spot fish.

- Be patient. If migrating fish feed (which is subject to some debate), they don't eat much. They're finicky, to say the least, and probably strike out of instinct or aggression. If you spot a group of fish in a pool below a set of riffles, stay with them. Sometimes you won't be able to see any but know from experience that a piece of water holds fish; repeatedly bounce your bait or lure deep through these sections. Do it over and over. You won't be likely to have a three-fish day on your first outing. Experience breeds success.

- Eliminate slack so you can feel the sometimes "soft" take. One technique used to probe for fish in runs is to fish with a short line hanging as vertically as possible, using a bright strike indicator. Keep your eye on the strike indicator.

- To cover a lot of water, use the across-and-downstream method of casting, using increasingly longer casts. Watch for strikes as the lure swings—especially at the end of the swing. For this method, a sink-tip line may work best.

- Try to fish early, at dawn's first light. You're more likely to be casting to fresh fish that have just come from the lake, and they seem to be less finicky. You are also less likely to spook the fish.

- Prepare to land the fish before you hook it. Before you wade into a precarious location, figure out how and where you'll fight and land a big fish. It usually requires some fast footwork, so don't get in a tough spot. Also wear felt-soled wading boots and insulated chest waders with a wading belt; cold water makes falling in even more dangerous.

Equipment/Tackle

If you're spin-casting for these big migrating trout and salmon

---

- **Rods:** 7- to 10-foot-long graphite.
- **Reels:** Heavy-duty spinning or bait-casting.
- **Line:** 6- to 10-pound monofilament. Check knots, swivels, and line often, because you won't get a second chance.
- **Lures or baits:** Plugs, spoons, jigs, and spinners. Popular brand names include Flatfish, Rapalas, Mepps, Cleos, Rebels, Bombers, and Shad Raps.

    A dependable favorite is a spawn bag, a sack of mesh netting filled with fish eggs. Use split shot or other sinkers to get the bait near the fish.

    Note: Some expert anglers use the spawn bag with a heavy-duty fiberglass fly rod and a monofilament-filled fly or spinning reel.

(continued)

If you're fly-casting

- **Rods:** 8.5- to 9.5-foot long.
- **Reels:** Multiplying reels that can hold at least 100 feet of backing are preferred by the regulars, but single-action reels with a dependable drag will work in most situations.
- **Line:** 30 yards of 8- or 9-weight floating lines with sink tip (optional); 6–10 pound tippets on 6–9-foot leaders for most situations. You'll have to vary these according to water conditions and whether you're fishing for leader-shy steelhead.
- **Fly patterns:**
  Beth's Best Bet (#4–12) tied with orange Glo-Bug yarn, gold chenille tinsel, and black saddle hackle.
  Single or double yarn egg imitations in bright colors such as orange, red, or chartreuse.
  Leech patterns in white, black, purple, or the bright colors above.
  Woolly Bugger patterns in the same colors. A combination called the egg-sucking leech is a popular fly.
  Bright-colored streamers with sparkling synthetics such as "flash-a-bou."
  Big mayfly, caddis, or stonefly nymphs. For a generic match, try a big Hare's Ear, sizes #6–10.
  Any western or Alaskan steelhead pattern.

Of all the fly patterns we've listed here, most fly-fishers use the yarn egg. Why? It's easy to tie, so if you lose one, it's not a big deal; it's also very productive. Simply put, these fish are attracted to fish eggs and their imitations. But sometimes it's not so much the fly as how it's presented. We've caught several big laker browns on a Yuk Bug. Don't be afraid to experiment. Another tactic: use the egg fly at the end of your leader with a dropper fly 12–18 inches from the end to double your chances of a hook-up.

These outfits will work for migrating salmonids anywhere in the world. But if you can't afford a trip to Alaska or Oregon soon, you might want to try Wisconsin's coastal waters. You could catch the fish of a lifetime.

6

Looking to the Future

MANY WISCONSIN trout streams have become better places for trout because of good conservation work. But traditional fish management often deals with only part of the management problem, and generally not on a comprehensive watershed basis. Today, integrated environmental ecosystem-based management is being extolled as a new approach to deal with ecologic complexity. These new, watershed-based strategies are a sharp departure from traditional natural resources management approaches, which have been largely reactive, narrowly focused, and disjointed. Former Wisconsin Department of Natural Resources Secretary "Buzz" Besadny believed that "a multidisciplinary, integrated approach to environmental stewardship may represent the most important scientifically and philosophically based management principle yet developed. Indeed, it may be the master key to our continued effectiveness. . . ." In simplified terms, one might think about this emerging strategy as trying to do the right thing, instead of only trying to do one thing right.

The current Wisconsin Department of Natural Resources was first formed in 1967 by merging the old Conservation and Resource Development departments, creating one of the nation's first environmental superagencies. Part of the rationale for the merger involved better coordination of related natural resources programs. It made sense to link an agency responsible for fisheries, forests, and other resources with one responsible for pollution control and environmental planning, and for the most part, the merger was highly successful. Wisconsin is consistently recognized as one of the leading environmental management states. Almost three decades passed before the WDNR was again reorganized in 1996, stressing a need to strengthen its environmental programs through two goals: a watershed-based integrated management focus, plus decentralization and greater local interest-group and community involvement in environmental stewardship. Trout and other

106

A healthy small watershed in the Kickapoo River drainage system. The steep valleys typical of the coulee country present challenges to watershed management. Photo by Harry Peterson.

anglers expressed some dismay that fishery management was being devalued in the agency, and worried that their concerns wouldn't be heard in the new organization. After several years of experience, the WDNR reorganized again. It will take time to assess ongoing changes, but we are convinced that fisheries will always be well served by a focus on watershed-based ecosystem planning and management that address the total health of the environmental system. If the watershed stays healthy, so will the trout.

No organization for managing resources is perfect. But we believe sound science bolsters professional management and its practitioners. The trend toward decentralizing management programs by placing significant responsibilities with local interests in watersheds represents a new wave of "grassroots" stewardship—one that appears to be embraced by fisheries managers in Wisconsin. Such an endeavor takes time. While state and federal regulatory programs have done much to improve and protect the environment, we believe those who live, work, and recreate in a watershed should become more directly responsible for its well-being. Watershed re-

DNR fisheries technician Scott Harpold with a monster brown trout captured during an electrofishing population survey—an essential management tool—on Mt. Vernon Creek. Photo by Kurt Welke.

sources can be protected and strengthened if government really does reach out to local conservation groups, businesses, and individuals to educate for, monitor, and plan conservation efforts.

Of all the changes happening in the world of trout—changes in resources, science, and management approaches—none is more far-reaching than the transformation of the trout-angling community. High-tech and easier-to-use fishing equipment, readily available educational materials, on-the-water instruction, and media hype have, for better or worse, changed trout fishing into an industry. This commercialization is a little hard for some of us to swallow, given that fishing for trout is necessarily a solitary experience. Nevertheless, the recreation and leisure-seeking public is taking to the streams in increasing numbers.

What might we expect from this new cohort of anglers? There are serious research studies that might help us answer this question. Trout anglers have long been the subject of social science researchers attempting to explore and understand the leisure world of trout fishers. Many older readers may remember being interviewed by Robert Jackson, a psychologist at the University of Wisconsin–La Crosse, who spent much of his career trying to characterize the behavior and values of Wisconsin trout anglers. What Bob and other researchers have found is that as skills and experience expand, anglers progress through stages. First they are occasional anglers who want to catch fish; next, active generalists who want to catch lots of fish; then, trophy hunters and technique specialists; and finally they join that exalted category of venerable old-timers—sometimes affectionately referred to as "old farts"—who are able to reflect on the aesthetics, culture, and philosophy of the sport. This body of research indicates that as anglers move through their fishing careers, not only do their angling preferences change, but so do their interests and perspectives regarding conservation: their concerns become habitat management, the environment, and contaminating wild-fish populations with hatchery-bred trout. They also become more receptive to progressive fishing regulations, including catch-and-release.

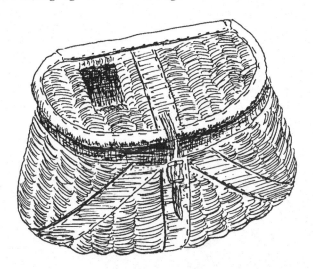

This characterization of the trout angler has been borne out in a major study in southwestern Wisconsin. Anglers surveyed in that study by University of Wisconsin–Extension researchers indicated that the most important attributes of their angling experience included good water quality, the experience of the catch, stream improvements, and the area's aesthetics. Least important was catching fish to eat. This was one of the significant differences in attitude between local and nonlocal anglers, which in some areas might lead to tension. But in general, today's trout anglers are shifting from an emphasis on fish consumption to preservation of the fishery, with increasing concern about the recreational nature of angling and the setting in which it is pursued.

As management approaches evolve and more reliance for long-range environmental stewardship is shifted to those who enjoy trout waters, we truly believe the environmental understanding exhibited by the growing numbers of anglers bodes well for protection of Wisconsin's cold-water resource. We wish you the best of luck and enjoyment on our irreplaceable trout streams. Release one for us.

PART 2

Pursuing the Trout

7

A Regional Guide to Wisconsin Trout Fishing

LOOK AT A trout stream map of Wisconsin and you'll see a distinct pattern. You can see major trout stream complexes along the coast of Lake Superior, along a line extending from Marinette to Madison, along the lower Wisconsin River, and along the Mississippi. In the middle of this circular pattern is a big hole, an area with few trout, that includes Marathon, Taylor, Clark, and Wood counties and much of the bed of the old glacial Lake Wisconsin—an area of heavy soils, some relatively level land, and few springs. What this pattern shows is that a trout fisher could do very well following the general outline of the last glacier to pass this way more than 10,000 years ago. This footprint or terminal moraine, often has the springs, groundwater recharge, and topographic slope necessary to form trout streams.

This method of finding trout isn't foolproof, however. There aren't many trout streams in the glaciated and hilly Kettle Moraine area of southeastern Wisconsin, but there are a bunch in the unglaciated, steep-sloped region of southwestern Wisconsin. So though we were tempted to organize the state using this twisty terminal moraine and the Ice Age footpath that follows it, we decided to divide Wisconsin into two trout-fishing regions—north and south. The dividing line for this north-south division is Highway 10. There is logic to this in addition to simplicity. Highway 10—stretching from Two Rivers in the east to Stevens Point in the middle of the state to Prescott in the west—is a dividing line often used by the Wisconsin Department of Natural Resources for separating natural resource zones. In addition, Highway 10 generally follows the snow line. North of the line you're more likely to find snow in the early winter and late spring, so streams north of this line are in a slightly different climate zone than those south of it. Vegetation changes north of this line, too; maples, aspens, birch, and evergreens dominate. South of the line, conifers are generally scarce and native prairies have given way to farms and grazing land.

The majestic Brule River in northern Wisconsin. Photo by Dick Berge.

More important for the trout fisher, insects emerge a little later up north than they do in southern Wisconsin.

Wisconsin's humid northern climate (with annual rainfall of 30 inches) and geology have resulted in a rich natural endowment of trout streams matched by few states. We have plenty of cold, oxygenated water in this headwaters state, from which waters flow in every direction. While brook trout and lake trout were the only native salmonids in the Badger State (and they're really members of the char family, not trout), brown and rainbow trout have found an environment in which they can thrive. Notwithstanding nature's occasional droughts and extreme winters, trout would get along just fine, were it not for man's activities.

Imposed upon a receptive geologic and soils landscape, these conditions have led to widespread trout stream complexes that range across the glacial terrain of Adams and Marquette counties in the south to Florence and Marinette counties in the northeast; across the northern tier of counties, many of which drain into Lake Superior; and through the hills and valleys of the unglaciated or "driftless" southwestern part of the state—our spring creeks. Trout streams are sparse in the heavy clay soil regions of the north-central part of the state, and in most of southeastern Wisconsin. The small number of natural trout streams in the southeast have been hit hard by development and urbanization, and few remain.

But trout are not forgotten. State officials, a team of students, and highway contractors helped create new trout habit for native brookies in Washington County's Allenton Creek. In the 1990s, road crews actually moved a section of trout stream, a tributary of the Rock River, to allow construction of a U.S. Highway 41 interchange near Slinger.

Our geologic and glacial heritage play a critical role in the formation of trout streams. High-gradient, fast-flowing creeks and rivers abound in those northern and northeastern watersheds where rainfall runs off the hills; such streams are also common in the southwestern part of the state, where the land forms deep valleys, or coulees. The flashiness of stream flow—that is, the rapid response of the streams to surface water runoff—is determined not only by rainfall characteristics and topography, but also by the geology of the watershed. Streams in geologic regions with limited infiltration to groundwater reservoirs are characterized by seasonal flows consisting largely of surface runoff. Heavy rains in these streams cause rapid runoff and short-term changes in stream levels and flows.

In contrast, other streams we profile are recharged by groundwater inflow. These lie in two areas: in the landscapes composed of permeable glacial sands and gravels that cover a substantial part of the state; and in regions underlain by limestone and dolomite bedrock rich in calcium and magnesium, sedimentary rocks deposited in shallow oceans during the Paleozoic Era more than 300 million years ago. Rather than flashy flows responsive to rainfall and runoff, these streams tend to have a more constant flow.

Knowing something about the variability of stream flow and the chemical properties of the water provides a clue to the geology of the area, and vice versa. When you see springs and seeps along a stream, you're looking at groundwater entering the surface water system. During the low flows of summer, the stream flow may come entirely from groundwater recharge. It is this influx of groundwater that results in the relatively constant flow and cool temperatures in some of our finest trout streams. Additionally, groundwater contributes key nutrients and minerals to streams, which is the reason for the enormous productivity of our spring creeks. Of course, groundwater flow can also carry fertilizers, pesticides, and other contaminants. Groundwater flow, largely invisible, is the lifeblood for most of our cold-water resources. The interested reader is encouraged to read a classic 1963 paper by WDNR fisheries specialists Bill Threinen and Ron Poff, entitled "The Geography of Wisconsin's Trout Streams."

In the following chapters we'll explore twenty well-known trout streams in the state. We profile ten rivers north of the general Highway 10 dividing line: the Bois Brule, Namekagon, White, Kinnickinnic, Peshtigo, Oconto, Wolf, Pike, Prairie, and the East Branch of the Eau Claire. Ten more fishing areas are

Reed's Creek, a charming small spring creek in southern Wisconsin. Photo by Jon Christiansen.

profiled south of Highway 10: the Tomorrow-Waupaca River, the Mecan River, Lawrence Creek, Black Earth Creek, Mt. Vernon Creek, Castle Rock Creek and the Blue River, the Big Green River, Timber Coulee Creek, Willow Creek, and the Kickapoo River system.

You may notice that none of our profiled southern Wisconsin streams is in the southeastern part of the state, where most of Wisconsin's five million people live. Most of the Great Lakes tributaries in this area are too warm for year-round trout populations, but they do get a mention in our "Don't Miss" chapter, in the section called Battling Big Salmonids in the Great Lakes Tributaries. In addition, the few trout streams in southeastern Wisconsin—mostly in the north and south units of the Kettle Moraine State Forest on the western fringe of the metropolitan Milwaukee area—are too tiny and fragile to be named. For sure, trout are there. We've seen them in tiny kettle spring ponds and in small streams that are easily leaped across. Part of this area is protected by being in a state forest, but development is spreading quickly.

If you can't stray too far from Milwaukee, we encourage you to try the pond at Paradise Springs, near Eagle, in Waukesha County. This spot, site

Sections of profiled streams described in Chapters 8 and 9

of an old resort, has very clear, very cold, spring water that flows at a rate of 30,000 gallons per hour at a constant 47 degrees. The pond is filled with manmade fish cribs of wood, and nature's own "hideouts," made of aquatic plants. Trout love this place. There is some natural reproduction here due to the WDNR's care and to strict regulations that require artificial lures and catch-and-release fishing. The WDNR also stocks some trout. At Paradise Springs, you can see some very big trout swimming in the clear water. They're hard to catch—college-educated, you might say. You'll have to take your tippet down to 6X or 7X, even if you're plying the bottom with a Leech or Woolly Bugger.

The area is treated like a state park, so you must purchase a daily or annual park sticker in order to park in the small lot. There is a paved trail around most of the pond, and a fishing pier for the disabled. The pier at one end and the old stone spring house at the other are two great places to watch the fish you can't seem to catch. But every now and then you can fool one or two. One of the great attractions of Paradise Springs is that the pond opens for fishing on January 1 each year, several months ahead of the regular season. It's a good place for stir-crazy anglers to visit on a nice winter day.

The catch-and-release, artificials only early season, which begins in early March, precedes the regular trout season, which begins on the first Saturday in May. Trout fishing during the regular season is governed by a regulation scheme that has been in effect since 1990. This scheme, based on five categories of trout waters, has a lot of science behind it and has yielded good results. The state puts out a thorough guide to the regulations each year. It contains superb maps and lists the regulations in effect for trout streams throughout the state. Be aware, however, that modifications are made from year to year, so some reaches of streams you fish may fall under different regulations, depending upon the condition of the resource. Signs have been placed at major stream entry points to remind anglers of the regulations; look in the WDNR guide for explanations of the stream categories.

Each of our stream profiles tries to tell a little conservation story while briefing you on proven methods that catch fish. Throughout each section we provide some information on interesting sidetrips and history—information we find useful when we're on a fishing trip. With each stream section we've also provided a map showing you basic landmarks, and a "stream snapshot" providing a quick overview of the river or stream. These items will enable you to find the information quickly that you'll need to help you decide where to fish.

When to fish? It depends on your tastes. Probably the most productive time is early in the season, when hatches are most prolific and before the freestone streams warm up. But there's plenty of good trout fishing available throughout the season, especially if you're partial to certain hatches, such as the White Mayfly and the Trico.

Our stream descriptions also give you the seasonal range in stream flow, usually with an indication of average daily flows at times when you're likely to be on the stream. Stream flow conditions for many Wisconsin trout streams now are available on the Internet, so you can decide from your computer station whether a visit to your favorite stream is worthwhile after

Winter reveals a totally different portrait of a trout stream. Photo by Brent Nicastro.

a recent rain or dry spell. Even if your stream doesn't have a gauging station, a nearby stream may have one that can be used as an indicator. The hydrologist's measure of flow—cubic feet per second (cfs) —may not be part of your daily vocabulary, but it's not difficult to learn and use. Throw a leaf or twig, even a grasshopper, on the stream, and see how long it takes to float a foot (or better, 10 feet). Divide the elapsed time into the distance the object has floated and you have the stream's velocity. A foot per second is not uncommon. Estimate the average width and depth of the stream—say 20 feet wide and 2 feet deep, which yields a cross section of 40 square feet. If the velocity is 1 foot per second through this cross section, the stream flow is approximately 40 cubic feet per second. Soon you'll be able to visualize the numbers we've provided. Incidentally, we've noticed that grasshoppers often don't survive the full 10 feet. If you observe this too, tie on a grasshopper imitation and start fishing fast.

While we're on the subject of insects, we'll refer you to our insect chart (page 73). While the timing of emerging insects varies some from north to south, the kinds of insects that trout like don't vary much. To simplify the task of matching the hatch, we've constructed one general hatch chart that will serve you well no matter where you fish in Wisconsin.

To supplement this information, go to our Fishing the Web section.

A challenging lie on any trout stream—confusing currents, demanding casting for the "hoped-for" lunker trout living under the bridge. Photo by Jim Bartelt.

8

Trout Fishing
in Northern Wisconsin

Bois Brule River

STREAM SNAPSHOT
Bois Brule River

MILES OF TROUT WATER: Nearly 50

SETTING: Famous Lake Superior freestoner flowing through Brule River State Forest

TROUT SPECIES: Resident wild brookies and browns; migratory steelhead and salmon

REGULATIONS: Category 5 entire length in Douglas County with special regulations and limited kill

BEST FLIES: Hex and Trico (in season), stonefly nymphs, Adams, Sulphurs, Brown Drake

NEAREST COMMUNITIES: Brule, Ashland, Superior-Duluth

WHEN WE LEFT the river the whip-poor-wills were in full cry, their repetitious yet haunting song casting a surreal mood over us as we walked up the path to the road. It was a little past 10 P.M., and the intense starlight was enough to brighten the sky. Aurora borealis, the wonder of nature called the Northern Lights, was beginning to perform its night-time dance on the horizon. As we made our way up the trail and into a stand of balsam fir and spruce, we savored the refreshing aroma of these evergreens. The smell lingered with us for a few brief moments and then was gone—either the slight breeze carried the scent away or our senses had become accustomed to its barely discernible presence. Our reverent mood brought to mind what Gordon MacQuarrie said about the Bois Brule in *When the White-Throats Sing*, "Men who know me well . . . will tell you that I practically fall apart spiritually once I am within earshot of the Brule."

It had been a memorable evening on the Bois Brule—one that left us content and grateful for just being alive to take in the total experience of the river. We were very quiet as we continued up the path, each of us pondering the mystery of our shared experience. The quiet wouldn't continue; how could we keep silent about the excellent fishing we had just left in that wide part of the Bois Brule known as Big Lake? Several areas of the large pool were dotted with the rings of rising fish. We had caught and released a number of very nice Brule trout. We couldn't help wonder if Calvin Coolidge had the same experience during his sojourn on the Bois Brule, back in the days when a president of the United States could spend the summer working out of a residence on the banks of a trout river.

THE SETTING

The Bois Brule is Wisconsin's most famous river, and there are many reasons for its fame. It was first a prominent transportation route, used by the Indians and then European voyagers in their travels between Lake Superior and the Mississippi River drainage. The first tourists were the Ojibwa Indians (usually referred to as the Chippewas today), who came to Superior country hundreds of years ago from the St. Lawrence River valley, searching for better hunting grounds. Then came the French, looking for fur and potential converts to Catholicism. Some historians speculate that Etienne Brule may have been the first white man to visit the region, probably in the early 1620s. But the Bois Brule isn't named for him; *bois brulé* means "burned wood" in French, and the river was so named because of the many lightning-sparked fires that marked the valley. Other historians say the first white man in the region was Pierre Esprit Radisson, who is said to have spent the winter of 1659–60 in the company of the Lac Courte Oreilles Chippewas, near present-day Hayward. Still others say the first European visitor was French officer Daniel Greysolon, Sieur Du Lhut, a title which became the name for the settlement we call Duluth. He made peace between the Chippewas and the Sioux in 1679, and then traveled to the Mississippi River valley via the water route—the Bois Brule to the St. Croix to the Mississippi. These and other explorers found that the Indians knew what they were talking about when they sometimes referred to the headwaters of the Bois Brule as "Moschettoe country." A British explorer, Jonathan Carver, wrote: "I never saw or felt so many of those insects in my life."

While the explorers did not come for the fishing, many people have since. A wagon trail in the 1850s from St. Paul to Bayfield allowed people to discover the outstanding brook trout fishery of the river. In the late 1800s several more wagon trails provided access to the river; and finally, two railroad

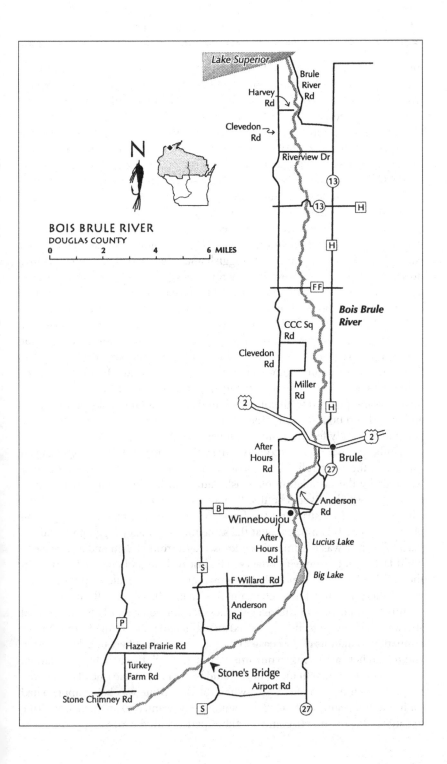

Lake Superior

Brule River Rd

Harvey Rd

Clevedon Rd

Riverview Dr

13

13   H

H

FF

BOIS BRULE RIVER
DOUGLAS COUNTY
0   2   4   6 **MILES**

Bois Brule River

CCC Sq Rd

Clevedon Rd

Miller Rd

2   H

After Hours Rd

2

Brule

27

B   Anderson Rd

Winneboujou

After Hours Rd   *Lucius Lake*

S

F Willard Rd   *Big Lake*

Anderson Rd

P

Hazel Prairie Rd

Turkey Farm Rd   Stone's Bridge

Airport Rd

Stone Chimney Rd

S   27

lines were built between Bayfield and Duluth, hastening the influx of people. Legions of anglers came on the railroads to fish for the coaster brook
trout, even as it was on the decline because of aggressive timber cutting and
overfishing. The coaster—a beautifully colored speckled trout commonly
weighing 4 to 5 pounds—spends some of its life in Lake Superior, and some
in the cold-water tributaries where it spawns. Fishermen each year ganged
up on the fish as they prepared to run up the Bois Brule and other Lake Superior tributaries to spawn. One state conservation commissioner reported
that in 1894 a single fisherman shipped more than 2,700 trout he had caught
on the Bois Brule to three Superior restaurants.

"Years ago the decrease was noticed, but nevertheless the pools were visited by anglers in greater numbers than before, some fishermen taking in a
single day a hundred pounds of sluggish and inactive fish, and often salting
down the surplus for winter use," wrote George Shiras III for the National
Geographic Society, in a report believed to have been written in 1927. Shiras
made a plea to stop the killing of these spawning fish, for "it is the same as
killing a bird on the nest." Shiras said that according to records covering 65
years, the largest speckled trout taken on the south shore of Lake Superior
before 1890 weighed 5.25 pounds; a much larger number varied from 4 to
5 pounds; and the minimum weight was about a pound. "Including the in-
dentations, the shore line of Lake Superior totals about 1,000 miles, and in
former years speckled trout could be found around all the rocky points, reefs,
and gravel and boulder beds. Today the story is a different one, for they have
become relatively few in numbers and are much scattered."

Timbering was also a problem. In 1890 the timber harvesting began in
earnest in the river valley, and most of the virgin timber was cut. The river
was hurt by the installation of splash dams and by the actual movement of
the logs down the river. The flooding and scouring of the river bed and the
siltation caused by stripping the forest cover severely limited the migration
of the coasters. It is ironic that at the same time the heavy logging was taking
place, the river was becoming well known as a trout stream and as a place to
build fashionable summer cottages. The last real runs of coaster brookies in
the Bois Brule ended about 1940, but by then the Bois Brule's reputation as a
great fishery was fixed in anglers' minds. Smaller brookies still inhabited the
far upstream portion of the river, as they had for eons; and later, introduced
species, such as the steelhead, revived an annual migration run of trout. Native
remnant populations of the coaster brookie remain elsewhere in Lake Superior,
and researchers are trying to nurture the coaster back to a fishable population.

The coaster rehabilitation effort would be for naught had one ill-conceived
proposal been implemented. Just when the Bois Brule was being appreciated
for its natural beauty and excellent fishing, some wanted to open the Bois Brule
to barge traffic in order to connect Lake Superior with the Mississippi drainage.

Trout fishing on the Bois Brule River, ca. 1900. Wisconsin Historical Society, WHi-2206.

In 1894, after $10,000 was spent on a study of this plan, it was estimated that the proposed 207-mile-long Bois Brule canal would cost $10 million. Luckily, the proposal was buried in the halls of Congress, and the beautiful tamarack swamps of the upper river were never excavated to create the artificial lakes the engineers of that day had envisioned to accommodate the lumber and grain barges.

It was about the turn of the century that the elite made the Brule its playground. The Winneboujou Club, a group of wealthy midwesterners from Milwaukee and St. Paul who joined in a landowners' association, was established, and the first buildings at the Cedar Island estate were erected. The estate, located on a Bois Brule island in the upper part of the river, began as the personal hunting retreat of Frank J. Bowman, a notorious poacher, gambler, and lawyer from St. Louis. After Bowman died, the island was owned by Henry Clay Pierce, an associate of Bowman's who also hailed from St. Louis. Under Pierce's direction, the estate grew into the showplace it is today. It was at this time that Cedar Island saw the building of its own commercial fish hatchery (in its heydey, the estate had barns for livestock, its own power plant, and even a zoo). The spring ponds on the estate, which formed the basis for the hatchery, were cut off from the main river in 1905, contributing to the decline of the brook trout population. However, Cedar Island brook trout fry were shipped all over the country, and full-grown trout were sold to the Duluth hotels and restaurants.

The Bois Brule and the Cedar Island estate became known to the nation when Calvin Coolidge was the guest of Pierce in the summer of 1928 and the estate was referred to as the "summer White House." The president set up an office in a Superior school building, but he spent a lot of his time relaxing on the Bois Brule. He took to the local customs, apparently. President Coolidge, according to a Duluth newspaper report, "has foresworn his customary fish bait by disdaining worms and using flies during his angling expeditions from the summer White House." Not all locals were enthralled with the Washington celebrity, who brought with him 60 soldiers, 14 servants and 10 Secret Service agents. Of course, the national press—about seventy-five in number—were in tow. One fisherman wrote that when he learned of "the threat to our traditional Brule peace and solitude" he took his family out of town. He also wrote that the local guides reported Coolidge's "predilection for the 'Barnyard Hackle' or 'Hum Dinger,' as the lowly angle worm" was called locally. Herbert Hoover, a fly-fisher, later wrote of his predecessor: "Being a fundamentalist in religion, economics, and fishing, [Coolidge] began his fish career for common trout with worms. Ten million fly-fishermen at once evidenced disturbed minds. Then Mr. Coolidge took to a fly. He gave the Secret Service guards great excitement in dodging his backcast and rescuing flies from trees. There were many photographs. Soon after that he declared he did not choose to run again."

Other presidents—Grant, Cleveland, Hoover, and Eisenhower—also fished the river, giving rise to the reputation of the Bois Brule as the "river of presidents." In 1947, Ike fished the Bois Brule out of Cedar Island Lodge, where he and his brother Milton were guests of St. Paul businessman John Ordway. Eisenhower liked northern Wisconsin so much that he almost bought a retirement home there, according to his biographer, Stephen Ambrose, but eventually settled in central Pennsylvania instead. Others in the federal government were drawn to the relaxing environs of the Bois Brule. James Angleton, the famed CIA spymaster, sought refuge from the pressures of the Cold War by fly-fishing for trout on the river. The chain-smoking Angleton was said to fish alone at night in his canoe. He knew what he was doing. Some locals like to use a fly pattern called "the Angleton," devised by the spymaster himself: a mouse pattern made of deer hair and saddle hackles. Many people—from every station in life—have loved the Bois Brule.

MANAGEMENT HISTORY

The Bois Brule originates on a high ridge in an area of conifer bogs known as the pine barrens, a large sandy glacial outwash plain. From there, the river

President Calvin Coolidge fishing at Cedar Lake Lodge on the Bois Brule River, in the summer of 1928. Wisconsin Historical Society, WHi-2093.

twists and falls nearly 50 miles down the Superior escarpment to Lake Superior, a 420-foot drop in elevation. These geologic features have created an infiltration area responsible for providing the uniform spring flow that enters the upper part of the river, ensuring cool, stable flows throughout the year. This spring flow, with its moderating influence on the temperature, helps keep the river free of ice in the winter and improves spawning success. Preservation of this spring flow is essential, and that's why many say the greatest conservation event in Brule history was a lumber baron's gift. The Brule River State Forest was created in 1907 when the Weyerhaeuser family donated 4,320 acres of land to the state; the gift was conditioned on the state's banning dams on the Brule. Expansion over the years has brought public ownership in the forest to 40,000 acres. Today this state forest protects the riparian corridor of the Bois Brule.

River lovers have kept the Bois Brule a treasure. One of the most prominent preservationists in the Bois Brule's history is Joe Lucius, a guide and the inventor of the Brule River Boat. This boat, which resembled a canoe in its general design, was built in lengths up to 24 feet and had a live well and sliding seats for better weight distribution. It was more likely to be poled than paddled. In 1887, Joe first guided a party for a ten-day fishing trip. As testament to his importance in the history of the Bois Brule, one of its lakes is named after him. Lucius left the Bois Brule in 1911 to work in the state's forestry service, where he left his mark with the construction of the steel forestry towers still found in the state today, the first nursery, and many "log cabin" ranger stations throughout the state.

Today, private landowners and organizations such as Friends of the Brule River and Forest, Brule River Preservation, Incorporated, the Nature Conservancy, and the Brule River Sportsmen's Club play key roles in complementing the conservation activities of the Wisconsin Department of Natural Resources. There are occasional differences in philosophy. The Friends of the Brule River and Forest, who convened in 1992 to protest WDNR-sanctioned clearcutting in the state forest, celebrated a victory in 1996 with the signing of a state law that demoted silviculture from its previous role as the primary purpose of state forests. The "biodiversity bill," as it was called during the legislative debate, balances state forest uses. The law got its start in the mid-1980s, when the Lake Minnesuing Association objected to timber-harvesting practices in the state forest; now state forests throughout Wisconsin and all of us who use them benefit because "native biological diversity" has been made one of the purposes of state forests. Recreation and the long-term health of the resource finally are on equal footing with timbering.

But mostly there is cooperation, often spearheaded by WDNR fisheries biologist Dennis Pratt, a native of the area who was born in Ashland. Under Pratt's supervision, the Brule River Sportsmen's Club and other conservation organizations conducted an extensive project to enhance and actually create spawning habitat in various sections of the Bois Brule. The Wisconsin National Guard helped airlift gravel by helicopter to eight remote spawning sites, creating almost 5,000 square feet of spawning habitat. This kind of cooperative effort is an example of the joint efforts that have gone on for years as people have banded together to protect and improve the river.

These kinds of management efforts are necessary because of the decline of the brook trout fishery—a shadow of its former self, in part because of the elimination of the coaster brookie. The present-day brook trout fishery is largely confined to the upper river, where extensive spring flow exists. While the Brule has the largest population of brook trout of all the Wisconsin streams that flow into Lake Superior, the brookie is nevertheless the least common of the salmonids residing in the river.

One of the Bois Brule's success stories has to do with steelhead, largely responsible for the Bois Brule's rebirth as a trout fishery. These lake-run rainbow trout were introduced in 1892, and today are the most abundant salmonid in the river. It appears that all the rainbow trout in the river are migratory—that is, they are born in the river, where they spend a year or two, grow up in the lake, then return to the river to spawn. Even though the best areas of the river for spawning success are in the upper river above U.S. Highway 2, more spawning occurs in the rapids and rips of the lower river downstream of this highway. But the spawning area in the lower river is more susceptible to spring flooding, which can decimate the eggs and fry of the rainbows. This accounts for wide variations in the number of young that survive the smolt period of their life, descend to the lake, and eventually return to the river as steelhead. There appear to be two distinct runs of steelhead—an autumn run and a spring run; the autumn fish overwinter in the river. Some biologists, however, speculate that there is really only one continuous run, interrupted or slowed by the cold temperatures and low flows of winter.

In the late 1970s the steelhead fishery of Lake Superior tributary streams—including the Bois Brule—began to decline. Overharvest was the suspected culprit, both in the stream and in the lake. Protective regulations were enacted downstream of U.S. Highway 2, eliminating the open winter season and limiting the harvest of rainbow trout to one daily, with a minimum size of 26 inches. In addition, eggs gathered from wild steelhead are hatched artificially, and the young are released back into the river as smolts (71/2 inches long) to bolster the stock of wild fish. The goal calls for the annual release of at least 50,000 smolts. Fish managers in Minnesota and Wisconsin are closely watching the progress of these steelhead recovery efforts.

Brown trout weren't introduced to the Bois Brule until the 1920s, and stocking was discontinued in the mid-1970s. They are common throughout the river, with two genetically distinct populations present—resident and migratory Even though they are theoretically able to spawn more than once, most migrating browns only make one spawning trip. It seems that either the actual spawning run or associated disease problems contribute to a high mortality rate among the migratory fish. The resident browns are the mainstay of the trout fishery in the upper river between the town of Brule and Stone's Bridge, and some huge resident browns are known to inhabit the lake stretches of the river.

Two species of Pacific salmon, the coho and the chinook, have become established in the Bois Brule in quite fishable numbers. A small number of pink salmon have also been recorded, but biologists don't believe they will ever occur in any significant numbers. Interestingly, these salmon populations became established from releases in the province of Ontario and neighboring states, which shows how closely linked the Bois Brule fishery is to the entire Lake Superior aquatic ecosystem. The first documented evidence of both coho and chinook salmon occurred in 1973. Coho, although the number of spawners ascending the river from year to year varies, extensively utilize the smaller tributaries in the upper Bois Brule for spawning. Chinook have made a slow but steady increase in their use of the river for spawning and juvenile salmon development. At first their use of the river was confined to Blueberry and Nebagamon creeks and main stem riffles near where those tributaries enter the stream. As glorious as they are, these migrations may have a downside; some people believe the spawning salmon disrupt the habitat for resident trout.

ANGLING OPPORTUNITIES

We have found both variety and solitude on the Bois Brule. You can fish the upper reaches for brookies, the meandering reaches in the middle section for browns, or the lower river casting for steelhead among powerful rapids and pools. The solitude is everywhere. The river is generally talked about in two sections: the upper and lower, with U.S. Highway 2 as the dividing line. Upstream—or south—from Highway 2 (the river flows north to Lake Superior) are familiar landmarks such as the Brule Trout Hatchery, the Winneboujou Bridge, the three lakes, Cedar Island, and Stone's Bridge.

First, the migratory fish. The Bois Brule is highly valued among Wisconsin fisheries because it doesn't rely on artificial stocking to maintain the populations of brown, rainbow, and the salmon, and provides angling for migratory fish in both the spring and the fall. Steelhead are the most highly acclaimed, and the Bois Brule has the relatively uncommon fall run. Most steelhead anglers concentrate on the lower river. Although standard patterns such as the Spring Wiggler, egg patterns, Comets, and the like will work, steelhead regulars prefer using more subdued, natural patterns. Many fish are taken with a weighted imitation of the large Black Stonefly, common in our larger freestone rivers and streams. Fishing in the fall will also occasionally yield the trophy brown trout, chinook, or coho that has returned to the river to spawn. (For tackle and techniques applying to migrating trout, see the Great Lakes section in our "Don't Miss" chapter.)

The lake-run fish attract many anglers, but the Brule also has a dedicated following of anglers who pursue the resident browns and brookies. You can still find relatively good brook trout fishing in the upper headwaters, but when it comes to fishing the hatches, most of us are after the brown trout. We like to fish the water upstream of Highway 2, considered the most productive water.

The first hatch of the season is the Hendrickson, which begins most years about the time the general fishing season opens on the first weekend in May. The hatch lasts for approximately two weeks. Patterns of choice are the standard Hendrickson, the Red Quill, and various emerger patterns. The next major hatch is the Sulphur, which generally starts during the last week in May. Sulphurs provide excellent action for a couple of weeks. Since these are usually known to hatch in the quieter areas and pools, we prefer to use less heavily hackled flies, such as no-hackle and parachute patterns.

The Brown Drake hatch normally begins in the middle of June. It's one of the most spectacular hatches on the Bois Brule, especially in the wide and slow reaches of the river from Big Lake down to Winneboujou landing. For this hatch, and some of the others as well, it really pays to fish the river by canoe. The soft sediments of clay and marl provide excellent habitat for this burrowing mayfly, and patterns such as a Brown Drake Parachute and emerger imitations work well. The spinner fall in the evening can be colossal. We've waited patiently for the descent of thousands of spinners hovering scores of feet above the stream, knowing their fall would trigger a feeding frenzy.

On the heels of the Brown Drake, Hexes begin their emergence in the slower, more placid reaches of the river. Again, the lake areas have the most prolific Hex hatches. This hatch can be very perplexing, as a night with a heavy emergence frequently will be followed by one or even two light hatches on succeeding evenings. The spinner fall can occur simultaneously with a heavy hatch, or even when very few flies are hatching. Carry imitations of both the dun and the spinner, and consider stocking nymph and emerger patterns as well.

The next major hatch, the Trico, occurs in late July and extends well into August. This is when the Brule takes on some of the angling character of a spring creek. The slower-moving reaches with abundant aquatic vegetation are the best habitats for this insect, and thus provide the best fishing to this hatch. It's imperative that you have the proper imitation—preferably sizes #20–24 Trico spinner imitations. A 7X tippet is the norm for this kind of delicate angling. These insects emerge as duns, then quickly fall as spinners very early in the morning, so be prepared to begin your fishing shortly after dawn. The most successful way to fish this hatch is to select a solidly rising trout and then, after approaching your quarry carefully, execute well-timed casts over and over. The secret is to keep your fly on the water. Many anglers will cast downstream, putting just enough slack line on the water so the fly will be the first thing to drift over the fish. Beware: the hatch can be suppressed by dark and cold weather.

The Bois Brule also harbors abundant populations of caddis and stoneflies. Be alert for hatches of these insects, especially when you are between mayfly hatches. With its excellent water quality, the river contains several species of caddisflies, and they can hatch simultaneously. Most anglers use various sizes and colors of the Elk Hair Caddis (#12–18). However, be prepared to use more exact imitations of the natural in the slower sections of the river when the trout become more selective.

During nonhatch daytime periods, we've had success floating a #16 Royal Coachman or Pass Lake in the riffle sections leading to slower water. Ron Manz, a well-known guide on the river, likes to fish his March Brown soft hackle during these slack times. Casting far back under vegetation, Manz can lure out brookies and browns on even the slowest days.

The river harbors a variety of stoneflies, and while they do not provide reliable hatches to fish to, the angler should not be without several nymph imitations of these insects. If you're fishing riffle areas in a no-hatch situation, try a stonefly nymph, such as the Brooks Stone (#6–8), or local tier Dick Berge's stonefly imitation. Look for stonefly water downstream from the Winneboujou Bridge, especially in the lower river north of Highway 2, with its numerous rapids and runs.

The lakes upstream from the Winneboujou Bridge can also be fished during summer nights. Favorite patterns to lure large browns include big mouse imitations in both natural deer hair and white.

One of the best ways to fish the Brule is by canoe, especially in the section between Stone's Bridge and Highway 2, where access from the road is limited as the river winds through many private estates. But don't canoe below Highway 2 unless you are experienced; the river gets much tougher downstream. Lacking a canoe, access the river at the numerous road crossing, pullouts, or angler parking lots. As always, anglers should be sensitive to the rights of private property owners along the river.

Migrating trout run up many Lake Superior tributaries in addition to the Bois Brule. For other inland trout fishing, try the Iron River, the White River, and the Namekagon River. During your travels, you may encounter some interesting town names, such as Oulu, a reflection of the strong Finnish heritage in the region. In these parts, a backyard sauna is more popular than the backyard pool. As a tribute to the Finns, try your luck at the wide part of the Bois Brule known as "Finlanders' Delight," just upstream from County Highway FF.

The Bois Brule River also is one of the best canoeing rivers in the state, with several reaches of the river offering exciting Class 1 and 2 rapids. Access points and bridges are conveniently spaced so that most floats can be accomplished in five to six hours. Several canoe liveries are located near Brule.

Namekagon River

STREAM SNAPSHOT
Namekagon River

MILES OF TROUT WATER: 21

SETTING: National Wild and
Scenic Riverway preserves a
natural freestoner

TROUT SPECIES: Brookies, rainbows, and browns, some
reproduction

REGULATIONS: Category 5 in
Sawyer County; artificial lures
only

BEST FLIES: Cap's Hairwing, stonefly nymphs, Sulphurs, Tan
Caddis, Hare's Ear, Gray Drake
(in season)

NEAREST COMMUNITIES: Hayward,
Cable, Eau Claire, Twin Cities

The Namekagon could be counted as
a great trout river for its beauty alone.
Be prepared to be overwhelmed by the
Namekagon; towering white pines and
balsam firs, bald eagles overhead, its
wild character, and—oh yes—its fishing. Gordon MacQuarrie wrote lovingly of the Namekagon in his story
Now, in June: "The best trout streams
are the ones you grow up with and then
grow old with. Eventually they become
like a familiar shotgun, or a faithful old
setter, or a comfortable pair of shoes.
You develop a profound affection for
them, and you think maybe before you
die you will even understand a little
about them." The Namekagon will do
that to you.

THE SETTING

This northern part of the state is generally regarded as musky country, and if
you doubt that, look south when you're on the main drag in Hayward; you're
likely to see one of the tallest structures in town—a giant musky that's part
of the National Fresh Water Fishing Hall of Fame. Climb up into Mr. Musky's
mouth and take in a grand view; the monument is a fitting tribute, given
the many warm-water lakes that dot this boggy region of the vast and wild
Chequamegon National Forest. The area is the heart of Wisconsin's Northwoods, where every bar has a fish on the knotty pine wall and where Chicago-
land families (and occasionally gangsters) have vacationed for decades. The
area is also home to the Lac Courte Oreilles band of Lake Superior Chippewa
Indians, to a growing elk herd, to the Lumberjack World Championships
(every July in Hayward), the World Championship Snowmobile Derby (every
year in Eagle River) and the marathon American Birkebeiner cross-country
ski race (every February, between Hayward and Cable).

But fishing is perhaps the most frequent pursuit of visitors. You can certainly fish for musky and other warm-water species in the Namekagon and
its flowages downstream from Hayward, but we trout anglers concentrate on

the 20 miles of beautiful water upstream, even though sometimes that trophy brown on the end of the line turns out to be a northern pike. The surrounding forest is composed of a mixture of hardwoods and evergreens. Tall, stately white pines, balsam fir, maple, birch, and basswood, and an occasional open meadow provide a wonderful setting. One of the joys we've experienced is being startled in the midst of fishing by a bald eagle cruising the river, soaring at treetop level. This section of the Namekagon has been praised by some of the greatest names in American trout fishing, including Ernest Schwiebert, A. J. McClane, and our own Gordon MacQuarrie.

Schwiebert, in his short story "Night Comes to the Namekagon," recalls fishing the Giant Mahogany Dun hatch during a visit to Hayward. While most anglers seemed to be gripped by musky fever, Schwiebert and a companion found big Drakes fluttering down in the swift current past some deadfalls. He recounted a wonderful series of hook-ups. "The first fish was rising methodically against the logs. The cast cocked the fly nicely and it disappeared in a quiet, self-satisfied swirl. The trout was well hooked," wrote Schwiebert about what would be a 6-pound brown. "The others were still rising steadily. The first was working tight against the jam, and it lunged sideways to engulf the fly. The second fight echoed the first, except for a clumsy jump that ended in a heavy splash. Finally it surrendered, threshing heavily in the meshes." We've also seen big Namekagon trout go crazy over big mayfly hatches, sometimes jumping entirely out of the water to snatch one of the big bugs. Everytime we visit the Namekagon, we come away amazed.

Around Cable, the river seems at times like one long riffle as it speeds downstream. The mostly tame, swift but sweeping sections typical in this reach make for a lovely and easy canoe ride in the spring and early summer when there's enough water. This isn't a bad way to fish the river, but we prefer to absorb the peaceful surroundings by wading in the sunlight as it filters through the overhead thatch of pine branches. Wading allows us to pause, stretch out on the shaded banks, sip from a canteen, perhaps puff on a cigar, and watch a belted kingfisher sky-diving for dinner. McClane says simply that the Namekagon "has the potential to satisfy the desires of almost any angler." A. J., we couldn't agree more.

MANAGEMENT HISTORY

You can thank federal action for the undisturbed nature of the Namekagon. The Namekagon, over 60 miles in length, is included in the St. Croix National Scenic Riverway. It begins at the outflow of Lake Namekagon in Bayfield County east of Cable, and winds through Sawyer, Washburn, and Burnett

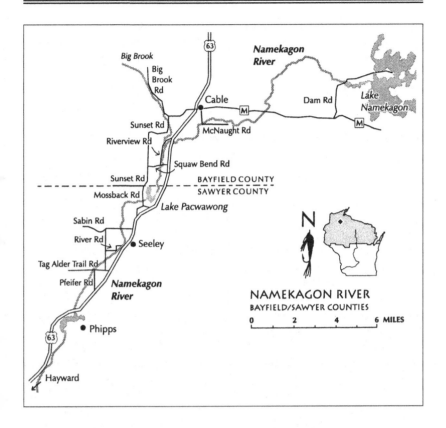

NAMEKAGON RIVER
BAYFIELD/SAWYER COUNTIES

0   2   4   6 MILES

counties before joining the St. Croix River at Riverside. The stretch from the dam at Lake Namekagon to Hayward has been classified by biologists as trout water with some natural reproduction. The river in this vicinity is good-sized; most of the time flows exceed 135 cubic feet per second. Below Hayward, the river is considered marginal for trout. Brook trout are found in the upper reaches of the river, with rainbow and brown trout distributed throughout the rest of the trout water. The Namekagon has a varied set of regulations, including a special regulations section—along Highway 63 from the dam at Lake Pacwawong downstream to near Phipps—designed to enhance fishing opportunities for larger trout. In addition, the river downstream from Lake Hayward has an extended season; check the regulations handbook for details.

Since the Namekagon's inclusion in the federal Wild and Scenic River System in 1968, the surrounding shorelands have been given protection to preserve them in their present undeveloped state. The Namekagon was one of the original rivers listed in the enabling federal legislation. Former U.S. Sena-

tor Gaylord Nelson, born in nearby Polk County, and other environmentalists feared development would ruin the wild character of the Namekagon and
the rest of the St. Croix system. Northern States Power Company pitched in
with a big land donation. Thanks to this farsighted protective designation
and National Park Service policy, signs of man are blessedly hard to find as
one ambles along the banks or floats the river by canoe. Because of the Wild
and Scenic River designation, little structural or in-stream work has been
done to improve the fisheries habitat, and what does exist was installed before the river was added to the program.

Long before the Namekagon was given this protection, the river was the
scene of a controversial fight to keep it free-flowing. This environmental battle
profoundly influenced the way Wisconsin upholds one of its most cherished
conservation legal institutions—the Public Trust doctrine. From the Northwest Ordinance of 1787, when Wisconsin was part of the Northwest Territory,
the riverways were declared "forever free." This is derived from Wisconsin's
State Constitution, and actually had its origins in English common law.

The test came when a dam was proposed on the Namekagon in Washburn County, supported unanimously by the county board and approved by
the state Public Service Commission. The anti-dam fight was led by Virgil
Muench, an ardent conservationist from southeastern Wisconsin who was
then president of the still-powerful Izaak Walton League. With a lot of help
from colleagues, the state attorney general's office, and the old Wisconsin
Conservation Department, Muench brought the case to the state Supreme
Court in 1951, setting up a landmark water rights case, *Muench vs. The Public
Service Commission.*

The Wisconsin Supreme Court ruled in favor of denying the permit to
build the dam, holding that preserving the river in its natural state was more
valuable than producing electricity. The court held that any stream is navigable if at some season of the year it is capable of floating any boat, skiff, or
canoe of the shallowest draft used for recreational purposes. The court also
said clearly that the Public Trust doctrine pertains to recreation and scenic
beauty, and that even though Muench wasn't from the region and had no di-
rect financial or land interest in the area, he had a right to his day in court. The
bottom-line interpretation from water rights experts: if you can float a canoe
in the water or if a trout can swim in it without turning on its side, it's a navigable waterway in Wisconsin, open to the enjoyment of any citizen. So as you
fish your way along the Namekagon, know that you're not far from where our
public rights in rivers and streams were boldly contested and secured for all.

Still, there are some small impoundments on the Namekagon. Although
they serve to stabilize flows and trap sediments, they also warm the river
downstream, and contribute to water temperatures reaching 80 degrees be-

low Lake Pacwawong. The angler should be aware of this problem with water temperature and adjust fishing strategies accordingly. The river does have areas of spring inflow that can be recognized by occasional growths of watercress at places along the banks of the river. It's a good idea to fish around these areas during hot spells.

ANGLING OPPORTUNITIES

While not a brawling, whitewater river like the Wolf, the Namekagon is big in our minds. It's one of the few large rivers in Wisconsin with sizable populations of naturally reproduced trout. The river ranges in width from 50 to 150 feet, allowing the angler to stand thigh-deep in a sweeping run and execute a big downstream-and-across wet fly swing with a long line. This type of fishing for stream trout is hard to find in Wisconsin. The nature of the river's flow also makes it popular with canoeists. The upper river above Hayward isn't used as much as the lower portion because low flows sometimes limit the ability to canoe. If the "aluminum hatch" bothers you, limit your fishing time to early mornings or late afternoon and evening. That's probably going to be the best fishing anyway. When you do fish, you'll find that getting around is pretty easy, especially in the area between Hayward and Cable. Wading is generally safe. Many roads cross the river, allowing easy access, and most of this land is in public ownership, with a network of fisherman's trails providing additional access to the river. There are still private inholdings within the Wild and Scenic River boundaries, so be careful to avoid trespassing. Detailed maps are available from the National Park Service.

The Namekagon is a productive fishery. The upper 8 miles from Lake Namekagon to Cable contain a small population of native brook trout, in addition to browns and rainbows. The river here is a rapid stream that winds through alders and forested reaches; it is small and intimate, with access at highway bridges. While it may not harbor trout in the sizes found in the lower reaches, the opportunity to tangle with spirited brookies is well worth the effort. Immediately below Cable the river picks up speed and has several fast-water rips, pools, and lots of pocket water. Where Big Brook enters the river, several access points are available. Below this confluence the volume and width of the river increase, and it starts to take on the character most frequently associated with the Namekagon. Here you'll find big sweeping bends and long pools.

Below Lake Pacwawong, the river is characterized by riffle sections interspersed with long pools. This is the special regulations stretch, with a slot limit designed to improve the holdover of trophy fish. This section is known as the big-fish water of the Namekagon. Many areas of the river may seem barren, so the angler adept at identifying trout habitat and lies will do best. Since the river has many areas of broad shallow flats, water with subtle changes in depth or current will sometimes hold surprisingly large fish. Moreover, while deep holes, logjams, and undercuts are obvious places to fish, don't neglect the deeper areas of long riffles. The soft-hackle addict will fall in love with these riffles—especially during a hatch. So will the spinning angler. Spin fishers also catch many fish in this section wading and casting Rooster Tails and Rapalas—upstream and across, and downstream and across. There is good angling all the way down to Phipps.

Prime time to be on the Namekagon is May and June, but the best advice we can offer is to get there whenever you can during the fishing season. The only exception to this rule is when the temperature is excessive. This is the Achilles heel of the Namekagon. Although it isn't as susceptible to high summer temperatures as the Wolf River in east-central Wisconsin, the same factors plaguing the Wolf also affect the Namekagon. Several springs and seeps flow into the Namekagon, but they aren't sufficient to keep the temperature low during the hot days of summer. Water temperatures can quickly reach 70 degrees even in May, and by June and July the river gets so warm that fishing shuts down during the day. At this time of year you should pay special attention to the early morning and evening hours—and use your stream thermometer. MacQuarrie's beloved "Mr. President" character noted that the unenlightened "will be city fishermen who don't know any better than to fish for Namekagon browns in broad daylight. They will be sore at the river. They will tell me there ain't a brown in the water—never was! They will go away from there, leaving it to me just when I want it, as the fishing gets good." Be sure to take Mr. President's advice. However, if you can't heed this admonition and must be on the river during the middle of the day, try fishing around Cable, where the river isn't as adversely affected by the dog days of summer.

How to catch fish in non-hatch situations? The angler has several strategies to choose from. First, learn to recognize the prime water and concentrate on it. One of the best bets is to dredge the depths of the pools, riffles, undercuts, and rips with a big nymph. The Namekagon has excellent populations of stoneflies, so imitations of the large nymph stage are a good bet. Perhaps the stonefly most anglers associate with the Namekagon is the Giant Black Stonefly nymph. When we say large, we mean it—at the end of three years the mature nymph will measure a full 2 inches in length just before hatching. Closely related to the famed salmonfly of the West, this stonefly does not emerge in an explosive hatch. The angler should concentrate on fishing a heavily weighted nymph in the deep runs, at the heads of pools, and in the deeper riffle sections. Take your time and make sure your fly is on the bottom—and don't neglect the chutes under the bridges. The Brooks Stone, Kaufmann Stone, or Yuk Bug in sizes #4–8 will usually be effective. Our fishing pal, Dick Berge of Iron River, fishes his weighted #6 Black Stonefly imitation with great success. He talks excitedly of the spring day when he took three brawny fish in a short burst; the fish ran from 18 inches to more than 21 inches. These dark and powerful rainbows fell victim to his Stonefly, worked deep through the boulder-strewn, well-oxygenated sections of the river.

Standard patterns such as the Hare's Ear, Prince Nymph, or March Brown Nymph are also good searching patterns in sizes #12–14. Another technique that lends itself to fishing the Namekagon is casting wet flies in the classic manner. The river is broad enough to allow the angler to cover a lot of water with wet flies cast down and across, and allowed to swing with the current. This strategy works with streamers as well. We often wade the river with a streamer or Woolly Bugger, casting to logjams, undercuts, and any other likely looking lies. Fishing upstream or down, maximize the amount of water you cover. In addition to a Woolly Bugger, try a Sculpin, or even a Leech. Don't forget to cast to debris, half-sunken logs, and brush when you are fishing the water; you may entice the trout that is tucked away in cover, waiting out the daylight hours. Spin-fishermen also are known to use some of these techniques as well, but they substitute Rapalas and other floating lures instead of flies. The really serious spin anglers are on the river at night.

In the summer, terrestrials can be effective when you find fish searching for them. Try Grasshoppers or Crickets, and cast to specific lies along the shore such as brush or logs fallen in the water. Watch for trout sipping ants under tree limbs, too.

These are all dependable methods of catching fish, but the fly-fisher is especially attracted to the Namekagon because of aquatic insect hatches that are not quickly forgotten. Listen to McClane: "Often in the summer, an angler will fish the Namekagon by day, and swear that it is a barren river. He will return as the trees begin to shade the water and stare with disbelief as the water begins to boil with the rises of fish he would not have thought could be sheltered in the stream. It may require several visits before you see a 'superfeed' and you may have to catch a major hatch or spinner fall, but once experienced, you'll be a Namekagon devotee for life. There are big fish here that would do a river anywhere proud. They are not dumb, and they do not come easy, but trying for them is a pleasant effort in this beautiful spot."

The Namekagon's hatches are similar to many other larger freestone rivers in Wisconsin, such as the Wolf and the Bois Brule. The first hatch to appear is the Hendrickson, usually in the first two weeks of May. Be prepared to fish a nymph or emerger pattern in the hours preceding the hatch. The nymphs are quite active during this period, and a well-fished Hendrickson Nymph is deadly. You may have to move around to locate a good riffle area where the flies are hatching. Well-hackled imitations are effective in the faster water, and no-hackle and parachute patterns should be used in the flatter, quieter water. The Sulphur hatch also occurs on the Namekagon, usually in late May and early June. Angler entomologists all agree that the Sulphurs you encounter could be any one of three species—and we should not really care which, because an effective imitation will work for any of them. The late Jeff Carlson, a superb northern Wisconsin trout angler, counted this among his favorite hatches because it lasts for a full two weeks or more.

In late May, the Gray Drakes emerge and the angler will probably not even notice the hatch, because the nymphs swim to quiet shallow areas, emerge as duns, and are largely unavailable to trout. However, the fly-fisher should prepare for the outstanding and exciting fishing soon provided by the spinner fall. At dusk huge swarms of adult mayflies will gather over the riffle areas of the Namekagon and perform their mating ritual. Be sharp, because the spinners can occur quite unexpectedly. The trout will key in on this and will eagerly wait for the spent insects to fall on the surface of the water. A large Spent-Winged Adams or a Cap's Hairwing (both in size #12) will usually do the trick.

In June, with warmer weather and greater periods of daylight, the hatches and spinner falls will occur in the evening or in the morning. This is especially true of the night-time Hex hatch, when spinners may still be on the water in the early daylight hours. Collectively we have experienced hundreds of nights fishing this famed hatch—you can never quite get used to that spine-tingling "slurp" that pinpoints a large fish greedily sucking in duns. Look for this large, silt-loving mayfly in the slower reaches of the Namekagon during late June and early July. While it may not have quite the hatch of the more famous Hex rivers, Hexes emerge in sufficient numbers to provide pretty good fishing. But the hatch is relatively short—only one to two weeks. There are many Hex patterns that work, and we imagine that experimentation among the faithful will continue into eternity in search of the perfect Hex pattern. Use one that is big (#6–8), durable, buoyant, and visible, usually a pale or bright yellow. Pay special attention to the fact that a spinner fall can occur in the dark, concurrent with a hatch of the duns. The trout will frequently focus on the easier-to-obtain spinner.

Two other mayflies deserve mention for late season anglers: the Trico and the White Mayfly. The Namekagon isn't noted for having outstanding hatches of these two late summer mayflies (late July and August), but the angler should be aware of their presence.

The Namekagon has almost constant caddis hatching during May and early June; more than likely you'll encounter a fishable hatch every day. Since caddisflies don't usually have the concentrated hatching periods that mayflies do, it isn't possible to pinpoint emergence times. The species found in the Namekagon are very diverse, as is the case with many freestone rivers. The Grannom, Tan Caddis, and many other species are found here. When caddis hatching activity begins, the Namekagon is a wonderful place to use soft-hackled flies or caddis pupa imitations on downstream-and-across drifts in the larger riffle sections. You can cover a lot of water this way, the fishing can be quite good, and the Namekagon lends itself perfectly to this type of fishing. We've experienced thick caddis hatches in which the egg-laying caddis mistakenly dive for our waders instead of vegetation. When we see this, we tie on an Elk Hair Caddis or a Gary LaFontaine Diving Caddis. We cast above rising fish, and jerk the fly underwater to imitate the diving insects.

The Namekagon is in the heart of one of northern Wisconsin's favorite vacation destinations. Most of the resorts, inns, and motels cater to those on vacation seeking walleye and musky, or a simple family getaway. Excellent accommodations are available in a wide range of comfort and cost levels.

Many of the resorts harken back to an era when families from the Twin Cities, Chicago, and Milwaukee, took an annual weekly vacation at their longstanding favorite resort with complete facilities including restaurant, lodge, activity programs for the kids, and badminton lessons for the grownups. Nowadays tribal casino gambling—the Lac Courte Oreilles Casino is located south of Hayward—has changed the face of Wisconsin's tourism industry, but the old-fashioned family resort can still be found. If you're camping, the closest available campground is at the Perch Lake Campground in nearby Chequemagon National Forest, just north of Drummond.

Other recreational locales abound in these parts of the Northwoods. You can canoe just about anywhere—there's that much water. There also are many hiking trails, including a National Scenic Trail called the North Country Trail that runs more than 50 miles through the Chequamegon Forest. Of course, you can always go to Hayward when the trout aren't biting and climb into the mouth of Mr. Musky.

White River

MILES OF TROUT WATER: 36

SETTING: Big water with much variety: brushy headwaters, Bibon Marsh, whitewater below

TROUT SPECIES: Wild brookies and browns

REGULATIONS: Categories 2 and 5 in Ashland and Bayfield counties

BEST FLIES: Hex and Hex Nymph (in season), Adams, Elk Hair Caddis, Woolly Bugger

NEAREST COMMUNITIES: Drummond, Ashland, Superior-Duluth

Around the turn of the nineteenth century, northern Wisconsin's great white pine forest was being decimated to feed a growing country's desire for timber. This vast resource was almost gone by 1910, leaving much of the Northwoods looking like a war zone. "The cutover," old tree stumps and slash left over from the orgy of tree cutting, burned and burned for 60 years—up until about 1930. So most of what you see today is second growth. But when you hack your way into the wild, remote sections of Bayfield County in search of trout, you may also stumble upon some of the virgin pines that loggers passed by. These ancient, gnarled trees tower above the forest floor, the old logging camps, and the feeder streams that create one of Wisconsin's most beautiful trout havens: Bayfield County's White River. Trout anglers often speak of the White in almost reverent tones, because it harkens back to a day when Wisconsin was on the country's frontier. You can still experience a little of that frontier danger by venturing into the sprawling and spooky Bibon swamp, one of the largest undeveloped marshlands in the state, and casting for big trout. Even if you don't get lost, you'll probably have a good fish story to tell.

THE SETTING

The dominant stream in Bayfield County, the White River is one of the largest trout streams in Wisconsin. Flows at Mason typically exceed 140 cubic feet per second, and several tributaries are good trout fisheries in their own right. Including these tributaries, the White has well over 60 miles of prime wild trout water. The waters of the White River originate in several spring ponds and lakes; rain and melting-snow water percolate rapidly through the porous, sandy soils of these headwater regions. Although this groundwater-based spring flow maintains the needed cool temperatures, the water is of relatively low productivity. Further downstream, several springs in the vicinity of

Sutherland add to the White's flow. In general, these springs have year-round temperatures below 60 degrees, which means that the stream stays open for much of the winter, an aid to natural trout reproduction.

The river corridor, lying mostly inside the boundaries of the Chequamegon National Forest, is largely undeveloped. The river is surrounded by many large tracts of marsh and moist forest of black spruce, tamarack, and aspen. In the headwaters region, you may find old logging camps and Indian artifacts. In the main stem, the river becomes deep, wide, and murky-looking as it goes into Bibon Marsh, a swamp so vast that once you embark on a trout-fishing expedition by canoe, you're committed to paddling and fishing until you reach a take-out point several miles downstream. Only Highway 63, a north-south road, cuts through this 8,000-acre marsh, and only then at the lower end of the swamp, so don't take the commitment lightly. Along the way, you may encounter bears, turtles, muskrats, mink, and a variety of marsh birds, including wrens, and bitterns. We've had reports of moose and timber wolf sightings, but those are rare. We hope you'll also encounter some of the big brown trout that prowl these waters.

Below the Bibon, the river turns into whitewater as it tumbles through a ravine towards its junction with the Bad River near Odanah. The 10-mile stretch between the Bibon and the dam at Highway 112 is as remote as the upstream stretch.

MANAGEMENT HISTORY

The White River system is managed for inland trout from its headwaters downstream to near the Highway 112 dam. In 1961, the White River Fishery Area was established by the Wisconsin Conservation Commission. The first land acquisition was the Delta Brook Trout Resort in 1962. This private fishing lodge was located on the South Fork of the White River, and included several impounded springs along with hatchery facilities, a main house, and an airstrip. As of 2013, more than 15,000 acres were protected as state-managed lands. Parking lots, access trails, and habitat projects were developed; moreover, several dams were removed from impounded springs in the headwaters, significantly improving water quality downstream. Water temperatures became lower in the summer and higher in the winter; in addition, the dissolved oxygen levels improved. Because of these improvements, brook trout have expanded their range downstream several miles.

Both brook and brown trout are found in the headwaters; farther downstream brown trout predominate. Although the stream was stocked on a regular basis, stocking has been discontinued because natural reproduction appears to

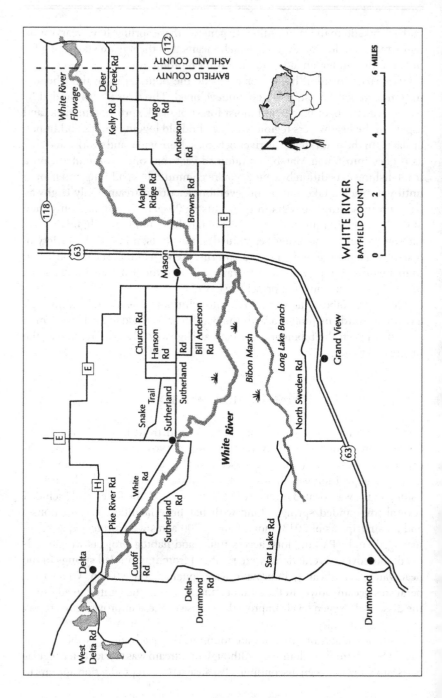

WHITE RIVER
BAYFIELD COUNTY

0   2   4   6 MILES

be adequate. But fish managers are concerned that beaver dams on key spawning tributaries may hurt brown trout populations. That's in part because brown trout are known to migrate up to 30 miles to get to these spawning areas.

ANGLING OPPORTUNITIES

The upper part of the river, from Delta to Sutherland, offers some first-rate brook trout angling for those willing to bushwack in to beaver ponds along the White. But perhaps the most unusual aspect of the White River fishing experience is the trip through the Bibon Marsh. In addition to soaking up the wilderness experience, anglers can search for big trout. A Wisconsin Department of Natural Resources study showed that the White River, and in particular the Bibon swamp reach, has one of the state's highest densities of trout over 12 inches. We've caught several trout over 20 inches and know many others who have done the same. Fortunately, much of the stream is covered by special regulations designed to protect the valuable spawners and to prevent over-harvest of the larger fish. One way to fish this area effectively is from a canoe. The trip from Sutherland to Mason takes about six hours if you don't stop; most people make an afternoon and evening of it. The fact that black bear inhabit the area and the occasional wolf can be heard enhances the allure of a Bibon Marsh float. Some choose to make an overnight camping trip out of the float, but we know of only one area of high ground on the trip that's suitable for camping—and it's stretching the definition of high ground. Some anglers opt to put in their canoe, fish upstream or downstream, and then return to their original point of departure. If you do .venture on a canoe trip—or go into the fringes of the swamp—take plenty of bug dope. Having been lost at night in this wild region ourselves, we'd recommend you take a compass along, too.

Downstream from Mason to the White River Dam at Highway 112, the river changes in character with a dramatic increase in gradient and with many riffles and rapids. With the substrate of the river more rocky, the species of mayflies, stoneflies, and caddisflies increase in number. This part of the river offers a pleasant diversion from the slow meanders of the Bibon Marsh.

The White is best known for its outstanding Hex hatch, perhaps one of the best in the Midwest. The big mayfly begins its emergence about the last week of June and continues well into July, but the Hex hatch is well known for happening off schedule, and the White River hatch is no exception. The hatch is generally regarded to be best downstream from the Pikes River Road Bridge, with the highest population between Sutherland Bridge and Mason.

Other hatches offer excellent fishing. Sulphurs and Brown Drakes make their appearance around the first of June. In addition, the Black Quill inhabits the White River and can provide some exciting, but localized, fishing. Besides mayflies, the river boasts large populations of other aquatic insects, including caddis and midges. When no hatch is present, we use Woolly Buggers, Leeches, and Crayfish—get your imitation down and into the deeply undercut banks. In the summer, try terrestrial patterns such as Grasshoppers and Crickets. Cast tight against those undercut banks.

Nearby trout-fishing options abound. The Bois Brule and Namekagon are within easy driving distance. The Iron River and the Marengo River are also worthy stops. In the spring and fall, you can also try for migrating trout and salmon moving up the Lake Superior tributaries.

Ashland is also the gateway to Wisconsin's beautiful Bayfield Peninsula and the Apostle Islands National Lakeshore. Bayfield, near the tip of the Bayfield Peninsula, is a quaint maritime resort community with many bed-and-breakfasts, restaurants, galleries, and a glorious harbor. A nearby ski hill is transformed every summer into an entertainment facility called Big Top Chautauqua.

Prairie River

STREAM SNAPSHOT
Prairie River

MILES OF TROUT WATER: 43

SETTING: Medium-sized freestoner with great mix of water flowing through wetlands, forest, and wild terrain

TROUT SPECIES: Wild trout (mostly brookies) above Dudley; some brown, rainbow, and brook stocking

REGULATIONS: Category 4 in Langlade and Lincoln counties

BEST FLIES: Hare's Ear, stonefly nymphs, Woolly Bugger, Griffith's Gnat

NEAREST COMMUNITIES: Merrill, Wausau

It's no surprise that so many Wisconsin anglers have a print entitled "Prairie River Solitude" hanging in their dens or fly-tying rooms. Artist Tim Johnson's painting captures the heart of every angler who has ever fished the Prairie. Perhaps we were charmed as much by the name of the painting as by its theme. This popular north-central Wisconsin stream offers variety, scenic beauty, and challenging angling. But, we're sorry to say, it probably offers less solitude than many anglers would like. Only a short trip from Highway 51 and just a few miles northeast of the city of Merrill, this fabulous stream receives heavy fishing pressure. Fortunately, anglers' affection for the Prairie translates into an active conservation constituency, which is the reason the Prairie is the site of one of the most successful dam removal and trout stream restoration projects ever undertaken in Wisconsin.

THE SETTING

The Prairie River originates in northeastern Langlade County as the outlet from Minito and Pine lakes. As it traverses the 12 miles to the Lincoln County border, the river flows over poorly drained glacial outwash soils, gaining flow from groundwater and spring pond discharge. The area is characterized by wetlands, wild terrain, and a diversified forest. In wet areas, the forest includes swamp conifers, hardwoods, thick alder, and lowland brush. Higher and better-drained areas include aspen, hemlock, and northern hardwoods. This part of the Prairie, upstream from the little community of Parrish, is difficult to access; but it offers many possibilities for the small-stream afficionado willing to cut through some tough country in pursuit of wild brook and brown trout.

In Lincoln County, the Prairie flows more than 31 miles through scenic rolling hills, a mixed landscape of forested recreational and agricultural lands. The river merges with its major tributary, the North Branch, about a mile upstream from County Highway J, and ultimately joins the Wisconsin River at Merrill. Above the hamlet of Dudley, the stream is trout water with self-sustaining fish populations; below Dudley, the Prairie has some natural reproduction. From Parrish downstream, the river is paralleled for most of its length by State Highway 17, and access is excellent at numerous crossroads, bridges, and public access points. Anglers and other recreationists are the beneficiaries of a major land acquisition program initiated by the Wisconsin Conservation Department in 1959, when the department approved the designation of the Prairie River Fishery Area. Over the years, the boundary and acreage goals planned for the area have expanded. The Wisconsin Department of Natural Resources presently owns about 1,840 acres of public land in Langlade and Lincoln counties. Between fee ownership and easements, more than 75 percent of upper Prairie River frontage is publicly owned or controlled.

The Prairie is a good-sized river. Where it hasn't been improved by habitat enhancement projects, the average width of the river exceeds 60 feet; these widespread areas tend to be quite shallow, often less than a foot or two in depth. Along its path, the river can exceed 100 feet in width, or be less than 15. Daily mean flows range from a low of 35 cubic feet per second to 4,200 cubic feet per second during peak runoff periods. Long-term records from the U.S. Geological Survey gauging station northeast of Merrill indicate that flows exceed 76 cfs 90 percent of the time. Because of significant groundwater inflows in its upper reaches, the upper Prairie tends to exhibit rather stable levels throughout the angling season. The Prairie is a low-gradient stream, generally less than 5 feet per mile. Much of the stream bottom is sand and gravel, with some big stone pocket-water sections; some long pool areas have a siltier substrate. There's an abundance of wildlife in the area, and the sharp-eyed angler may catch a glimpse of a black bear or an otter sharing the stream.

MANAGEMENT HISTORY

Like many other Wisconsin rivers and streams, the Prairie River was used to float logs down to the mills along the Wisconsin River. Remains of some of the old logging dams can still be seen along the stream. In the middle part of this century, cattle grazing and other agricultural activities led to stream bank erosion, sedimentation and shallowing of the stream, and other problems. Habitat improvement projects conducted by the WDNR, in cooperation with local conservation groups, have rehabilitated large segments of the Prairie. But without question, the most dramatic change in the Prairie River environment in recent years was the removal of the Prairie Dells Dam and the ongoing restoration of

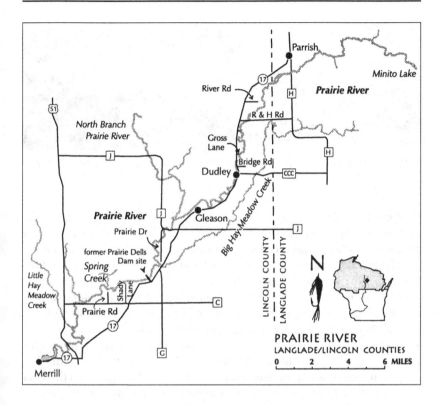

PRAIRIE RIVER
LANGLADE/LINCOLN COUNTIES
0   2   4   6 MILES

the stream. Given the increasing recognition of the potential for restoring many degraded river systems by removing dams, no trout fisher should miss visiting the location of this symbolically important conservation event.

The Prairie Dells Dam site is about 7 miles northeast of Merrill and roughly 3 miles southwest of Gleason (which on an old weathered sign lays claim to being the "Trout Fishing Capital of the World"). The dam was a 60-foot-high masonry structure built in 1904 to generate power for a downstream paper mill. In testing, the generator never produced the required power and was reinstalled elsewhere, so the dam never served its hydropower objective. But it did create a 126-acre lake, later reduced in size, which was used for log transportation. Over the years, the impoundment came to be appreciated by people in surrounding communities for fishing, boating, swimming, duck hunting, picnicking, and general sightseeing. Long-time Trout Unlimited activist Gordon King, of Merrill, recalls his avid trout-fishing friend Otto Krueger reminiscing about what a wonderful trout stream the Prairie was before the in-

The Prairie River dam and power house. Wisconsin Historical Society, WHi-76969.

trusion of the dam. Yet, most area residents had no appreciation for the Prairie River in its free-flowing state. In fact, the county built a wayside and park area and made other recreational improvements to this popular locale.

The private owners of the dam deeded it to Merrill in 1953, which in turn sold it in 1967 to Lincoln County for $1. In 1980 the dam was inspected by the U.S. Army Corps of Engineers, who declared it unsafe. A long history of contracting and negotiating with various engineering consulting firms ensued, but the perpetually escalating cost estimates for repairing the dam always far exceeded estimates for its removal. Sides were taken. A local interest group, the Society for the Preservation of Prairie Dells Dam, formed to support maintenance of the dam. Professional fishery biologists and the local Trout Unlimited chapter favored dam removal. Largely driven by economics and the potential liability associated with dam failure, Lincoln County, amidst much controversy, sought to abandon the dam. A state permit was granted, and with financial assistance from the WDNR, the dam was removed in 1991. The county estimated that the dam controversy cost it about $1 million over a decade; about $200,000 was spent on physically removing the dam.

To nearby communities, removing the dam represented the loss of a widely used warm-water fishing lake and regional recreational resource. But clearly there were environmental problems associated with the dam and impoundment. The pond behind the dam destroyed important trout-spawning areas. Furthermore, the dam was located on a portion of the Prairie where temperature conditions threatened the cold-water fishery. Changes in stream temperatures, documented by WDNR, hurt trout.

Upon removal of the dam, a new problem emerged—how to deal with the nearly twenty feet of sediment that had accumulated behind it. State fisheries personnel, working with the local TU chapter, dug a sediment trap extending across two-thirds of the stream. This trench was two hundred feet long, forty

The free flowing Prairie River after removal of the dam; the river rushes through the narrow canyon at the former impoundment site. Photo by John Exo, courtesy of the River Alliance of Wisconsin.

feet wide, and eight feet deep. In its first year of operation, it was emptied four times, twice yearly after that, and dredged only once in 1995. An estimated 40,000 cubic yards of sandy sediment were removed from the river. From all early appraisals, the trout population has benefited greatly.

To get to the former dam site, follow an inconspicuous roadway on the north side of Highway 17, just before the County Highway G intersection, and take a short hike from the loop road parking area. At the site, you can look into the steep gorge and see a mile of remarkable new trout stream uncovered through this chain of events. As the years go by, anglers marveling at the scenery and fishing should pause to thank those conservationists who led the long battle to restore this reach of the Prairie River.

One of Wisconsin's earliest habitat improvement demonstrations was undertaken in 1950 along approximately a mile of the Prairie River near Gleason. In the streamside corridor, livestock were fenced out from stream banks, trees were planted, and rock wing deflectors were installed. The WDNR and local conservation organizations have continued an intensive habitat improvement program on the upper Prairie. Bank riprapping and the installation of stream improvement devices have led to better habitat and hiding places for trout. A particularly good stretch to see the results of this work (as well as to enjoy some fine fishing) can be found above Dudley between Hackbarth and R & H Road.

While trout populations, especially brook trout, are naturally sustaining in the upper part of the Prairie River above Dudley, supplemental stocking has been carried out lower down in the stream since the 1960s. Retired WDNR area fish manager Max Johnson reports that annual stocking has been fairly consistent in the 1990s: 1,000 yearling brook trout, 4,500 yearling browns, 3,000 fingerling brown trout, and when available from hatcheries, thousands of rainbow yearlings. Supplemental stocking has resulted in a good fishable population of trout in the Prairie, with indications that the brown trout in particular are getting the opportunity to grow. Although scientists aren't sure why, the brown trout population in the Prairie appears to respond very positively to habitat improvements, in contrast to brook trout. It should be noted that the Prairie River trout fishery is very susceptible to drought conditions and thermal warming. The 1988-90 drought, which adversely affected trout streams, over much of Wisconsin, resulted in losses of more than half the trout population at selected monitoring reaches, according to Johnson.

Throughout the 1970s and 1980s, it became increasingly apparent to fish managers that brook trout were being overfished. For this and other reasons harvest regulations on the Prairie have become more restrictive, but several small tributaries offer larger bag limits for those anglers thinking of the frying pan. Additionally, one segment of the Prairie above Dudley was designated for trophy angling, where only artificial lures were used; the bag limit was two fish, with a minimum size of 20 inches for browns and 14 inches for brook trout. This special regulations section attracted anglers seeking larger fish, and WDNR personnel noted that fishing pressure on some parts of the Prairie sometimes rivaled that on some of Wisconsin's most intensively fished streams, including Castle Rock Creek and Timber Coulee Creek. Given the heavy angling pressure on the Prairie, increasingly protective harvest regulations may be necessary to prevent over-exploitation of the fishery.

ANGLING OPPORTUNITIES

The Prairie is a joy to fish. Access is excellent and, for the most part, wading is easy. Competition from canoeists is minimal. The river offers an enormous mix of water types, from big slow pools and classic riffles to boulder-and-rubble-packed water at Yankee Rapids, the Prairie Dells gorge, and from Bridge Road to Gross Lane north of Dudley.

The Prairie has healthy populations of mayflies, caddisflies, and stoneflies. Prominent mayfly hatches include Blue-Winged Olives both early and late in the season; Hendricksons; Light Cahills during early June; Brown Drakes, a superhatch on the river that normally occurs during the first half of June; the Hex hatch, which follows the Brown Drake and usually begins around June 5; and the White Mayfly, early to mid-August. Good populations of caddis exist, and Hare's Ear Nymphs or caddis nymph imitations are always a good choice. After a long cold spring, caddis hatches can be explosive; we remember an incredible hatch of #14 Tan Caddis one early June day. Oxygenated, rubble-strewn substrates have good populations of stoneflies, from the Giant Stonefly to smaller Brown and Golden stoneflies. Montana or Brooks Stonefly Nymphs, or Borger's Red-brown Nymph, or even a big black Woolly Worm or Girdle Bug (#4 or #6) can produce well. In May, in no-hatch situations, we've tried the Hornberg streamer with good results. An abundance of crayfish inhabit the river, and a good crayfish imitation or Woolly Bugger is always worth tying on, as is a Muddler Minnow or other sculpin replica. In long quiet pools, such as above and below Yankee Rapids, trout commonly are found sipping midges, and small #22-24 imitations like the Griffith's Gnat can be effective. Small spinners and Rapalas are quite deadly in many stretches of the river, especially when fished in the long and deep pools next to cover.

Every angler's goal—a big brown trout in the net! Photo by Jim Bartelt.

The Prairie can be difficult fishing, and we've had our share of slow days. But if you connect with one of the stream's great insect emergences or spinner falls—the Brown Drake or White Mayfly hatches are favorites— you'll be back. While we have a strong aversion to guidebooks with detailed step-by-step instructions to particular holes along a stream, we'll make one exception here for beginning or youthful trout fishers. There is a wonderful and easily wadable stretch of water above the Gross Lane pullout and access where, after crossing a dilapidated bridge, you can often find splendid early to mid-May daytime dry fly fishing for beautiful little brook trout and the occasional brown. We've hit the Hendrickson hatch here on several occasions, and most standard imitations and fly styles will work fine, including a #14 Adams. While the fish are small, the fishing is straightforward and the environs are scenic. It's a great place to introduce beginning fly-fishers to Prairie River solitude!

There are numerous other streams to fish nearby. Big Hay Meadow Creek, a Prairie tributary which joins the river near the Highway 17–County Highway G junction, is a lovely little stream. As its name implies, it's open meadowland fishing that can even be good during the dog days of summer. The Prairie's major tributary, the North Branch, also offers some good angling potential, as do many of the small creeks in the immediate area. Within an hour's drive are the Hunting River (covered in our section on the Wolf River), the East Branch of the Eau Claire near Antigo, and the Big and Little Plover rivers near Stevens Point.

Peshtigo River

STREAM SNAPSHOT
Peshtigo River

MILES OF TROUT WATER: More than 30

SETTING: Freestoner featuring whitewater, large boulders, natural terrain

TROUT SPECIES: Brookies, browns, and rainbows; limited reproduction

REGULATIONS: Categories 3 and 5 in Forest and Marinette counties

BEST FLIES: Adams, Elk Hair Caddis, Drakes, Muddler Minnow, Royal Wulff, Pass Lake

NEAREST COMMUNITIES: Crivitz, Dunbar, Crandon, Antigo

Summer seems like the time to head up north, and what better destination than the Peshtigo River, a big and brawny northern river that flows through cool forests on its way to Lake Michigan? But we've discovered an awful truth about the Peshtigo's beautiful waters: they're too warm in the summer when vacation time is readily available. They aren't as hot as in 1871, when the great Peshtigo wildfire raced along its banks, sending people, cows, and assorted other creatures into the waters to fight for survival. But they're warm enough to send the trout—so prevalent in May and June—to spring holes, tributaries, or some other part of the river known only to the fish. The same is true for many of our favorite northern streams. Dams, flow-ages, and northern Wisconsin's hydrologic system—dependent on lakes and wetlands that heat up in the summer sun—are to blame.

So you can still head to the Peshtigo, wade into one the state's first fly-fishing-only section and make all the right casts, but we bet you'll catch few if any fish. Come instead in the spring or the fall, and leave the summer Peshtigo to the whitewater rafters. If you must visit during the heat of the summer, be content to explore the small upper tributaries, where brookies and the occasional bigger trout can be located.

THE SETTING

The Peshtigo River is a huge system, originating in the central portion of Forest County and flowing through Marinette County before it empties into Green Bay, a distance of about 100 miles. The headwaters start at one of the highest points in northern Wisconsin, in the Nicolet National Forest north of Crandon, and the water flows rapidly in most stretches. Unfortunately, this high gradient also made the Peshtigo a prime target for hydroelectric development. The four dam sites on the river above Crivitz are at Caldron Falls, High Falls,

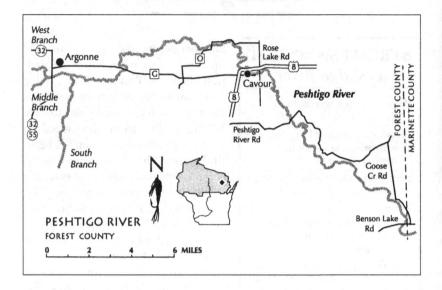

West
Branch
—32
Argonne
Middle
Branch
32
55
South
Branch
N
PESHTIGO RIVER
FOREST COUNTY
0   2   4   6 MILES

Rose
Lake Rd
8
Cavour
8
Peshtigo River
Peshtigo
River Rd
FOREST COUNTY
MARINETTE COUNTY
Goose
Cr Rd
Benson Lake
Rd

Johnson Falls, and the Sandstone Flowage. Trout water is designated up-stream from Sandstone Flowage to about Spring Rapids.

The upper Peshtigo is a maze of small tributaries and feeder streams in a near-wilderness setting. Access is plentiful as the river flows through public lands, including the Nicolet National Forest. Three branches come together near Argonne, in Forest County, to form the main stem of the Peshtigo. The river flows in a generally southeastern direction through the forest into Marinette County. Peshtigo River Road traverses a good portion of the river in this region, and provides a number of access points. The stream is medium-sized and fast-flowing in this region, with flows in the range of 50–100 cubic feet per second. In Marinette County, the river flows through Goodman County Park and McClintock County Park—among the most scenic county parks in the state. Waterfalls abound, and fishing at their base can be excellent as well as aestheti-cally invigorating. Much of river is fly-fishable in this area. The river continues to flow southwest until it crosses County C, where the impoundments start.

The lower Peshtigo starts below the Johnson Falls dam, which also marks the beginning of the five-mile fly-fishing-only waters, established in the fif-ties. This is big water, and fishing difficulties are compounded by water re-leases from the dam that can raise the water level rapidly, making it unsafe for wading. The river continues on its generally southeastern direction down to Crivitz; but trout water is absent from a little upstream of Crivitz to Peshtigo. From the city of Peshtigo to the mouth at Lake Michigan's Green Bay is a good stretch of water for migrating trout species that has excellent steelhead fish-

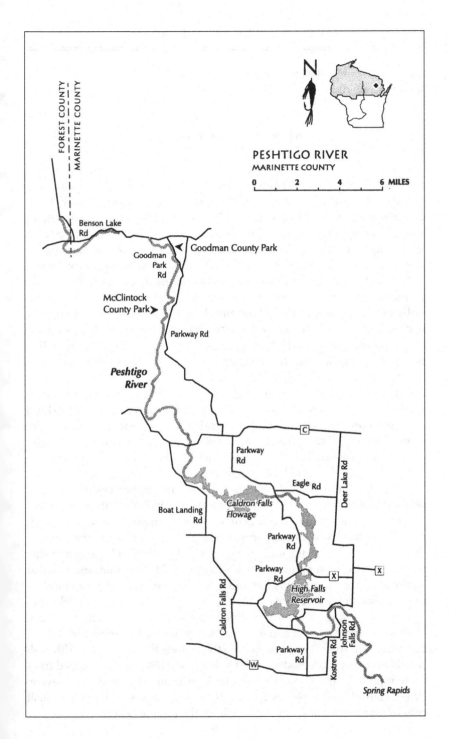

N

PESHTIGO RIVER
MARINETTE COUNTY

0   2   4   6 MILES

FOREST COUNTY

MARINETTE COUNTY

Benson Lake
Rd

Goodman County Park

Goodman
Park
Rd

McClintock
County Park

Parkway Rd

*Peshtigo
River*

C

Parkway
Rd

Eagle Rd

Deer Lake Rd

*Caldron Falls
Flowage*

Boat Landing
Rd

Parkway
Rd

Parkway
Rd

X

X

Caldron Falls Rd

*High Falls
Reservoir*

Kostreva Rd

Johnson
Falls Rd

Parkway
Rd

W

Spring Rapids

ing. Lake-run browns and even some brook trout also can be found during the spawning runs.

MANAGEMENT HISTORY

The five-mile stretch of the Peshtigo below Johnson Falls was one of the first waters in the state to be designated fly-fishing-only. Stretches of the Peshtigo and the Wolf River were given these tackle restrictions in 1955. Lyle Kingston, an engineer with the Wisconsin Public Service Corporation, which operated the Peshtigo dams, is credited with promoting the Peshtigo fly-fishing-only section. He convinced the utility to grant an easement to the Wisconsin Conservation Department (now the Wisconsin Department of Natural Resources) for the purpose of restricting this water to fly-fishing. At the time it was a successful experiment. Today this stretch is still specially regulated; only artificial lures may be used, and only two fish may be harvested per day. Unfortunately, erratic discharges from the Johnson Falls dam limit the quality of the fishing. Aside from the danger to those wading in rapidly rising waters, the changing water levels limit or even eliminate natural reproduction, so all the fish in this stretch are stocked fish. Brook and brown trout naturally reproduce upstream, and we're convinced natural reproduction could happen here, too. We wonder what would happen to local tourism in the summer if the lower Peshtigo were transformed into a cold, trout-friendly tailwater fishery, similar to those in the West. Trout angler visits during the summer would surely increase. Perhaps regulatory changes in operating the dam will lead to more fish-friendly flows on the Peshtigo.

Like other northern Wisconsin streams, the upper Peshtigo is also plagued by nature's dam-builder, the beaver. Beaver dams in the upper headwaters and feeder streams are difficult to control, simply because of the vastness of the area. By damming up a stream, beaver dams warm the water in the summer and allow the water to ice over and remain colder longer during the winter. The beaver ponds often lead to the build-up of nongame fish that compete with the trout, and greater fish densities can bring about an increase in predators and fish diseases. Most important, the reduced water velocities can ruin spawning sites for trout. Even after a dam is breached, the stream channel is often widened and water velocities are too low to remove the accumulated silt from the stream bed, so the damage is long-lasting. Although new beaver dams can produce good fishing for a few years as trapped trout grow rapidly in the flooded water, the long-term effect is usually severe. While controlling beavers is a major fishery management activity, a small fisheries management staff is no match for the prolific beaver.

ANGLING OPPORTUNITIES

Brook trout primarily occupy the headwaters of the upper Peshtigo, and fly-fishing can be tough in this country. But if you're a spin-fisher and don't mind doing some bushwhacking, some beautiful brook trout can be your reward. Panther Martins and other small spinners flipped upstream and retrieved just faster than the current are a good bet. Experiment a bit on the rate of retrieve and the size and color of the spinner.

The fly-fisher can succeed, too. Sometimes sticking a fly rod between tag alders and drifting a weighted streamer, like a Muddler Minnow or Woolly Bugger, downstream under banks and deadfalls can induce strikes. Brook trout are plentiful, and this is one of those situations where it doesn't hurt to harvest some fish. There are so many brook trout that competition for food limits their growth, so some judicious thinning of the population is desirable. Make sure to check the trout regulations for what you can keep.

Downstream from Cavour to the beginning of the reservoirs, you encounter rock-strewn pocket water reminiscent of the freestone rivers of the East. There are many access points along Peshtigo River Road, as well as Benson Lake Road. Goodman Park and McClintock Park are also good access points, but you're more apt to have company when starting at these locations; even so, blessed solitude can quickly be found.

Fly hatches are typical for a northern freestoner. Hendricksons can be a significant mayfly hatch in May. March Browns occur in late May and June; we use a large (#12) darkish mayfly imitation, like a Dark Cahill. Brown Drake hatches can be spectacularly large. Caddis, particularly Tan Caddis, occur throughout the spring and summer, and a heavily hackled pattern, such as the Elk Hair Caddis, is a good choice in the usually fast water of the Peshtigo.

Attractor patterns, such as the classic Royal Coachman, the Pass Lake, or the White Wulff, can be good throughout the season but especially early, when the fish are active and looking up toward the surface. In this fast water the trout are likely to grab anything that catches their attention because the swift current doesn't give them time to inspect the imitation. The Pass Lake is especially popular because it can be fished wet or dry. Regulars on the Peshtigo cast it upstream and let it swing below them, then retrieve it like a streamer. Big streamers can produce big fish on the Peshtigo. Try the Muddler Minnow, the Woolly Bugger, Zonker, or a Strip Leech. Weight them and keep them ticking along the bottom.

In the special regulations stretch below the Johnson Falls dam, the same hatches occur, but the timing of the hatches is less predictable, because of the varying flows. The caddis hatch, beginning in late afternoon, can be enormous in late May and early June. Try a darkish #14 or #16 Elk Hair Caddis with a brown body for this hatch. In September, when the water cools again, streamer patterns, such as a Clouser Deep Minnow, can be effective in the bigger holes.

In selecting a section of the Peshtigo to fish, anglers need to be aware that brown trout move with the seasons in search of optimum water temperatures. Scientists have documented fish moving as much as 12 miles during spring and fall; one trout moved downstream 10 miles in only four days.

There are many other fishing options in the "empty corner," a nickname for the sparsely populated northeastern portion of the state. The Oconto and Pike rivers are nearby (see separate sections on those waters). Many of the brook trout streams that feed the Peshtigo are unnamed. But one named creek in Forest County, Otter Creek, near Argonne, is specially regulated for brook trout. Remember also that fishing is available in the spring and fall for steelhead and other migrating fish making their way up from Lake Michigan.

When visiting the Peshtigo, camping at Goodman or McClintock parks will make your trip enjoyable even if the trout aren't cooperating. These county parks are very well maintained and are among the nicest camping facilities we have seen in the state. Built in the 1930s by the old Civilian Conservation Corps, the parks consistently fulfill our desires for a taste of the Northwoods. They are especially good for taking kids camping. The bridges that cross the rushing Peshtigo and the wooden walkways that lace the parks provide, to a child's eye, magical paths that lead into a mystical wilderness.

If you're curious about the great Peshtigo fire, visit the fire museum in Peshtigo. It tells the story of the worst fire disaster in U.S. history. We all know about the Chicago fire that burned through that city on the same windy day in October 1871, but Peshtigo and nearby settlements were even more devastated; in all, some 1,200 people died.

Oconto River

Drive west along Highway 64 between the tiny Northwoods communities of Mountain and Langlade, and you'll cross the North Branch of the Oconto, the First South Branch of the Oconto, the Second South Branch of the Oconto, and finally the South Branch of the Oconto. We and countless other anglers have been rightly confused, especially during our early visits when we were directed to fish the "north or south branch" of the Oconto. To make matters worse, even the North Branch flows south. "In this country you can hardly walk in any direction without having to cross some branch of the Oconto," says Tim Kinzel, a Madison dentist who grew up fishing the complex river system. Where to fish? Well, it's hard to go wrong, because there are trout in all the branches of the Oconto; this maze of streams forms one of the premier trout rivers in Wisconsin.

THE SETTING

The Oconto and its many branches, originating just east of the Wolf River watershed, flow in a generally southeastern direction. The main part of the South Branch comes together in northeastern Menominee County and then hooks up with the North Branch just above Suring in Oconto County. From Suring on down to Lake Michigan, these waters are called the Oconto River.

We like to fish the main South Branch, which begins about a mile west of Mary Lake in the Nicolet National Forest. Trout waters don't begin until below Setting Lake, near where the stream crosses Setting Lake Road. The main South Branch starts to pick up flow as it receives water from springs and tributaries on its travels back and forth between Langlade and Oconto counties, with flows in the range of 25–50 cubic feet per second. The river flows under State Highway

64 a few miles east of Langlade; from here it deepens and takes on the characteristics of a small but swiftly flowing freestoner. The South Branch flows west and then south until it crosses into Menominee County and the Menominee Indian Reservation, where public fishing is not permitted. After receiving water from its sister branches, the main South Branch flows out of the reservation and soon crosses County AA in far northwestern Oconto County. Most anglers devote their attention here. At this point the South Branch is a good-sized trout river, about 50 feet wide with an average depth of about 1.5 feet. The bottom is sand, gravel, and small rocks. Trout waters continue to the confluence of the North Branch, below Highway 32 and a few miles northwest of Suring.

While the undeveloped South Branch watershed receives relatively little pollution, the water is stained with dissolved organic matter received from the many natural wetlands it drains. Like other rivers in the northeast, the water has relatively low alkalinity and hardness, limiting fish growth and numbers. However, what it lacks in fertility it makes up for in sheer length, so the South Branch still holds a lot of trout. Above the reservation the South Branch is mostly brook trout water; below the reservation, both browns and brook trout are the fare, and there is considerable cultivated land in the watershed. Fortunately, the lower flood plain mostly contains northern hardwoods and conifers, so anglers still get the aura of the Northwoods. Below AA the river passes through the Oconto Fishery Area, which offers substantial public access.

MANAGEMENT HISTORY

Creel surveys show that two-thirds of the anglers fishing the South Branch are from the Green Bay area and the rest of Fox River Valley. Anglers from this region, organized through groups such as Trout Unlimited, have championed stream improvements and conservation efforts on the South Branch. Lack of habitat is a major limitation in many parts of the river, so much volunteer labor has been devoted to helping state fisheries managers create in-stream holding cover. Other major management activities on the South Branch include beaver control, construction of sand traps, and cattle fencing.

Another management activity somewhat ahead of its time was the implementation of special angling regulations for the popular stretch between Highways AA and 32. Fearing overharvest, angling devotees of the South Branch mounted a campaign for special regulations. Finally, in 1988 the trout take was limited to three fish per day, with a 10-inch size limit on brook trout and a 13-inch limit on browns. More significantly, no live bait angling was allowed. In 1990, new statewide regulations went into effect that included similar harvest restrictions. The years of discussions and debate that preceded the South

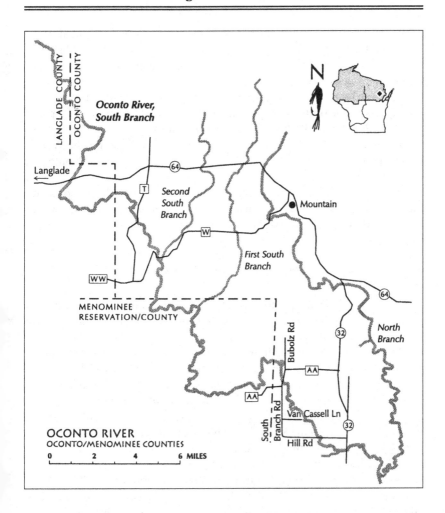

Branch regulations undoubtedly helped clear the way for similar regulations to be adopted statewide.

The Oconto has also been the site of some important trout fishery research. Wisconsin Department of Natural Resources fisheries biologists once tagged 2,000 brown trout and found they traveled vast distances. Beginning in the spring, many fish traveled forty miles or more upstream to smaller, cooler streams. Temperature appeared to drive this annual migration. As the water warmed, the tagged trout moved gradually upstream, displacing the smaller brookies, which in turn moved even farther upstream. After spawning in October, the brown trout often moved back downstream to larger, deeper waters.

Such a finding has many implications for the fisher, since those small tributaries and feeders could hold big trout during the summer, and the fisheries manager, for removal of headwater dams and obstructions could greatly enhance big trout populations.

The very lower reaches of the Oconto River, below the Stiles dam at Highway 141, was one of the most polluted rivers in the state because of a paper mill in Stiles. The mill closed in 1978 and a subsequent court settlement stemming from government legal action provided $600,000 for the WDNR to restore a fishery damaged since the 1890s. Today the lower Oconto is a vibrant fishery, prized for its warm-water species and its nearly year-round steelhead run. Stocking of lake-run browns and chinook add to the excitement in the spring and fall, and an agreement with a local power cooperative keeps the flows stable below Stiles.

ANGLING OPPORTUNITIES

Because of these clean-up efforts and the resiliency of the Oconto, trout can be found the length of the system. The WDNR and local fishing groups have helped ensure ample access, too.

Access is especially good in the upstream part of the main South Branch, as it flows mostly through the Nicolet National Forest. Be careful of wading above the reservation, because some spots are very mucky and one can get in deep trouble. Wading in the stretch upstream of County Highway W is particularly hazardous. There is a section downstream from Sauls Spring in the headwaters called the Mud Flats. This is serious muck, and can be fished only from a canoe or other watercraft.

A lot of access points can be found downstream from the Menominee Indian Reservation. There is a parking area on Hill Road west of Highway 32. The wading here is quite easy, though the current is swift. The South Branch and its tributaries can be easily fished with ultralight spinning tackle. Try a tiny jointed lure for brook trout. Make a down-and-across cast, and let it catch in the current and begin to wobble; then hold it as it swings. At the apex of its swing it should be right where you suspect Mr. Trout to be lurking. If the fish doesn't take right away, hold it in the current; sometimes the enticing motion of the lure will bring on a strike. This technique is similar to fishing a wet fly or streamer using a down-and-across swing, one of the oldest techniques around. Another spinning technique is to throw a spinner or wobbling spoon into some slower deep water, letting the lure fall to the bottom. Make your cast upstream. After the lure settles on the bottom, begin a slow retrieve just faster than the current. The lure will remain deep and will even scrape the bottom.

As a general rule, getting and keeping lures deep or right off the bottom will result in more strikes. Unfortunately, it will also result in many lost lures. Frugal spin-fishers, like fly-tying anglers, learn to make their own lures.

As in other northeastern streams, fly hatches aren't as predictable as they are in southern Wisconsin, but there's still plenty to interest the fly-fisher. In the spring, Blue-Winged Olives often lead to good dry fly action. March Browns can hatch towards the end of May and into June; a size #10 dry fly imitation is about right for this hatch. The Brown Drake is another big fly (#8 or #10) that can really excite the fish when it occurs in late May and early June. There is some Hex fishing on portions of the South Branch in the silty, mucky areas in late June. The mud flats mentioned earlier can have very heavy hatches of this giant mayfly, and it's quite an experience to see all the brook trout up on the surface gorging themselves. Caddisflies are active through most of the spring and early summer. Elk Hair Caddis, or other heavily hackled patterns, are usually effective. Streamers are good throughout the season, but particularly in August and September; we like the Muddler Minnow, Woolly Buggers in various colors, and the old reliable Mickey Finn. If you're determined to fish dry, Wisconsin's own Pass Lake is an all-purpose pattern that is easy to follow in the colored water.

A wild brown caught nymphing. Photo by Jim Bartelt.

It catches fish and we know of some highly accomplished anglers who use little else.

Warm water can be a problem in the summer, so the best fishing (and the most fishing pressure) occurs in May and June. But if you're on the Oconto in the dog days, remember the fisheries study and go into the headwaters region. In September, when temperatures start to cool, move back downstream. Past creel surveys show the highest catch rates (fish caught per hour) were actually in September, even though the fishing pressure was very low.

The tributaries of the Oconto and their feeders are all worth exploring. The Wolf River is nearby, and so is the Peshtigo (see separate chapters on those waters). Below Oconto Falls and the Machickanee Flowage, the Oconto's migratory fishery starts. Steelhead and salmon, and occasionally brown and brook trout, move into this water from Green Bay. The spring and fall fishing for these monsters, including some exciting surface feeding on small dry flies, can be spectacular. Popular access points include the Highway 141 bridge, the Highway J bridge to the east, and Suzie's Rapids upstream from the Highway 41 bridge.

Wolf River

STREAM SNAPSHOT
Wolf River

MILES OF TROUT WATER: 34 public; 27 nonpublic in Menominee Reservation

SETTING: Big, brawling, high-gradient freestoner flowing through hilly and wooded terrain

TROUT SPECIES: Browns, brookies, and occasional rainbows; fishery maintained by stocking

REGULATIONS: Categories 4 and 5 in Langlade County

BEST FLIES: Cap's Hairwing, stonefly nymphs, Woolly Bugger; Brown Drake and White Fly (in season)

NEAREST COMMUNITIES: Langlade, Antigo, Shawano

An 1880 map of the Wolf River and vicinity lists a fledgling community called Troutville, south of Langlade. No Troutville exists near the spot on the map where the present-day Wild Wolf Inn lies, but those early white settlers knew what they were talking about. Local tourism boosters have dubbed the Wolf River environs "Troutland." Whatever the name, the centerpiece of this famous Wisconsin trout country is the brawling and boulder-strewn Wolf River. The largely undeveloped and natural state of much of the Wolf's shoreland, along with its size and extensive stretches of whitewater, make fishing the Wolf as close to a "big river" western experience as Wisconsin offers. Waist-deep in this most untamed of Wisconsin trout waters, in the company of bald eagles and ospreys soaring high overhead, taking in the stately white pines that line the shore, it's hard to imagine a better place to be.

THE SETTING

From the outlet of Pine Lake in northeastern Wisconsin, some 25 miles south of the Michigan border, the Wolf River flows and grows southerly for 200 miles to where it enters Lake Poygan. Giant sturgeon from Lake Winnebago move into the warmer, slower parts of the river in the spring to spawn, but upstream is trout water. More than 34 miles of the river in Langlade County and 27 miles traversing the Menominee Indian Reservation to the south are classified as trout waters. The Menominee Reservation portion of the river is authorized as part of the National Wild and Scenic River System. You know why when you see it. It's especially picturesque, with old-growth forests and dramatic river scenes such as Big Smoky Falls. This part of the river, however, is closed to fishing by nontribal members. State Highway 55, which nearly overlays the 1830s

Military Road (the old Lake Superior trail), parallels and provides good access to the primary trout waters from the town of Lily down to the Menominee Reservation boundary. Being close to the reservation offers visitors the chance to drive through the one big piece of northern Wisconsin spared the massive timber clearcuts of an earlier time. Every time we're there, we stop to marvel at the big pines.

The Wolf's waters are slightly alkaline and colored light brown. The river averages more than 50 yards in width, partly the source of the Wolf's big trout water reputation. At Langlade, the average flow is slightly less than 500 cubic feet per second, ranging from about 150 cfs in low water periods to more than 2,100 cfs during periods of high spring runoff. With common-sense wading precautions, much of the river is wadable for most of the fishing season, although some rapids are extremely dangerous and a few are unwadable. Water temperatures range from 32 degrees to as high as 83 for short periods in the summer. During these times of high temperatures, which can be lethal to trout, the fish seek relief near the many groundwater seeps, rivulets, and springs entering the river. Pay attention to the temperature conditions, which are critical to finding good fishing opportunities on the Wolf.

While the upper Wolf from Pearson to Lily is relatively low gradient, with only three rapids over approximately 14 miles, the river descends more than 400 feet between Lily and the Menominee Reservation line. This stretch is characterized by sections of whitewater, with some 24 rapids and a gradient of 15 feet per mile. This rapid drop results in tumbling falls that attract rafters, kayakers, and other water-loving recreationists from all over the Midwest. So trout fishers must share the resource. Fortunately the potential for conflict has been substantially reduced by local ordinance and by the cooperation of the local rafting "industry" so that fishers have the undisturbed advantage of prime morning and evening trout fishing.

More than 90 percent of the watershed is forested or relatively undisturbed land. Northern hardwoods are the dominant tree types in the region, with swamp hardwoods and conifers, especially fir and spruce bordering the Wolf and its tributaries. The Wolf River flows over a Precambrian granite-type rock complex more than a billion years old. For the most part, these igneous and metamorphic rocks are buried under more than 100 feet of glacial deposits; you can see these rocks where the Wolf River channel has cut the glacial terrain overlying the bedrock.

We mention this geologic history because some of the gravest long-term threats to this marvelous resource stem from the geologic character of the Wolf River region. Several years ago the federal government listed

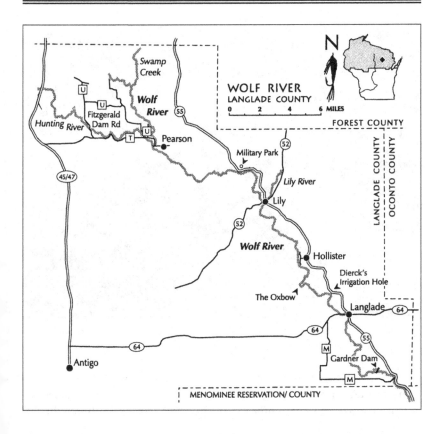

the region as one of several possible sites across the nation for the location of a permanent, underground, high-level nuclear waste site. The region has since been dropped from the list. But there have been other threats. The Crandon Mining Company, a subsidiary of two mining giants, Exxon and Rio Algom, proposed a major underground copper and zinc mining operation in the area. The plan for developing this mineral deposit, first announced in the mid-seventies as the largest sulfide deposit of its type in North America, was under review by state and federal environmental regulators during the mid-nineties. The mining company originally proposed discharging treated mining wastewater into Swamp Creek, a tributary of the Wolf, but was forced to consider other alternatives. The greatest potential long-term threat from mining involves the disposal of mine tailings. Such mining waste would have to be safely managed forever to protect the re-

The Hunting River—tributary to the Wolf River and a fine trout stream in its own right. Photo by Steve Born.

gion's groundwater quality and stream flows. Not surprisingly, a wide array of conservation and environmental organizations successfully fought the project.

The Wolf River has often been exploited for commercial gain. It played an important role in the mid-1800s settlement and economic development of the region, an economy which was largely built around logging. State government studies note that the five dams built in Langlade County by the Wolf River Improvement Company were used to ease the shipping of lumber to the mills on the lower river. From there, the tall and thick white pines of the region were floated down the river to Oshkosh, where historians note that some fifty sawmills prepared logs for shipment to Green Bay and Chicago. Few obvious signs of the dams and other remnants of the old lumber industry remain, but anglers still can connect to this bit of North Country history when they snag their lure on drowned logs from a bygone era. For a more conventional study of this era, take a mid-day break and visit the Langlade County Historical Society in Antigo.

MANAGEMENT HISTORY

Conservation and intense natural resources management have also been a big part of the Wolf's history. In 1966, the Wisconsin Conservation Commission approved the establishment of the Upper Wolf Fishery Area, with the major goal of providing fishing and other recreational opportunities while keeping the Wolf in its natural state. Since 1966, the Wisconsin Department of Natural Resources has acquired slightly more than 9,150 acres on the Upper Wolf at a cost of about $6.5 million. Ultimately, according to their master plan, the agency hopes to acquire 14,240 acres. In 1968, Congress designated the upper Wolf River as part of the nation's Wild and Scenic River System. While the Wolf isn't formally incorporated into that system, it is managed by the state in a manner generally consistent with the guidelines and spirit of the act. Land acquisition and the wild-and-scenic-river guidelines help ensure public access and scenic beauty. State laws also ban navigation improvements or dams on the Upper Wolf, thus assuring a wild, free-flowing Wolf River. In general, WDNR's management strives to manage the river corridor—extending at least 300 feet from the stream banks—to provide a high-quality recreational experience. Veteran WDNR Antigo-area fish manager Max Johnson, now retired, worked hard to restore river habitat for trout for several years, and the results of one such project, completed in 1994–95, can be seen about half a mile upstream from Hollister Road.

The WDNR classifies the Wolf River through the Menominee Reservation (also Menominee County) and north to Pearson as water than can sustain some natural reproduction and good survival and growth of trout. But these waters require supplemental stocking to maintain the sports fishery desired by anglers. The Hunting River, a major spring-fed tributary that enters the Wolf at Pearson, is also rated as having some natural reproduction. Several self-supporting streams enter the Wolf below Pearson. Brown trout are the heart of the fishery, but anglers will catch occasional rainbows in the riffles and rapids, and brookies near cold-water tributaries and springs. Small-stream angling for brook and brown trout is available on the tributaries downstream from Pearson.

Natural reproduction in the Wolf is limited, and Johnson indicates that 70 percent or more of the trout in the river are stocked fish. Fluctuations in fish populations are largely due to stocking success and to short-term weather conditions, such as drought or severe cold. The stocking program is carried out by WDNR, with the aid of Trout Unlimited and local conservation clubs. Separate seasonal stockings appear to provide greater assurance of stocking success and more consistent high-quality fishing. Johnson believed that the quality of fish stocked in the Wolf had declined over the years—the result of brood stock domesticated in hatcheries. Returns from stocking hatchery rainbow trout were so low that stocking them was discontinued. The agency has since been working with wild strains of brown trout secured from the Prairie and Oconto rivers, hoping to produce a better Wolf River trout.

Herb Buettner—the late long-time Trout Unlimited activist, proprietor of the Wild Wolf Inn, and 1960s pioneer of commercial rafting on the river— believed removal of beaver dams would go a long way towards improving the Wolf's brook trout fishery. Beaver dam removal on small spring creek tributaries would lower water temperatures, and there are some indications that natural reproduction is increasing in improved tributaries. Buettner also has been working with the Menominee Indians and others to raise a wilder strain of rainbows historically adapted to Wolf River conditions. Rainbows were once a significant part of the fishery but were overfished during the Depression, as the needy used any means (including dynamite) to put meat on the table. As Buettner nurtures the fingerlings in his small private hatchery, he looks ahead optimistically to these wild-gene rainbows someday reducing the river's dependence on stocking.

A 6-mile special regulations section of the Wolf has been set aside for fly-fishing, catch-and-release only. This area, known as the Oxbow, starts at the railroad trestle at Hollister and extends downstream to Dierck's Irrigation Hole. Interestingly, the Wolf joined the Peshtigo River in 1955 as Wisconsin's first fly-fishing-only waters, when more than 4 miles of the Wolf in Langlade County were designated as flies-only water.

ANGLING OPPORTUNITIES

Upstream from Pearson, the Wolf is a warm-water fishery. Downstream, particularly from Lily to the Menominee Indian Reservation line, the Wolf is a classic, big-water, freestone river, with challenging flats, runs, pools, riffles, and boulder-filled pocket water. Access to the river is good, with several highway bridges and parking lots between County Highway T west of Pearson and County Highway M just north of the Menominee line. Among the more popular access points are the Military Park wayside north of Lily (the best public facilities along the river), Hollister, the Irrigation Hole north of Langlade, the State Highway 64 bridge, the Gardner Dam Boy Scout Camp (stop and get permission from the ranger), and the County Highway M bridge. WDNR's land acquisition program has resulted in more than 25 miles of publicly owned stream frontage, a remarkable conservation heritage for Wolf River anglers. A bit of hiking will get you to some less-pressured water, but a rafting trip is an especially effective—and sometimes truly exciting—way to cover the more remote stretches of the Wolf. Trout anglers seeking solitude will want to avoid the mid-day hatch of rubber rafts, canoes, and kayaks on this heavy-use section (a dandy chart is available from local outfitters showing where and when anglers can fish undisturbed during normal rafting hours). However, we've had excellent daytime fishing working shoreline lies away from the main river flows; the parade of watercraft, which can disturb the tranquility, doesn't seem to affect the trout much. We recall catching five fish in the 15-inch range early one summer afternoon while working logs with a green-bodied Woolly Bugger.

May through mid June are the prime fishing months and offer the most consistent fishing. For the fly-fisher, hatches during this period are fairly dependable. Buettner notes that if conditions are right and river flows aren't too high, a good early season is almost guaranteed. Fishing and fish populations are ultimately controlled by weather conditions. If water temperatures are too warm, the trout will ignore even the heaviest hatches and spinner falls. We recall a bluebird June day a few years ago. Adult stonefly egg-layers were everywhere, crashing into the boulder-infested pocket water at the Boy Scout camp. Over a period of several hours we did not witness a single rise! The water temperature? Seventy-eight degrees. Temperature is the key to late spring and summer fishing opportunities on the Wolf. Anglers can cope with warm water by fishing in the cool of the evening and morning, or by locating cooler water below springs, tributaries, and seeps. During sustained very hot weather periods, when water temperatures can reach 83 degrees, consider pursuing non-fishing activities. In such scorching conditions, even if you succeed in connecting with some trout, the stress of the battle could well be lethal for them. In the fall, water temperatures cool and the fishing picks up again. There's an extended fall season on the Wolf, allowing the opportunity for a "cast-and-blast" adventure combining superb grouse hunting with trout angling.

Strategies for fishing the Wolf are varied. Spin-fishers do well on Panther Martins, Rooster Tails, and Mepps spinners, Rapalas, and numerous other lures fished through and around cover. When there's no hatch, fly-fishers can fish weighted nymphs deep around boulders, always prime holding lies in the Wolf. Big stonefly imitations (#4–6 Brooks or Kaufmann Stonefly Nymphs, black Woolly Worms and Girdle Bugs, and Golden Stoneflys), caddis larva replicas, and old standards such as the Hare's Ear and Prince Nymphs are always good choices. Tandem nymph rigs are effective and give the angler a chance to explore the trout's menu preferences. Fish a stonefly or similar weighted imitation on the leader, and a Serendipity or Hare's Ear as the point or dropper fly. Of course, the two-nymph set-up also doubles your chances for losing flies.

Wayne Anderson, a well-known local guide, favors a swinging wet fly, nymph, or streamer; he thinks the activated swinging fly is a key to successful searching for trout on the river. Anderson, by the way, has paired with Gary LaFontaine to produce an excellent audiocassette, "Fly Fishing the Wolf River" (available from Greycliff Publishing Company).

Various streamers can be enormously effective when worked around boulders and through fast currents. Jeff Smith, an avid Wolf River fly-fisher from Madison, says simply, "When in doubt, fish a Muddler Minnow," and a variety of muddler-like imitations have been the bread and butter of local experts like Buettner. Woolly Buggers, Blacknose Dace, and a local standby, the Artesian Green, are favorites. Because the Wolf has an abundance of crayfish, a crayfish pattern fished deep and retrieved in short strips is often productive. In fall, a swinging and activated White Marabou Streamer can be devastating. Local fly shops are well worth visiting to pick up some home-grown favorites.

One final word of advice regarding strategy: keep moving. While the Wolf is a good fishery, it doesn't support the fish populations of many rivers and streams. The abundant food supply and the diversity of habitats allow the existing fish population to spread out. What appear to be "can't miss" lies often don't hold fish. The angler must keep on the move, searching persistently for interested and willing trout.

Local expert anglers may argue about the best mayfly hatch on the river, but there's no disagreement about the excellent insect hatches and high-quality dry fly fishing. Anderson argues that the mid-May Sulphur hatch is the greatest fishing of the year. This hatch can start as early as 3:30 in the afternoon and will bring up the bigger fish. Long-time Wolf River angler Jim Curry thinks the Sulphur hatch is less dependable than the next superhatch, the Gray Drake, which usually begins hatching the last week of May. Others would argue for the explosive early to mid-June Brown Drake hatch and spinner fall. Gary Borger describes Brown Drake hatches on the flats of the Wolf "that appeared as a column 400 yards long, 200 feet wide and rising out of sight into the evening sky." We have witnessed such spectacular hatches, too, but they don't always bring the fish up. Such fish behavior is a constant source of angler angst on the Wolf.

Other hatches can offer splendid fishing. Curry likes the mid-May Hendrickson hatch, which he feels is the first fishable hatch before the emergence of the Sulphurs. A Yellow Drake hatch (matched with a #12 Cream Fly) comes off in the latter half of June and can provide good fishing, depending on water temperature. The Wolf also has a significant Hex hatch that generally starts in mid July The Hex here is not the fabled *Hexagenia limbata*, but a smaller, #8-hook-size cousin. Depending again on water temperature and related weather conditions, an angler prowling the siltier sections of the river for the emergence of the duns and the later evening spinner fall has a real opportunity to hook one of the Wolf's biggest browns (5 pounds plus) on a dry fly. In those years when water conditions have remained relatively cool, the White Mayfly hatch can furnish some of the best dry fly angling of the year. This hatch, matched with a #12 imitation, begins in early August and can produce evening blizzards of flies big enough to attract the larger fish.

The timing of emergences and their duration is, of course, subject to temperature and other natural factors that influence the internal clocks of insect populations. Ask around at the area fly shops for specific hatch information; you can check out local patterns developed to meet the Wolf's hatches at the same time. George Close from Kiel, who owned a cabin on the river, developed his Close Carpet Fly before Antron became a common fly-tying material. Close uses milled Antron rug fibers from a special source—his cabin's floor—to build up the thorax on this Comparadun-style fly. Fished flush in the film, the Carpet Fly is effective during the Drake hatches, and for George's favorite Wolf River hatch, the Sulphur, as well.

No discussion of the Wolf's fly-fishing and patterns can be complete without mention of Herb Buettner's deceased brother, Cap, master angler and designer of the Hairwing Adams. Cap's Hairwing (as it was rechristened in 1983 by Cap's master fly-tier Ed Haaga) has been a fast-water staple on the Wolf for decades. It is fished in various sizes throughout the Hendrickson and Brown and Gray Drake hatches, and also as a general attractor pattern. Locals argue about the origins, tying variations, and best tiers, but no fly angler should be on the Wolf without some of Cap's Hairwings in his flybox.

Although the Wolf is not known as a caddis stream, caddisflies can produce good fishing throughout the season. Green-bodied and other caddis are well matched with Elk Hair Caddis and flat-water No-Hackle Caddis in various patterns; local flurries of egg-layers and emergers can result in exciting fishing.

On rare occasions we've experienced some spectacular dry fly fishing for egg-laying stoneflies. One late May afternoon, as the last of the rafts and kayaks paraded by, stoneflies flew and were wind-blown from streamside vegetation into the side channel where we were wading, giving rise to a feeding frenzy of waiting browns. Stimulators or Hairwings (#8-10) drifted down the run to the watchful trout resulted in more than a dozen fish up to 15 inches, many with undigested stoneflies still dangling from their mouths! Smaller (#14-16) stoneflies, the Little Yellow Sallies, can also provide fishing opportunities during May. And on the many long flats of the Wolf, midge fishing possibilities exist throughout the season. A #20 Griffith's Gnat is always a good choice when the trout are sipping tiny flies.

The Wolf is an amazingly productive river. The angler will commonly encounter several species of mayflies, caddisflies, and other insects simultaneously. The insects may be in varied stages of emergence or egg-laying, giving rise to incredibly complex hatches. Such situations produce some of the greatest challenges (and often the highest levels of frustration) of our sport. The successful angler must adapt by changing his flies and techniques frequently in search of success. Trout can be very picky in these situations, and what may look like the obvious fish food of choice to the angler may not correlate with the trout's appetite.

Fishing the Wolf River is a beautiful experience. It can also be a dangerous one. Wading the rapids and riffles of the river, especially during higher flows, demands caution. A wading belt, boots with studs, and a wading staff are important pieces of gear for anglers who wish to make a return trip.

A wealth of options awaits Wolf River visitors. The spring-fed Hunting River joins the Wolf at Pearson, and adds more than 15 miles of fine trout waters with a healthy population of brookies and browns. The lower portion of the Hunting (upstream to Fitzgerald Dam Road) is under a restrictive harvest, artificials-only regulation. The WDNR has done some of its finest habitat restoration work on the Hunting, and for the smaller-stream fisher, it's a gem. One warning—don't forget your mosquito repellent.

The Lily River also offers several miles of small-stream pocket-water fishing, as do other Wolf River tributaries. There are also several small lakes

Springheads and tributaries of the Wolf hold jewel-like brook trout. Photo by Jim Bartelt.

and spring ponds in the region for the still-water angler, like McGee Lake, 2 miles south of Elton and State Highway 64. McGee is a 25-acre spring-fed lake which the WDNR stocks with some nice rainbows and brookies. After the crowds of the season opening, anglers can find elbow room here for a day of belly-boating. The Nicolet National Forest spans eastward from the Wolf into Marinette County, with many small streams supporting native brook trout. And the cousin of the Wolf, Waupaca County's Little Wolf River, has a watershed with well over 200 miles of trout water that will provide opportunities for any angling method. Also nearby are some of our other featured streams, including the East Branch of the Eau Claire, the Oconto, and the Peshtigo.

Pike River

STREAM SNAPSHOT
Pike River

MILES OF TROUT WATER: 66, including N. Branch, S. Branch,
Little S. Branch, and main stem

SETTING: Freestone Wild and Scenic River featuring waterfalls
and heavily forested terrain

TROUT SPECIES: Wild brookies and
browns, some rainbows

REGULATIONS: Category 4 in Marinette County

BEST FLIES: Hare's Ear, Elk Hair
Caddis, Muddler Minnow,
Royal Wulff, Pass Lake wet

NEAREST COMMUNITIES: Crivitz,
Dunbar, Marinette, Iron Mountain, Mich.

Sometimes in these parts of far north-eastern Wisconsin you feel as though you're in the remote Upper Peninsula of Michigan. After all, the land mass called the Upper Peninsula continues into Wisconsin. Only after you cross the wide Menominee River are you formally in the Badger State, but on either side of this rather arbitrary dividing line you find a similar kind of trout stream. It's usually a tributary to a much bigger river, like the Menominee. And it's full of waterfalls, where tea-colored water pours over ancient rocks, spilling, gurgling, and rushing to one of the big lakes.

Ernest Hemingway wrote about an Upper Peninsula trout stream in his stories about the Big Two-Hearted River: "shallows, light glittering, big water-smooth rocks, cedars along the bank and white birches; the logs warm in the sun, smooth to sit on, without bark, gray to the touch." The great Upper Peninsula native writer Robert Traver (*Anatomy of a Murder*), who grew up as John D. Voelker fishing these waters before he became a Michigan Supreme Court justice and a novelist, made this region's waters famous. He wrote once, in *Big Secret Trout,* about how he felt as a "middle-aged fisherman" coming back to his home waters pursuing "a great copper-hued trout" and recapturing his youth. ". . . There is fantasy in the air; the earth is young again; all remains unchanged; there is still the occasional porcupine waddling away, bristling and ridiculous; still the startling whir of a partridge; still the sudden blowing and thumping retreat of a surprised deer. . . . The sun is low, most of the water is wrapped in shadow, a pregnant stillness prevails. Lo, the smaller fish are beginning to rise. Ah, there's a good one working! Still watching, he gropes in the bunch grass for his rod case. All fantasies are now forgotten." Hemingway and Traver weren't writing about Marinette County's Pike River, but they could have been.

THE SETTING

The Pike River, a tributary of the Menominee, is wild, fast flowing, and adorned with inspiring waterfalls. This freestone river consists of two main branches, the North and South; both flow in a generally southeastern direction and are relatively narrow, 30 to 40 feet or less in some stretches. But they have many deep holes and pools that provide shelter for trout.

The main stem of the Pike is a big river, almost 100 feet wide in some areas. The upstream reaches of the Pike and its tributaries have lots of gravely riffle areas; downstream, the river bottom is mostly sand. The average flow a mile downstream from the confluence of the North and South branches is about 215 cubic feet per second. However, as in other streams in the northeast, the flow is highly variable. The Pike does have a more stable flow than the neighboring Popple and Pine rivers, but extreme high or extreme low flows can certainly spoil fishing on the Pike. During the drought of 1988–89 low flows and high temperatures severely reduced the Pike's trout populations.

The basin drained by the Pike is mostly forested and has sandy soil, so the Pike's watershed contains less swamp than the nearby Popple and Pine watersheds. This is significant, because wetland drainage tends to warm rivers in the summer, even in the North Country. The Pike contains native brook and brown trout, and the North Branch is a particularly good brown trout stream. The Pike's water is unpolluted, but it has the low alkalinity and hardness typical of other streams in the northeast. Therefore, despite the rugged and beautiful setting, the trout-carrying capacity of the Pike is limited. Fortunately, waterfalls prevent Menominee River warm-water species from moving too far upstream. Dave's Falls near Amberg is probably the upstream limit for warm-water fish, although trout are still found below the falls.

MANAGEMENT HISTORY

The Pike River, along with its sister rivers the Pine and the Popple, are unique not only within Wisconsin but throughout the nation. When Wisconsin enacted the first system of wild-and-scenic rivers in the nation by designating the Pike, Popple, and Pine rivers as special in 1965, it led the way for other states to develop wild-and-scenic-rivers programs. Wisconsin's action was also the forerunner of the federal Wild and Scenic Rivers program, which the U.S. Congress enacted in 1968. The Pike, Popple, and Pine, according to the Wisconsin statute, are to receive "special management to ensure their preservation, protection and enhancement of their natural beauty, unique recreational and other inherent values." Given this designation, development along these rivers

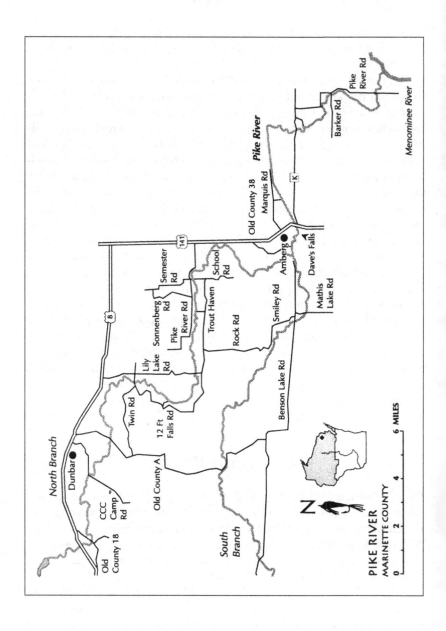

PIKE RIVER
MARINETTE COUNTY

0   2   4   6 MILES

North Branch

Dunbar

Old County 18

CCC Camp Rd

Twin Rd

Old County A

12 Ft Falls Rd

Lily Lake Rd

Sonnenberg Rd

Pike River Rd

Semester Rd

School Rd

Trout Haven Rd

Rock Rd

South Branch

Benson Lake Rd

Smiley Rd

Mathis Lake Rd

Dave's Falls

Amberg

Old County 38

Marquis Rd

Pike River

Barker Rd

Pike River Rd

Menominee River

N

has been held in check. Because of this foresight, these rivers will remain wild far into the future.

At the time of the designation very little was known about the natural history of these rivers. Information was needed to determine a benchmark for future protection and sound management, and so a series of valuable studies was funded by the Wisconsin legislature. Data were collected on the fish populations, the insect populations, the rivers' recreational value, and other topics; thus one of the inherent values of special designation is that it stimulates research and data-gathering on the rivers—the only way we can expect to be better able to manage these waters so future fishers can enjoy them as we do. If you ever get to the Pike to fish or simply to enjoy its wild beauty, take time to appreciate the special program that has helped keep this river an untamed treasure. We recommend canoeing the Pike, Popple, and Pine to get a feeling for the breadth and importance of the wild-and-scenic-river designation.

One possible downside to the wild-river designation has been the legal interpretation that habitat improvements are banned; the "development" or "alteration of natural conditions" isn't permitted. Beaver control has also been affected by the designation. Consequently, projects like developing in-stream habitat, which benefit most streams in the area, aren't being done on the Pike.

In the 1940s, 1950s, and 1960s, the North Branch of the Pike was stocked with brook, brown, and rainbow trout. However, Wisconsin Department of Natural Resources surveys showed that the stocking actually depressed the native trout population. As a result, stocking the North Branch has been discontinued, but some stocking does still occur in the main and South branches. Natural reproduction appears to be very good in the Pike, although the growth rate is slower than in streams farther south.

ANGLING OPPORTUNITIES

The Pike River is one of the better streams in the northeast to fish. It tends to be narrower and deeper than the Pine and the Popple, and the North Branch is particularly good. Trophy browns are taken every season, and brook trout are plentiful but don't seem to reach large sizes. The fish apparently move around quite a bit, so one area may not provide consistent fishing throughout the season. A good section of the main stem is from the confluence of the South and North branches downstream to the end of the trout water at Dave's Falls.

Pike River Road south of Highway 8 and west of the town of Amberg parallels the river for several miles and offers easy access; there are other access points at Eight Foot Falls, Twelve Foot Falls, and Eighteen Foot Falls. Farther upstream on the North Branch there is a nice stretch between Highway 8 and Old County 18. An unmarked road runs along the east side of the river. For the more adventuresome there are foot trails and old logging roads that provide access, but be careful; this is wild country, and that logging road you take may lead you astray.

The Pike River is a good spin-fishing stream, and many spin-fishers try their luck here. Cast a small Marabou Jig with ultralight spinning gear into some of the deeper holes. Cast upstream and slowly bring the jig back, bouncing it along the bottom. This technique can be potent.

The Pike has decent fly hatches, but the often cold spring weather and variable flow make the hatches unpredictable. For mayflies, the Blue-Winged Olives can provide some action early and late in the year. The Brown Drake is probably the premier big mayfly hatch, but it's hard to hit it right. The Mahogany Dun can be significant should you be so fortunate as to hit a hatch, usually late June or July. The Brown Drake and Mahogany Dun are large mayflies (#12), so a large attractor fly, such as a Royal Coachman or a Gray Wulff, is sometimes effective during nonhatch periods. Caddis also can provide action on the Pike; we like to use a darker caddis pattern earlier in the season, and go to a lighter pattern, as spring turns into summer. On the faster water, patterns such as the Elk Hair Caddis or the Henryville Special are generally good bets. For exploring when little else is happening, try a Woolly Bugger.

In the North Branch of the Pike, a streamer that imitates a minnow or juvenile brook trout, such as a Blacknose Dace tied in the Thunder Creek style, might just be supper for that big old brown. Actually, this style of streamer fly, which imitates small baitfish, was named after a northern Wisconsin brook trout stream. The inventor, Keith Fulsher from the state of New York, first put the flies to the test during a vacation in northern Wisconsin, and named his fly style in honor of the Wisconsin creek that yielded such beautiful brook trout. There are several Thunder Creeks in northern Wisconsin and we aren't sure which one should get the honors, but it doesn't matter. Blacknose Dace tied in the Thunder Creek style will work on both brookies and browns in a variety of streams in the area.

With about a quarter of Wisconsin trout stream mileage located in the northeastern corner of the state, there is no lack of other streams to try. We have mentioned the nearby Pine and Popple, and there are innumerable tributaries to these three wild-and-scenic rivers that provide outstanding brook trout fishing. In most cases, with the possible exception of Opening Day weekend, you'll only have to share your water with the mosquitoes. Locations of the tributaries can be found in the WDNR's *Trout Fishing Regulations and Guide*. Note that during warm weather these tributaries may harbor some bigger fish trying to escape the warmer temperatures of the Pine and Popple rivers.

A few of these tributaries and some other nearby trout waters deserve special mention. Woods Creek is the largest tributary of the Popple River, flowing through about 13 miles of heavily forested Florence County. It has an excellent reputation as one of the top brook trout streams in the north, and has received national attention from being featured in Gary LaFontaine's widely acclaimed book, Caddisflies, considered the primary treatise on these insects. Rock Creek, a tributary of the Popple, and Lepages Creek, a tributary of the Pine, are also worth attention.

The Pemebonwon River is another major river system that contains brook and brown trout. The North Branch and South Branch combine east of Pem-bine before the main branch flows into the Menominee River. The Brule River, located in northern Florence County (not to be confused with the Bois Brule in Douglas County), is another fine river. It forms the border between Michigan and Wisconsin for quite a distance before it joins the Menominee River north of Florence.

There are numerous campgrounds in the area, especially in the Nicolet National Forest in northwestern Florence County. For the Pike River, Goodman County Park along the Peshtigo River is as close as any place. For the northeastern corner in general, Lost Lake and Chipmunk Rapids are well-maintained campgrounds. Perch and Lauterman lakes provide walk-in camping. Homestead Park on Bass Lake might make a good central location. There are some good campsites along the Brule River.

East Branch of the Eau Claire River

STREAM SNAPSHOT
East Branch of the Eau Claire River

MILES OF TROUT WATER: 17

SETTING: Freestoner flowing through dairy farms, potato fields, and woods

TROUT SPECIES: Wild brookies, some browns

REGULATIONS: Categories 3 and 5 in Langlade County

BEST FLIES: Muddler Minnow, Mickey Finn, Pass Lake, Royal Wulff, Elk Hair Caddis, Adams

NEAREST COMMUNITIES: Antigo, Merrill, Wausau

Most Midwest residents have heard of the Wisconsin River Dells, but there's another great natural river wonder on north-central Wisconsin's Eau Claire River. A series of rapids roars for more than a mile through 25-foot-high rock outcroppings as the river drops more than 50 feet For years this gorge, called the Dells of the Eau Claire, has drawn local visitors to the site between Wausau and Antigo. There's another treat farther upstream: great trout water amid the acres and acres of potatoes growing in rich Antigo Silt Loam, the state's official soil. Not so coincidentally, the hub of this region, the city of Antigo, is the headquarters for Sheldons', Incorporated, the American home of the Mepps fishing lure. As the story goes, a GI back from Europe after World War H lent Sheldon a Mepps, a lure well known in France. One day, when nothing else was working on the nearby Wolf River, Sheldon pulled out a badly tarnished Mepps and bagged four big trout in two hours. It's worked wonders for a lot of American anglers since.

Three main tributaries of the Eau Claire River harbor trout: Spring Brook, the West Branch of the Eau Claire, and the East Branch. We've chosen the East Branch for its accessibility, its variety, its simple beauty—and its good fishing. Sometimes it's the simple pleasures that create the best memories. On trips to the Eau Claire we've spooked a young whitetail deer standing knee deep in the cool waters; just as often, we've interrupted our fishing to watch an ovenbird flitting among the springtime trilliums. And sometimes, a playful otter or slaphappy beaver has interrupted our fishing with its antics. These are all part of the Wisconsin trout-fishing package, and the East Branch of the Eau Claire is as good a spot as any to find these experiences.

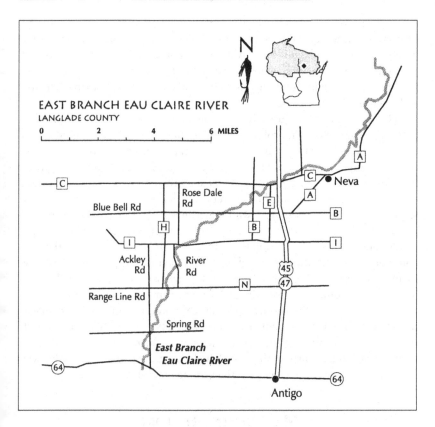

EAST BRANCH EAU CLAIRE RIVER
LANGLADE COUNTY

THE SETTING

The East Branch of the Eau Claire, about 8 miles northwest of Antigo, is in a transition zone between the Northwoods and Wisconsin's farm country. A little north of Antigo the elevation rises slightly, the vegetation changes, and you come upon the terminal moraine of the last glacier to pass this way some 15,000 years ago. The Ice Age Trail, a proposed 1,000-mile trail following this glacial footprint, is nearby. In this region, pockets of woodlands and wetlands, interspersed among the cultivated land, provide an ideal habitat for wildlife. In the untilled riparian zone are wildflowers of many varieties. Such a pastoral, open setting is unusual among brook trout streams, most of which are narrow and brush-covered, not conducive to casting a fly or lure. But that usually isn't a problem here.

The East Branch flows across old glacial Lake Wisconsin. The glacial deposits, subsequently enriched with the organic matter from prehistoric forests, resulted in a productive, level, silty soil called Antigo Silt Loam. This versatile soil, found chiefly in north-central Wisconsin, supports dairy farms, potato growing, and timbering. Antigo Silt Loam was chosen to represent the more than 500 soil types in Wisconsin and became the official state soil in 1983, after a major lobbying effort by University of Wisconsin–Madison soil scientist Francis Hole.

The river flows in a southerly direction, and has good water quality It has a slightly brownish color, probably owing to the wetlands that drain into it. It averages about 40 feet in width, and the typical summertime flow is about 30 cfs. The trout water in the East Branch of the Eau Claire starts above Highway 64, and extends for about 17 miles. Brook and brown trout naturally reproduce throughout the stream, but the best reproduction is in the middle 5–7-mile segment. Outside this segment, wild fingerlings have been stocked as part of an effort to increase the range of this strain of brook trout; the stream is unique in Wisconsin in that large brook trout, in the 12–16-inch range, are relatively common. Moreover, the number of brook trout per mile is probably as high as in any Wisconsin stream, and these brookies persist even though high water temperatures, sometimes exceeding 80 degrees, can occur in the summer. Max Johnson, the former Wisconsin Department of Natural Resources fish manager in charge of the stream, speculates that a temperature-tolerant strain of brook trout may have evolved in the East Branch environment. Brown trout density is fairly low, but large fish, in the 16–23-inch range, are present. Those browns probably grow big from feeding on the prolific brook trout.

MANAGEMENT HISTORY

In-stream habitat work in the 1980s resulted in major growth in the trout populations in the improved sections, and more improvement is likely to occur in the future, since this stream is an important resource for the area. Because of an extensive forage base that thrives in the high-quality water, the East Branch seems to have a very high trout carrying capacity and apparently is on its way back from the drought of the late 1980s, when it and other streams were closed to fishing because of the extremely low water. The major threats to the stream are common themes throughout Wisconsin. Agricultural runoff pollutes the stream, and although it's not yet "urban sprawl," residential development slowly eats away the streamside habitat. To combat these problems, the WDNR and certain landowners and river-lovers are working to establish a streamside corridor that will contain natural vegetative buffers. Such corridors impede agricultural runoff, and naturally filters out pollutants otherwise carried into the river. An effort has been started by local citizens to help protect and preserve the private lands necessary to achieve such a corridor. With the development of the stream corridor and future in-stream habitat work, this wonderful brook trout river will still be there for future generations of Wisconsin trouters and other outdoor enthusiasts to enjoy.

ANGLING OPPORTUNITIES

Although much of the stream flows through private land, many access points exist. Numerous town and county roads cross the stream. There are three WDNR access parking sites, and Trout Unlimited has also obtained some easements that provide access. Trout waters begin northeast of Neva, near Shaddick Springs. The stretch of water that flows southwest towards Neva runs through a marshy area approximately parallel to County Highway A. From Neva the river flows west along County Highway C, and near the intersection of County C and U.S. 45 there is a special-needs access site with restroom facilities. Shortly after the river crosses U.S. 45 it travels southwest, crossing a variety of roads. From Blue Bell Road to River Road, the East Branch of the Eau Claire is restricted to angling with artificials only. This special regulations stretch is excellent water, and a lot of the natural reproduction probably takes place here. There is a nice access site with a parking area where the river crosses County I, just east of the intersection of County I and River Road.

Because this stream is subject to some wide temperature fluctuations, fly hatches are difficult to predict. Hatches of Blue-Winged Olives can get the fish up, and these can occur pretty much throughout the season. Sulphur duns provide good small mayfly fishing from late May through June; try size #18 light-colored spinners at dusk. Look for March Browns towards the end of May and into June; the hatch seems to be best towards dusk, but can occur throughout the day. A fly similar to the March Brown, the Gray Fox, occurs about the same time of the year; use a size #14 instead of a size #10 or #12.

The Brown Drake is another big fly (#8 or #10) that occurs in late May and early June. It's hard to hit this hatch right, but if you do, it can lead to spectacular fishing. The Eau Claire also has a Hex hatch; the peak Hex fishing occurs about mid-June most years. Caddisflies are active throughout the spring and early summer; fish an Elk Hair Caddis pattern in the riffles, but on flatter water use a pattern that sits lower in the surface film. Various caddis emerger patterns can also be the ticket when fish refuse standard dry fly patterns but are obviously feeding on the surface. The White Mayfly will provide action should you hit it right in late July and August. Trout get excited about this mayfly—try the warmer reaches in the lower, or marginal, trout water.

When there's no hatch on, don't despair. We've had great success with small streamer patterns, such as the Muddler Minnow and the Mickey Finn. During several morning encounters in midsummer, we've caught brookies in the riffles by merely swinging a weighted streamer through the fast water on a down-and-across cast, or by hanging the fly in the current. Weight the streamer enough to get it scraping the bottom. Terrestrials—Hoppers, Crickets, Beetles, and Ants—are a good bet throughout the summer and early fall.

The spin-fisher also will find the East Branch rewarding. Brook trout, the predominant fish, generally are very receptive to small spinners, such as the Mepps. But other artificial lures will work, too; try a small, wiggly-action lure like the Flatfish when the fish don't appear active. Retrieve this lure downstream just barely faster than the current. Sometimes the enticing, seductive action of such a lure will tempt trout from the safety of their lies.

The West Branch of the Eau Claire is also a trout stream, but not nearly as renowned for big fish. Spring Brook, another Eau Claire tributary that runs through Antigo, has a long stretch of artificials-only water starting south of town (below County Highway X). There are also many worthwhile streams not far from the Eau Claire: to the east is the Wolf and its tributaries, to the south is the Plover River, and to the west is the Prairie River (we feature the Wolf and Prairie rivers elsewhere in this book). In addition, many spring ponds, kettle holes filled with clean, cold water, abound in Langlade County; they are fished from shore or from a small boat or float tube with all of the lures that are used in stream fishing.

Kinnickinnic River

STREAM SNAPSHOT
Kinnickinnic River

MILES OF TROUT WATER: 25

SETTING: Spring creek with a lot of variety: riffles upstream, broad meanders downstream

TROUT SPECIES: Wild browns and brookies

REGULATIONS: Categories 2 and 5 in St. Croix and Pierce counties

BEST FLIES: Hex (in season), Trico (in season), Blue-Winged Olive, Elk Hair Caddis, Scud

NEAREST COMMUNITIES: River Falls, Hudson, Eau Claire, Twin Cities

It's only 45 minutes away from the traffic, congestion, and corporate towers of Minnesota's Twin Cities, but when you slip into a secluded, shady bend of the meandering "Kinni," it feels as though you're a million miles away. The Kinnickinnic River, one of Wisconsin's most enchanting, most productive trout streams, is a haven for the hassled office rat, a place to unwind with a #16 Blue-Winged Olive mayfly imitation attached to a fly line.

If this sounds like a commercial for a real estate company and you're looking for an inexpensive retreat, it's too late. The Kinni, like so many other prized fisheries within calling distance of America's cities, has been discovered . . . and discovered . . . and discovered.

Now those who love the Kinni are frantically trying to preserve the river before it's too late. The folks at the Kinnickinnic River Land Trust are hoping that instead of buying pieces of this exquisite valley for themselves, people will help them protect a piece for everyone. Radio personality and humorist Garrison Keillor, a land trust supporter, had a home in the Kinni watershed, where all the land, as he might say, is above average. Another supporter is Doug Swisher, the famous fly-caster and author who used the Kinni as a base for his early fly-fishing schools. "It is frightening to think how dramatically it will change if development continues unchecked," says Swisher.

THE SETTING

The good news for anglers is that the Kinni has stood up pretty well so far under all the pressure, because of the loving care it has received from conservationists since the 1940s. A little care will go a long way on a river like the Kinni. The river has been equipped by its creator with a wondrous array of natural attributes, which have accumulated since the time 450 million years ago when Wisconsin was covered by a shallow sea.

The Kinni has it all. Generous groundwater recharge, typified by its springs and spring-fed tributaries. Cool, clean water with the right chemical balance, due largely to the dolomitic limestone that can sometimes be seen in highway outcrops, seeping through the bedrock under its cover of glacial till. Aquatic vegetation. Bald eagles and osprey overhead, and wood ducks nesting in the woods bordering the river. A variety of animals and plants, including oak savannas and other rare habitat; the Kinni's 140-square-mile valley is home to more than forty species of rare and endangered plants and animals, according to the Kinnickinnic River Land Trust. In the lower river, where the Kinni cuts a canyon 200 feet deep in places, you can spy a rare piece of nature: boreal forest. This habitat of balsam fir, yellow birch, and yew is commonly found far to the north, but here it has survived on shadowy north-facing cliffs. A biologist who mapped the river called the corridor a "rare gem."

Oh, did we mention trout? There are many, many brown and brook trout, and they're reproducing naturally. The Wisconsin Department of Natural Resources hasn't stocked trout here since the 1970s, because it found the conservation work paid off. The Kinni's trout numbers rank it among the most productive in the state, about 8,000 per mile in the upper reaches. In the lower, more-fertile reaches, brown trout are bigger and less frequent, but still plentiful—several thousand fish per mile. "It has everything you could ask for: it is challenging, scenic, productive, and easily accessible," Swisher says. Because of these natural attributes, the Kinni has the attention of state government. It is the state's only "outstanding resource water" flowing through a city of 10,000 people, and it has been chosen for a state priority watershed project that will help improve water quality by fighting non-point-source pollution coming from urban and rural areas. "It's healthy right now, but we want to see it stay that way," says Marty Engel, a WDNR fisheries biologist, who worries about the rapid development.

The Kinnickinnic River (named after an Indian smoking mixture made of tobacco and dogwood bark) originates about 2 miles north of Interstate 94, where groundwater bubbles through glacial sand and till. Major springs bolster the stream south of the interstate, and brook trout become noticeable. Then it flows in a southwesterly direction until it reaches two small hydropower dams in the rapidly growing city of River Falls, home to a University of Wisconsin campus. There, the river turns west, flowing through Pierce County until it enters the St. Croix River at lovely Kinnickinnic State Park, ending a 25-mile journey. All but the half-mile at the very lower end—a "transition zone" where the St. Croix backs up into the Kinni—is managed as trout water. The water warms and slows considerably below the Highway F bridge as the river broadens and takes on a sandy bottom, but the 20-mile section upstream from the bridge is considered to be prime trout water.

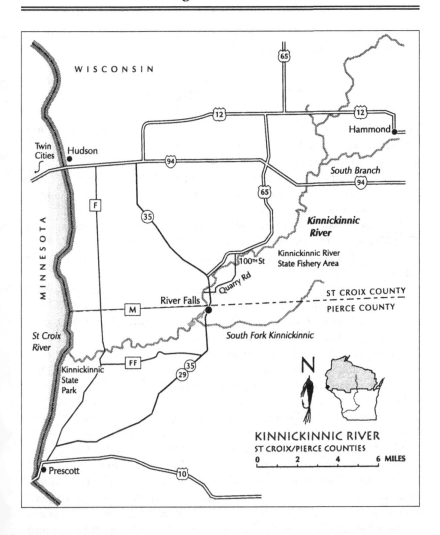

KINNICKINNIC RIVER
ST CROIX/PIERCE COUNTIES

The upper part of the river, in St. Croix County, flows mostly through farm land, despite the rapid residential development of the 1980s and 1990s. The area upstream from River Falls is the most heavily pressured by development because it lies closest to the interstate, which allows fast access to a little piece of Kinni heaven. The lower section, flowing through land untouched by the last glacier, is a different kind of river. After leaving the River Falls dams, it goes through a gorge, and then broadens and winds past high bluffs on its way to the St. Croix. Development pressure has been less in this section because a few farm families control large pieces of the riparian land. But this part of the river isn't immune from development; big houses are rising in the agricultural uplands.

MANAGEMENT HISTORY

Thankfully, conservationists have been paying a lot of attention to the Kinni. The attention has paid off in many ways, but most noticeably in the cold water and natural reproduction. According to WDNR records, some of the first stream-improvement work occurred in the 1940s, when the River Falls Rod and Gun Club spent an estimated $5,000 and dedicated several hundred volunteer man-hours to make the Kinni a better place.

Wisconsin state government followed up in 1950 with a program called "The Kinnickinnic River Watershed Stabilization Demonstration Project," implemented by the fish management division of the old Wisconsin Conservation Department. The department secured many twenty-year leases from upper river landowners to allow improvements that included stream bank fencing and installation of in-stream structures to speed water flow, prevent siltation, and provide more cover. This continued until 1957, with the department spending more than $140,000.

Then, in 1957, the department began a land-acquisition program to ensure public access to the river and to protect its watershed; today, much of the upper river's 15 miles are lined by conservation easements and other public lands. Wastewater treatment, hydropower restrictions, and improved land management and farming practices—all good things—followed. Since then, state government, in partnership with groups such as the KIAP-TU-WISH Chapter of Trout Unlimited, has kept up the good work. Much of it has focused on building in-stream structures and providing cover, stream bank fencing and stabilization, installation of cattle crossings, tree planting, and de-brushing. De-brushing involves clearing out some of the extensive growth of tag alders and box elders along the fenced stream banks, necessary because overhanging branches slow the current, causing a buildup of silt and preventing sunlight from reaching the water. Less sunlight means less aquatic vegetation, which decreases the amount of food and cover for trout. The de-brushing is selective, so there's plenty of cover for woodcock, grouse, and ducks.

A recent player in the Kinni's conservation history is the Kinnickinnic River Land Trust, founded in late 1993. It is a nonprofit, tax-exempt group operated by a volunteer board of directors led by one of the founders, Rob Chambers. Based in River Falls, the trust works to permanently protect land in the valley through the use of conservation easements and other devices. These easements limit development, but allow a full range of uses for agriculture, recreation, and open space; landowners can donate or sell a conservation easement to the group, protecting the land from development while keeping most of the rights and benefits of private ownership. The trust doesn't own the land; it ensures that the restrictions against development are observed by future owners. Current owners who grant a conservation easement may sell their land, but the restriction goes with the deed. In the mid-1990s, Chambers and his St. Paul family donated a 22-acre conservation easement to the trust to set an example for others. One of the major features of the land is an area of oak savanna, a patch of never-farmed land containing ancient oaks and prairie plants. These savannas are increasingly rare—fewer than thirty original stands are said to exist in the entire state. But progress by the trust has been slow: as of mid-1996, the trust had protected roughly 300 acres, and only about a third of those through the desired conservation easements. Handshake agreements with more than a score of other river-lovers, however, indicate the possibility of more success if the new idea takes hold in the valley. It will take time and patience. Many valley residents are wary of protection efforts, having been soured by previous heavy-handed government efforts.

The land trust has joined the WDNR and a big group of active players, including representatives of St. Croix and Pierce counties, the University of Wisconsin, and Trout Unlimited, to implement a watershed improvement program. Begun in 1995, this program will bring millions of dollars into the Kinnickinnic River valley for water quality improvements. One of the key early strategies was to attack suspected thermal pollution originating in the city of River Falls. Trout populations fall off dramatically below storm sewers that funnel warm street runoff into the river after big rains. These runoff discharges, which also contain sand and silt that smother trout habitat, add to problems created by two city reservoirs that slow down and warm the Kinni before it goes into the gorge, limiting natural reproduction. Above River Falls, trout densities are high, up to 12,000 per mile, according to the local TU chapter; in the lower Kinni, densities are about 3,000 fish per mile. The lower river made a comeback after World War II, and now there are increasing numbers of 12–16-inch trout in the canyon section. Some tributaries in the Kinni canyon even harbor brook trout, but heavy loads of sand—from past bad farming techniques—still plague the upper and lower sections of the river. "The Kinni is alive and well," Engel says. "The whole issue is how to keep it that way."

Among the options: change older street sewers so they go into slow-draining retention basins and not directly into the river, monitor Kinni tributaries, and do a better job of planning for housing and street development. Another option is removal of the two River Falls dams, but that potentially expensive and controversial action seems a long way off. Some changes are already being made, showing that there is a constituency watching out for the Kinni. But time is short. As one river-lover observed in the land-trust newsletter: "Preserving a trout stream so close to a major metropolitan area involves the same sort of trust it would take to curl up and sleep beside a fitful elephant—if it rolls over, you're history."

ANGLING OPPORTUNITIES

One of the best things about fishing the Kinni is the variety and change of scenery; in one day, you can fish two different rivers—the upper and lower sections.

The upper, St. Croix County part of the river and its tributaries are classic rapid-flowing spring creeks rarely getting much wider than 20 feet. Much of the upper Kinni is managed as part of the Kinnickinnic River Fishery Area, which stretches upstream from Highway 35 near River Falls to a little north of the interstate; in all, there are about 15 miles of trout water in the upper Kinni's watershed. In this stretch the water is cold and the bottom is sandy, with some gravel. There's plenty of in-stream cover due to vegetation, undercut banks, and many deadfalls propped up on the 6-foot-high silt banks; cast to that cover and you'll find success. Water temperatures rarely exceed the low 60s, even in summer. The water temperature is about 10 degrees cooler than in the late 1940s, when the river was heavily stocked with trout, according to Wisconsin Department of Natural Resources records. Good conservation practices and constant, cool groundwater are responsible for that significant temperature drop. An indication of the healthy recharge: upper river base flows of 38 cubic feet per second have been recorded in August. This cold water and constant recharge result in a lot of trout—brookies in the headwaters, and native browns downstream. But the cold water also limits the number of forage fish, such as minnows and sculpins, so the brown trout never get all that big here, topping off in the 14-inch range. Access points are plentiful, with a few on the main road between the interstate and River Falls. You can also access the stream when you arrive at River Falls; enter the river at several bridge crossings, or by using a trail from Glen Park to the foot of the second dam.

The lower section—all special regulations water—takes on the nature of a freestone stream, with 40-foot-wide boulder-strewn water flowing in the dark shadows cast by high bluffs. The banks of the lower Kinni are often steep, and its access points hard to find. The best spots in this special regulations section are upstream from the Highway F bridge; and via a trail from the end of River View Road on the north side of the river, a little below the second dam. But the rewards for exploring and bushwacking are good: bigger trout, which feed on forage species in the slightly warmer water, are found in the 8 miles of prime trout water downstream from River Falls. The prevalence of minnows means that spin-fishers will do well on this section. There's plenty of room to cast, so fly-fishers, too, might prefer this section to the narrower, brushier confines of the upper river. We don't recommend fishing the marginal trout water below the Highway F bridge; trout are few and far between in this sandy-bottomed section. You're more likely to catch a bass. But if you're on a canoe trip, the limestone outcrops and 50-foot-high sandy bluffs between the bridge and the Kinni's junction with the St. Croix River are worth seeing.

You can sample three of our favorite Wisconsin hatches on the Kinni. The Hendrickson kicks off the regular season in May; then both Hexes and Tricos serve as trout food during the summer, with the Hex mostly confined to the upper river. Both emergences start in late June, but only the Tricos (#20–24) go all the way through the season's end in September. There appears to be no best time of year to fish the Kinni; there's usually something emerging. Little mayflies, typified by the Blue-Winged Olive (#18), hatch all season long on the Kinni. So do varieties of caddis (we recommend the usual Adams and Elk

Elk Creek, Chippewa County—unpredictable spring weather in northern Wisconsin can make for challenging fishing. Photo by Duke Welter.

Hair Caddis in sizes up to #20) and midges (we usually tie on the standard Griffith's Gnat in a size #22). There's also a lengthy Light Cahill emergence starting in early June and going through September.

Being so close to Interstate 94, the area has access to many kinds of lodging, food, and tourist attractions, as well as to other popular trout streams, such as the Rush River, the Apple River, the Clam River, the Trempealeau River, Elk Creek, and the Buffalo River. The Bois Brule and the Namekagon (featured elsewhere) are also within easy driving distance.

Accommodations are plentiful. You could stay in the Twin Cities, or across the St. Croix River in Hudson, Wisconsin, or camp in Kinnickinnic State Park. But to get a feel for the area, stay in River Falls. River Falls also has a variety of lodging places and eateries. There are two very comfortable bed-and-breakfasts, Knollwood House and Trillium Woods. A nice sidetrip is the nearby community of Prescott, where the St. Croix meets the Mississippi. From Prescott, you can drive south along the Great River Road to Lake Pepin (a dammed-up part of the Mississippi River) and the town of Stockholm, settled by Swedish immigrants. This is a great trip for the "antiquer" in the family. Primitive camping is available in the nearby Upper Mississippi River National Wildlife and Fish Refuge, which begins at Nelson.

9

Trout Fishing in Southern Wisconsin

Tomorrow-Waupaca River

STREAM SNAPSHOT
Tomorrow-Waupaca River

MILES OF TROUT WATER: 38

SETTING: Medium-sized free-stoner with high hardness and alkalinity; woods and farms

TROUT SPECIES: Browns, rainbows, and brookies; some reproduction

REGULATIONS: Categories 2, 4, and 5 in Portage and Waupaca counties

BEST FLIES: Hex and White Fly (in season); Griffith's Gnat, Brooks Stone, Cap's Hairwing, Sulphurs

NEAREST COMMUNITIES: Iola, Amherst, Stevens Point, Waupaca

A S WE STOOD at the bridge looking upstream, we could see dimpling fish in the long, flat pool above us. A brief conversation ended with the declaration that they were most likely feeding on midges, it being a little too early in the season for the Trico hatch. Those fish would definitely be worth trying. It was very early in the morning and all of us were groggy from the night before. The Tomorrow had been good to us, yielding several good-sized browns during an almost supernatural Hex hatch. Our dulled senses were no doubt due to the fact that our bodies had yet to purge the tobacco toxins consumed in the form of cheap cigars that we used into the early morning hours to repel pesky mosquitoes. But our spirits lifted and energy returned as we were refreshed by the sight of the clear water and by the coolness of the river against our legs. We each found our little bit of solitude and began fishing to separate groups of midging fish. This delicate fishing was quite a contrast to the aggressive, heavy-duty fishing we had experienced scarcely eight hours earlier. Again, the river was good to us. A satisfying evening and morning on the Tomorrow. We wondered what tomorrow would bring.

THE SETTING

This river with the wonderful name flows 55 miles through some of the prettiest countryside in Wisconsin. The river originates between Stevens Point and Rosholt, in an area that taps into a vast groundwater reservoir underlying the Central Sands region of the state, and ends up in the lower Wolf River east of Waupaca. The sandy loam soils characteristic of the headwaters region provide good conditions for infiltration of precipitation and storage of groundwater. Numerous springs and seepages supply the river with abundant cool water. In addition, the groundwater inputs help offset the warming effects of the flowages located on this river. However, during the summer's hot weather, water temperatures may reach the upper 70s—tough conditions for trout.

The Tomorrow becomes the Waupaca River as it flows east from Portage County into Waupaca County, changing its name when it crosses the county line. It ranges in width from 10 feet at the headwaters to up to 50 feet 30 miles downstream in Waupaca County. In the Nelsonville area, flow is about 20 to 30 cubic feet per second during the fishing season. In its upper reaches the Tomorrow is a clear, groundwater-dominated stream that takes on some characteristics of a spring creek. It has gently moving stretches with abundant aquatic vegetation and silt-loving aquatic invertebrates like a spring creek; yet the river also has reaches that contain classic riffles and runs and the high-gradient characteristics of a freestoner. It is relatively large as Wisconsin trout streams go and is quite properly referred to as a river, so the angler has plenty of room to move around and avoid fishing competition. The river corridor is very scenic, given its location in a region of the state where northern and southern tree species both occur (referred to as the tension zone). While not in a truly wild setting, the Tomorrow-Waupaca provides the angler with that all-important restorative sense of being alone while fishing, surrounded by a seemingly continuous canopy of trees that rarely interfere with your casting.

MANAGEMENT HISTORY

In all, the Tomorrow-Waupaca system has about 38 miles of trout water. In the part of the system upstream from Nelsonville lies the Richard A. Hemp

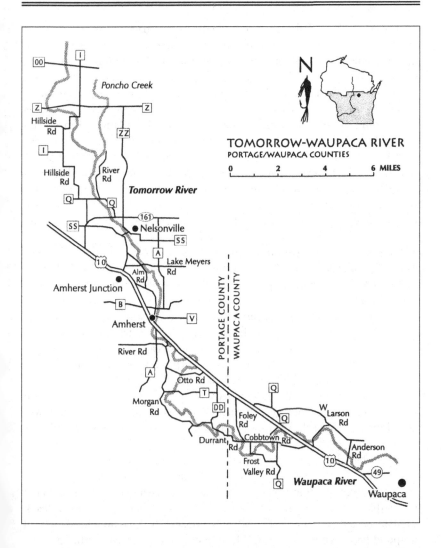

TOMORROW-WAUPACA RIVER
PORTAGE/WAUPACA COUNTIES

Fisheries Area (previously known as the Tomorrow River Fishery Area before being renamed in honor of the late trout-fishing Natural Resources Board and Conservation Hall of Fame member). This area, covering just over 2,000 acres and including about 1,200 acres in state ownership, protects vital headwater springs and seepages, including Poncho Creek, a major tributary of the Tomorrow.

The upper Tomorrow above Nelsonville has naturally reproducing populations of both brook and brown trout. Both rainbows and browns are stocked in the lower reaches of the river, especially in Waupaca County. About 24 miles of the river are considered fully or partially self-sustaining. The scatter-planting each fall of thousands of trout, including longer-surviving wild fingerlings, may ultimately lead to fully self-sustaining waters.

Trout Unlimited, the Izaak Walton League, and high school groups have worked to improve the fishery on the Tomorrow through such activities as de-brushing to prevent excessive shading and the installation of in-stream habitat devices to provide more cover for trout. One of the most prominent river-lovers has been Nancy Rose, a Chicago public relations person who fell in love with the Tomorrow-Waupaca River and bought a cottage and 30 acres of riverfront in 1982. She dove into conservation efforts, getting grant money for stream restoration and helping to organize the Waupaca-Tomorrow Watershed Association that successfully lobbied for state help in cleaning up the 300-square-mile watershed. The result: state-landowner cooperation in curbing animal waste runoff and other non-point-source pollution. Rose also is a key player in the local Federation of Fly Fishers and Trout Unlimited groups. The river is a better place because of dedicated conservationists like Nancy Rose.

Even before this recent conservation initiative, a couple of dramatic steps had been taken to enhance the fishery. The first occurred in 1971, when the Nelsonville-to-Weyauwega stretch of the stream was treated with fish toxicant to eliminate an overpopulation of carp, suckers, and minnows. The trout were removed and held for restocking in the river. Most people agree the trout fishery improved immensely after this radical action. Locals still recall the many big trout over 20 inches that were picked up in the lower part of the river after the chemical treatment—testimony to the capability of the river to support large fish.

The other significant event occurred when the mill dam at Nelsonville was acquired by the state and removed. The dam had been built in the mid-1860s to power a grist mill, the last commercially operated and licensed grist mill in the state. But when the economic benefits could no longer be realized, the dam became a liability. The adverse impacts of the dam and associated millpond had been acknowledged for many years: excessive warming of the stream in summer and cooling in winter, plus algae blooms in the summer, which lowered oxygen levels in both the pond and the river. In 1984, the Wisconsin Department of Natural Resources acquired the dam for $38,000; another $62,000 was spent on removal of the dam. The river channel was then stabilized with riprap and vegetative cover. The entire former bed of the mill-pond is now covered with wetland and prairie plants, and a variety of trees and shrubs. Trout Unlimited and many private citizens played key roles in making this project happen. On a statewide basis it is significant because many trout streams and rivers are adversely affected by old millponds. Removing dams can help restore these rivers to their free-flowing state.

ANGLING OPPORTUNITIES

The Tomorrow River has three separate categories of trout-fishing regulations. Big fish can be found anywhere below Nelsonville, but more large trout reside in the Waupaca River stretch. Jeff Smith, a friend of ours from Madison, often fishes this lower part of the system, and captured a true lunker one July day. Smith sighted some nervous water in a deep pool, and after two casts with a grasshopper imitation and some heavy lifting, he hauled in a 25-inch brown trout. After a quick photograph, he released that trophy back into the deep, dark pool.

The angler should easily find a piece of fishable water no matter what the weather, because precipitation readily infiltrates through the sandy soils and it would take a lot of rain to create unfishable water. Summer heat would suggest that one fish the cooler headwaters, or invest in those cheap cigars we've referred to earlier and become a nocturnal citizen of the stream.

Spin-fishing can be very productive, especially in the lower stretches where you can cover a lot of water quickly. The usual Panther Martin, Mepps, and Rooster Tails are standard fare. However, for the really big fish many veteran spin-fishers use Rapalas at night.

Fly-fishers will find a very diverse array of aquatic invertebrates throughout the stream. The first major hatch is the March Brown, which starts in the middle of May and runs through early June; the spinner fall at dusk probably produces the best action. The Sulphur hatches, in late May through June, frequently bring about heavy feeding activity by good-sized fish. A #16 or #18 Sulphur Comparadun and parachute-style dun are excellent imitations. Progressing to bigger and better things we come to the Brown Drake, which hatches in late May or the beginning of June, is a sporadic hatch but can bring up large fish on good nights. Brown Drake spinners, the choice of many anglers in early June, serve as a prelude to the Hex.

The Hex brings out everything—anglers, fish, and mosquitoes. Usually by mid-June this hatch is in full swing. Arrive in plenty of time, be courteous to fellow anglers, and take care to select a good beat. This hatch excites big fish, so prepare well. Throughout its long length the river harbors excellent Hex populations, but be sure to figure out which part of the river has the hatching activity before you select the section you plan to fish; the best way to do this is to ask around. To many people, especially those who don't share our addiction to trout fishing, the huge Hex is the only mayfly that exists, so asking where are the mayflies hatching is likely to elicit some valuable information.

After the Hex comes the tiny, tiny Trico, hatching in late July, August, and September in the early morning. The White Mayfly also hatches during this time in the warmer, lower sections of the river. This fly, like its relative the Hex, hatches as dark falls; the White Mayfly can be every bit as exciting as the Hex if you hit it right. We like any bushy White Fly in sizes #12 and #14, but sometimes the fish don't respond even while swarms of White Mayflies go through their rapid transformation.

Don't count out caddis hatches for providing excellent fishing during the early part of the season. Terrestrials can be productive during the early morning in late summer when the fish aren't taking Tricos or midge imitations. Grasshoppers and Crickets can be deadly in the meadows sections of the river. Nymph imitations, including beadheads, Hare's Ear variations, and stonefly imitations, are also productive on this river. The larger riffles in the lower part of the river are excellent places to use the down-and-across wet fly swing with a soft-hackled fly or a big streamer.

If you should get to where you have mastered the Tomorrow or simply need a change of scenery, try the Plover River, just east of Stevens Point, or Emmons Creek, a few miles south of the Tomorrow.

Nelsonville Dam removal, new culverts, and stream restoration on the Tomorrow River in Amherst. Photo by Duke Welter.

Mecan River

The Mecan River, in the heart of the geologic region known as the Central Sands, is one of the Badger State's most popular streams. Over the years, the Mecan has acquired a national reputation for its brown trout fishing—probably less for the size of the fish than for the quality of the angling experience. The haunting quality of the Mecan after dusk is unforgettable—sponge-like wetlands collapsing underfoot, luxuriant ferns, assertive frogs, and black nights. Day or night, the Mecan is a trout fisher's haven; accessible, relatively wide and shallow, and delightful to wade. In June, the stream explodes with thick hatches of the Hex mayfly, stirring trout and trout anglers. The intensity of the mayfly explosion is a surprise, but nothing like the surprise that greeted Opening Day anglers in May 1994. A dead, 1,700-pound hippopotamus was found in the stream near Neshkoro. It hadn't migrated from tropical climes, but from a local "zoofarm." We can't guarantee such a discovery on your trip to the Mecan, but we're pretty sure you'll take away an exotic fishing experience.

THE SETTING

Events going back tens of thousands of years set the stage for trout angling in this part of Wisconsin. The fingerprints of the Ice Age are beautifully displayed on the landscape of this region. The Mecan and other nearby small streams, including Wedde, Chaffee, and Tagatz creeks, have their headwaters on the eastern side of a northerly trending glacial moraine. These streams flow southeasterly into the Fox River drainage basin, and collectively are a major tributary of the system that ultimately discharges into Lake Michigan. Streams originating on the western side of the hilly moraine topography flow across flat, sandy, outwash plains deposited by the glaciers, and into the Wisconsin River. Thus the prominent hills left behind by the glaciers are a major surface water divide.

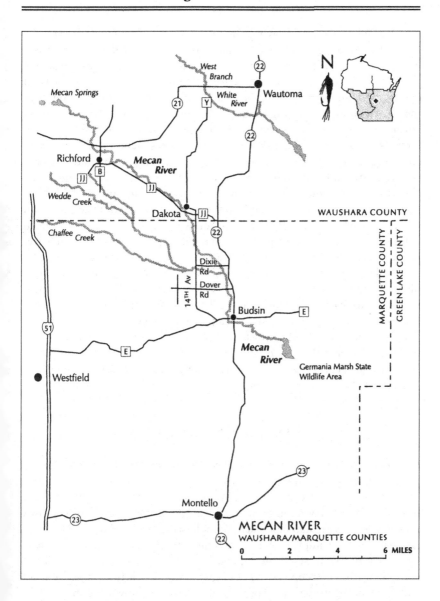

These glacial features can be seen particularly well as one drives north on Highway 51 towards Portage County. In the Mecan River watershed, the national Ice Age Trail follows the westside uplands overlooking Mecan Springs, a testimony to the scientific significance of the area.

The Mecan River begins at Mecan Springs in Waushara County and glides into Marquette County, flowing almost 17 miles before entering the Germania Marsh, a state wildlife area flooded for waterfowl. The Mecan is a hard-water stream draining a watershed of about 200 miles. It has a relatively low gradient, dropping less than 2 feet per mile along its course. Several spring ponds and springs form the headwaters and are the source of much of the Mecan's flow, accounting for the high water quality of this clear-flowing stream. The upper reaches consist of small pools with longer riffle-and-run sections; stream bottoms consist of sand and gravel suitable for fish spawning and reproduction. Farther downstream the bottom is largely sand, with extensive peaty banks covered with grasses, sedges, speckled alder, and choke cherry In-stream aquatic vegetation is quite sparse. The stream width averages about 30 feet. The sandy soils in the area favor rapid infiltration of rain and snow-melt, limiting flooding. Groundwater discharge into the stream helps stabilize summer low flows, which range from about 10 to 20 cubic feet per second at Richford to 75–100 cfs at the Highway 22 bridge.

While most of the area's native oaks have been cut down, the mixture of plantation pines, remaining hardwood woodlands, and fields provides great scenery, and it's not surprising that the demand for recreational cottages and real estate has been high for many years. Tamarack swamps and other low-lying wetland areas border substantial parts of the stream. There are large numbers of deer in the region. The Mecan Springs are a refuge and migration stop for Canada geese, as well as other waterfowl. The observant angler also has a good chance of seeing sandhill cranes, bald eagles, and ospreys.

MANAGEMENT HISTORY

In 1957, the Wisconsin Department of Natural Resources' predecessor agency began acquiring lands for what is now the Mecan Fishery Area. Several separate areas on the Mecan, Chaffee, Wedde, and Little Pine were combined into the present-day management area in 1985; the Mecan Fishery Area now includes more than 6,000 acres, purchased at a cost of over $2 million. Extensive habitat improvements, including boom covers, deflectors, half-log structures, bank stabilization, and de-brushing, have been carried out since the early 1960s on several key reaches of the nearly 50 miles of trout stream included in the area. Some of this good stream work, done in close cooperation with the local Trout Unlimited chapter, is deteriorating because of age; even so, the stream work is helping trout. Access to the river is generally excellent, with some three dozen small parking areas located along the length of the streams. Excellent highway access via State Highways 51, 21, and 22 make this area, with some of the finest small trout streams in the state, readily accessible and within a three-hour drive for millions of people.

The WDNR land-acquisition program in the Mecan Fishery Area has been contentious, particularly during the 1980s. In the Mecan watershed, local government officials and some private property owners organized to stop state land-buying, claiming that public-land acquisition reduces the local tax base (University of Wisconsin studies, however, indicate the tax impacts are generally minimal to nonexistent). Landowners were also concerned about the heavy use of public lands in the area, complaining about serious littering and trespass problems. Today's anglers, along with increasing numbers of canoeists and tubers, often have little knowledge about the controversies associated with acquiring these sensitive natural resources for the public. Mecan River anglers owe a debt of gratitude to the professionals who secured public access and protection of the area from rampant land development; at the same time, given the history, fishers should be especially sensitive to the rights of local landowners, many of whom have long been responsible resource stewards.

Of the 49 miles of trout streams in the management area, there is good natural reproduction in about 31 miles. Brook, brown, and rainbow trout spawn successfully in the upper 6.6 miles of the Mecan River, and though brown trout are the dominant species and rainbow populations are small, it's worth noting that the Mecan is one of the few stream systems in Wisconsin with a naturally reproducing rainbow population. As many as 6,000 fingerling brown trout were stocked in the lower Mecan as recently as the early 1990s, but WDNR area fish managers noted that less than 2 percent of the stocked fish survived. Moreover, excellent natural reproduction was occurring, with all year-classes well represented in their fish population surveys. In 1992 stocking was halted, and a wild brown trout fishery now thrives the length of the Mecan River. From 14th Avenue downstream, fishing regulations allow artificials only, with bag and size limits aimed at a high-quality recreational fishing experience.

ANGLING OPPORTUNITIES

Aquatic invertebrates are the primary food for Mecan River trout, although shiners, sculpin, and other forage fish are present. The most eagerly awaited angling event is the annual Hex hatch, which begins in early June and continues until the later part of the month. A local pattern called the Hart Washer, a large Wulff-type dry fly developed by one of the sages of central Wisconsin trout angling, Arling Erickson, is the sentimental choice of many anglers who knew him. But a variety of Hex patterns, from emergers to spinners, fare well. The extensive peat and silt banks along the Mecan harbor huge numbers of Hex nymphs, and the hatch and later spinner falls seem to bring up every fish in the stream. Brown trout exceeding 20 inches are caught every year, but the fisher should be happy to connect with several 10–14-inch fish. Of course, we all hope for that trophy, and from time to time, the Mecan delivers. One June night we left one of our team, who was on crutches from a sports injury, at a popular bridge crossing, while the rest of us dispersed to more remote and secretive Hex fishing destinations. After a perplexing and sweltering evening, we returned to find him still grinning about the two 20 inchers he'd lured from tag alder snags right by the bridge.

The river can have good Hendrickson hatches, although they often precede the opening of the traditional fishing season. In May, before the Hex hatch, anglers fishing a heavily weighted Hex Nymph tie into some big ones. Later on during the Hex hatch, other smaller mayflies are commonly dancing over the stream before sunset. A #14 Light Cahill or parachute-style Sulphur dry fly can be extremely effective at such times. These flies and #14–18 Elk Hair Caddis are good searching patterns throughout the season when there is no surface activity. The old reliable Muddler Minnow, swung close to deadfalls and overhanging branches, is always a good choice for fishing your way slowly downstream, exploring every possible lie. Terrestrials, especially smaller grasshopper imitations in sizes #12–14, have their moments later in the summer.

The small-stream angler should try the Lawrence (described in the following section), Chaffee, Wedde, and other area creeks, which support good trout populations. Hopper fishing in late summer along the upper Chaffee can be unsurpassed small-water sport. We also recommend the nearby White River in Waushara County. The White River State Natural Area is a wonder to behold. It has rare natural communities, including oak barrens, wet prairies, calcareous fens, and elements of the Atlantic coastal marsh community. More than 100 rare plant and animal species have been found here, including the Karner blue butterfly.

Lawrence Creek

STREAM SNAPSHOT
Lawrence Creek

MILES OF TROUT WATER: 3.4

SETTING: Fast-flowing, spring-fed Central Sands creek feeding Lawrence Lake and West-field Cr.

TROUT SPECIES: Wild brookies

REGULATIONS: Category 2 in Mar-quette County

BEST FLIES: Blue-Winged Olive, Pheasant Tail, Adams, Royal Wulff, Scud, various caddis, Muddler Minnow

NEAREST COMMUNITIES: Westfield, Montello, Portage, Stevens Point, Madison

We bushwhacked through the second-growth pine woods to get a view of Lawrence Creek before grabbing our gear. It was mid-June, and while we had worked up a sweat, it was one of those magnificent late spring Wisconsin days—a bluebird sky, and temperatures pushing 70 degrees. Our eyes were fastened on the ground as we stepped over deadfalls and avoided encounters with thorny raspberries. Suddenly we stopped in our tracks. Before us was a rare sight: several patches of the rare pink lady slipper, one of Wisconsin's largest native orchids. Pink moccasin-flower, as it is sometimes called, aptly describes this beautiful Wisconsin native. Appropriate, we thought, to find the lovely lady slipper in the watershed of one of our favorite Wisconsin trout streams, Lawrence Creek. This gorgeous little stream in central Wisconsin's Adams County harbors a healthy population of native brook trout.

But spotting pink lady slippers was not our only surprise of the morning. Walking back to the car, we noticed another car arriving at the pullout. A man got out and began peering around inquisitively. As we got closer, we recognized him to be none other than Ray White, an old friend who has become one of the leading trout biologists in the country. White did his master's and doctoral studies at the University of Wisconsin–Madison, and his dissertation focused on wild trout and their habitat in Wisconsin streams. Much of his early learning came from work on Lawrence Creek, and he had returned to check out how the stream was faring. He marveled at how the vegetation surrounding the creek had changed. "There used to be a cow pasture surrounding the stream," he remarked. "And now the vegetation has really filled in." Just the way it was supposed to. White's work had helped make Lawrence Creek one of the shining gems among Wisconsin's many trout streams.

THE SETTING

Lawrence Creek is a narrow stream, averaging about 10 feet in width. It originates from several small springs at the end of a glacial terminal moraine in Adams County, and flows over sandstone bedrock for about 3 miles through a watershed typified by cropland, pasture, and mixed leafy and pine forests. Flow is relatively stable throughout the year (about 15 cubic feet per second), and the gradient is less than 10 feet per mile. The water is moderately hard with little detectable pollution. The stream bottom is predominantly sand with gravel and cobble in the few riffles; there are flat bottoms in the straight stretches and deep holes and artificial undercut banks at the bends. High grasses and cattails grow on the banks and hang over the water. Lawrence Creek ends at a millpond in Marquette County called Lawrence Lake, a warm-water pond that has good bluegill and bass fishing.

Lawrence Creek is typical of many of the small, even-flowing, virtually riffle-free creeks found in the sand country of central Wisconsin. The creek flows through part of the Lawrence Creek State Wildlife Area, which has many attractions other than the showy lady slipper to interest the nature enthusiast.

MANAGEMENT HISTORY

Perhaps no Wisconsin stream is more important from a fisheries management perspective than little Lawrence Creek. The creek was the site of a unique longterm study by the Wisconsin Department of Natural Resources, which operated a year-round research station here from 1955 through 1967. Studies were done on a variety of topics, such as improving the living conditions for trout through habitat development, and an evaluation of experimental angling regulations for wild brook trout (including catch-and-release fishing, and fly-fishing-only regulations). This research effort was among the most detailed ever done, and the results continue to be used here and across the country.

Bob Hunt, who was one of the key WDNR biologists participating in the Lawrence Creek project, wrote a book titled *Trout Stream Therapy* in which he describes his work. Hunt's work showed the benefits of helping trout streams help themselves through installation of devices that speed up the current, stabilize stream banks, and create more in-stream cover for trout. The man-made devices created a stream characterized by 75 percent runs and 25 percent riffles, with sweeping bends. Although Hunt found that increased fish populations sometimes lag behind the improvements, the result today is impressive: a naturally reproducing, unstocked brook trout stream that has good quantities of mayflies, stoneflies, and caddisflies; desirable aquatic vegetation such as

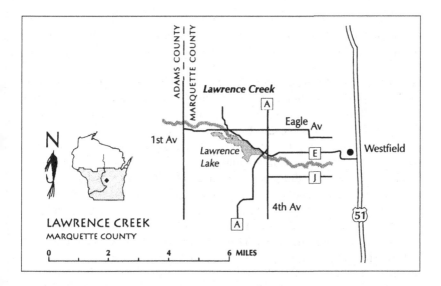

LAWRENCE CREEK
MARQUETTE COUNTY

watercress and *Elodea;* and stable banks that prevent erosion. In effect, White, Hunt, and others have used trout stream therapy to provide a better, longer-lasting home for wild trout.

Although it doesn't hold trophy fish, Lawrence Creek should still have a special place in the hearts of Wisconsin trout anglers. For those interested in fisheries management, this little brook provided much of the information that is guiding trout stream managers in the Midwest and elsewhere. You can still see some of the structures put in the creek during the fifties and sixties. Lawrence Creek today is perhaps more a shrine than a fishing destination, and it doesn't get fished as much now as in past years. Nevertheless, this little gem of a creek has played an important role in Wisconsin's trout-fishing heritage.

ANGLING OPPORTUNITIES

The stream is full of wild brook trout. Although hardly trophies (the average size is probably about 6 inches), they are beauties. Fly-fishing is possible along much of the stream, as the marshy vegetation doesn't hinder backcasts. The stream is narrow enough, however, so that presenting a fly properly without spooking the fish is always a challenge. The water is usually crystal clear, so the angler must be very wary.

Flies for the stream are typical of those recommended for other sand country streams. Brook trout are usually not the hardest fish to fool, but there are days when even brook trout can give you the blues. Nymphs, scuds, midges, and streamers will produce all year. Various caddis patterns will work when caddis are active, and mayflies like the Hendrickson and little Sulphurs can be the ticket if you hit one of these springtime hatches. Ants and Beetles are often productive during the summer, although the angler usually has to work hard to get fish with these. Attractors, such as the Royal Coachman or the Royal Wulff (in small sizes, such as #16), are more likely to produce on brook trout waters like Lawrence Creek than on brown trout waters.

Anglers visiting in July and August will find a consistent Trico hatch; the spinner fall is usually during the mid-morning hours. Tiny *Baetis* mayflies hatch in the fall, providing good surface activity. Fishing this hatch can be quite a challenge, especially when it's cold and windy. Use the Tiny Blue-Winged Olive. The bugs tend to hatch under low light conditions, such as late afternoon or even rainy or snowy days. These flies are small, sizes #22–24 and sometimes even smaller. These are among the most difficult hatches to fish. The water is usually very clear, and the fish are easily spooked. It's fun to keep trying—especially on a stream like Lawrence Creek. Sometimes a #22 Adams works if the brookies are up feeding on duns. If they're slashing under the surface, try small mayfly nymphs and emergers.

If you're spin-fishing on the Lawrence, it's important to keep the spinners small. But more important than the lure or fly pattern on this clear, sandy-bottomed stream is to make a presentation that doesn't scare the fish.

For another creek similar to Lawrence, we recommend Chaffee Creek, located in the northwestern corner of Marquette County. For bigger water, try the Mecan River or the White River near Wautoma. The Mecan is featured elsewhere in this book.

Interestingly, John Muir grew up in Marquette County not too far away from Lawrence Creek. You may want to visit the John Muir Memorial Park on County F between Montello and Portage. Some 60 acres of his family's original 160-acre homestead, Fountain Lake Farm, are within the park. In honor of Muir, who was an inveterate walker, you may also want to take a hike along the Marquette Trail, which runs along the Fox River a little north of Portage.

Research done on streams like Lawrence Creek is vital to ensure good fishing for the next generation of anglers. Photo by Duke Welter.

Black Earth Creek

STREAM SNAPSHOT
Black Earth Creek

MILES OF TROUT WATER: 12

SETTING: Spring creek threatened by development; farms, small towns, and expanding suburbs

TROUT SPECIES: Wild browns, stocked rainbows, and occasional brookies

REGULATIONS: Categories 3 and 5 in Dane County

BEST FLIES: Scud, Cressbug, Griffith's Gnat, Woolly Bugger, Tiny Blue-Winged Olive, Adams

NEAREST COMMUNITIES: Cross Plains, Black Earth, Middleton, Mt. Horeb, Madison

Flowing through the rapidly suburbanizing farm country west of the capital city of Madison is a spring creek of such renown that Trout magazine named it one of the nation's top 100 trout streams. Black Earth Creek, at first glance, may seem too slow and muddy for trout. Busy Highway 14 paralleling most of the creek may also give you pause. But don't be discouraged. Black Earth Creek's cool, spring-fed, limestone-enhanced waters, deep undercut banks, and watercress islands provide wonderful habitat for naturally reproducing browns.

Alas, like Pennsylvania's Letort, the secret is out. Anglers from nearby Madison, the Milwaukee and Chicago metropolitan areas, and throughout the Midwest are regular visitors, especially during the *Hexagenia* mayfly hatch that starts in early June. But Black Earth Creek still harbors its own secrets, such as wily 20-inch brown trout in hidden lairs that resist even the well-presented lure. It is a place where anglers often must resort to a #22 fly on a 7X tippet in order to claim success. Sometimes even that doesn't work on this temperamental stream. And the angler may feel privileged to survive a silt-slogging night fishing trip, having snared what we jokingly call the "Black Earth Creek Grand Slam"—a bat, a muskrat, a red-winged blackbird, and a chub, or the rough fish of your choice. We and our compatriots have managed to hook all of these species on our fly lines and talked about it later over an Esser's Best brew.

Even frequent visitors are kept guessing when fishing this prized piece of south-central Wisconsin water, where the sounds of summer softball, car traffic, and the occasional freight train provide an inviting small-town backdrop to interesting and challenging fishing. It's why nationally known writer-angler Tom Wendelburg characterizes it as a "friendly wilderness" that "beckons you to take your time." Take your time on Black Earth Creek, and you'll certainly be rewarded.

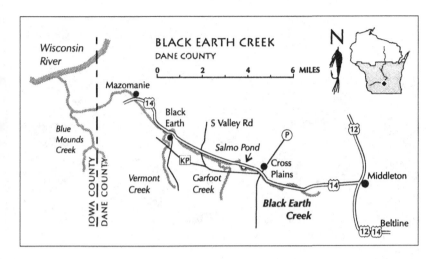

THE SETTING

These waters originate in a marsh, but soon get their rich quality from springs that bubble from beneath the remnants of the last glacier, which passed over much of present-day Wisconsin more than 10,000 years ago. The glacier stopped a little west of today's Madison and nearby Middleton, providing the geologic setting that makes Black Earth Creek so special. Starting about 15 miles west of central Madison, the stream drains approximately 107 square miles on its way to the Wisconsin River. In that area lies some of the most productive wild brown trout water in the state. The creek officially becomes trout water a little east of Cross Plains at a major spring complex, and flows generally along Highway 14 through Black Earth. Most anglers end their search for trout at Lake Marion, just east of Mazomanie. Splendid habitat improvements below the community of Black Earth will make the lower reaches a prime destination for trout anglers. In all, Black Earth Creek's trout water measures more than a dozen miles, not counting its tributaries.

The scenic valley cut by the creek contains some of the most desirable land in Dane County. Despite the increasing pressure from developers, recreationists still stream to the rolling hills, steep ridges, and rich plains of the creek's valley. The Ice Age Trail passes nearby, testimony to the area's glacial history. Planners from the Wisconsin Department of Natural Resources, the National Park Service, and the Ice Age Park and Trail Foundation have begun to lay out a 1,000-mile-long hiking trail across the state, following the terminal moraine left by the last glacier. Part of this geologic preservation effort is exemplifed

Picture perfect Black Earth Creek, where there are many trout and many anglers! Photo by Steve Born.

by the Cross Plains Ice Age Reserve, one of nine units in the Ice Age National Scientific Reserve, and one of the state's best examples of the contrast between Wisconsin's glaciated and unglaciated terrain. This unit is located at the very upper edge of the Black Earth Creek watershed, south of Highway 14 between Cross Plains and Middleton.

The creek is loved but endangered. Development marching westward from Madison poses a threat to the pure springs at the headwaters and to Black Earth Creek's spring-fed tributaries; water experts say development on the ridges could hurt the groundwater recharge that maintains the stream's spring creek qualities. Erosion and barnyard runoff are still problems downstream. State environmental programs seek to limit the damage, but local environmentalists fear the programs won't be able to stop all degradation. Proposed construction of a new printing plant that would have been located just feet from the stream at Cross Plains was stopped in the mid-1990s, but only after the threat of legal action from the local chapter of Trout Unlimited. Madison attorney and trout fisher Peter Peshek, honored for his efforts to stop the plant, later said: "It was the Trout Unlimited members who had the vision, commitment and political sophistication to make the victory possible. . . . Members of Trout Unlimited can help bridge and encourage the creation of wise stewardship of land and water, without sacrificing the identity or singular purpose of Trout Unlimited."

Those kinds of conservation efforts protect the lifeblood of Black Earth Creek—its springs. The springs feeding Black Earth Creek maintain a constant flow of clear, cold, mineral-rich water. The water, which flows through dolomite-sandstone bedrock, is high in alkalinity, and it is this chemical property that spurs the abundant growth of plant life and aquatic organisms, providing shelter and food for a flourishing trout population. The excellence of this trout stream, state biologists say, is due to the combination of ample groundwater, a mostly gravel-rubble bottom for spawning, good gradient, a diverse insect population (mostly mayflies, caddisflies, scuds, and cress-bugs), and an ideal pool-riffle ratio.

MANAGEMENT HISTORY

History shows that Black Earth Creek can mend itself if given a little help. The creek has changed dramatically from the low-production, stocked fishery of yesteryear, a change that occurred because of caring individuals, conservation groups, and government agencies. Members of local groups, such as the chapters of Trout Unlimited and Federation of Fly Fishers, have adopted the stream and devoted hundreds of hours to stream improvement projects, like stabilizing and fencing banks, and shaping stream contours to speed flow and reduce silting of spawning areas. One observer explained the local anglers' devotion this way: "Fly-fishing is a religion. And Black Earth Creek is an area of worship." State resources have helped, too. The old Wisconsin Department of Conservation began one of the state's first stream habitat improvement projects on Black Earth Creek in 1949. The state agency has been actively involved ever since. Over the years, the stream has bene-fited from a variety of state-sponsored measures, including aggressive land acquisition, removal of two mill dams, habitat improvement, and controls on water pollution and livestock. In all more than $2 million in private and pub-lic monies have gone into making Black Earth Creek a better place for trout.

Many studies laid the foundation for this action, and in 1987, the state selected Black Earth Creek for a priority watershed project, in recognition of the threats to this valuable resource. This project, which involves the state, local landowners, and communities, makes money and other resources available to limit pollution caused by non-point sources such as runoff from construction sites and feedlots. In addition, creek advocates brought together trout anglers, farmers, and community leaders in the Black Earth Creek Wa-tershed Association to deal with environmental issues.

Black Earth Creek has a good temperature range, which peaks at about 70 degrees. It is never very wide, averaging 20 feet, but it can carry a lot of water during big summer storms. In July 1954, the U.S. Geological Survey gauge at Black Earth recorded a peak momentary flow of 1,750 cubic feet per second. The instantaneous low flow, the opposite end of the scale, has been recorded at less than 5 cubic feet per second. It is during such low summer flows that heavy in-stream vegetation and low oxygen levels threaten trout. Fish kills are rare, but many trout in one lower stretch died during the 1988 drought. Efforts to improve the stream's health, particularly those efforts to stem animal manure runoff, are helping it cope better with these stressful spells.

Like streams in the rest of Wisconsin, Black Earth Creek once contained a naturally reproducing population of native brook trout. Those are gone, but they've been replaced by a healthy, self-sustaining population of wild brown trout, and recent counts estimate the population in some reaches as high as 2,300 trout per mile. Brook trout are stocked in an upper Black Earth Creek tributary, Garfoot Creek, and some find their way into the main stem. The good news is that brook trout are starting to reproduce naturally in Garfoot and densities are increasing, according to state fisheries personnel. In the lower stretches, rainbow fingerlings are stocked in the fall but in lesser numbers than they used to be. These rainbows are stocked for diversity and to boost the fish density, which averages 1,500 fish per mile. The stockers are providing some worthy angling, and there are even some signs of rainbow reproduction. Stream improvement projects on these lower stretches are also providing more homes for trout. Fisheries managers say the stream is holding up to the pressures of development, but they worry about the future. "If we don't protect the groundwater sources, all of that habitat work isn't going to mean much," says the WDNR's Scot Stewart.

ANGLING OPPORTUNITIES

The trout of Black Earth Creek are wary. So come prepared to slip quietly among the watercress and spend some time on your hands and knees in cautious pursuit of these selective fish. Luckily there are plenty of access points, giving fishers sufficient routes to get away from the most heavily pressured parts of the stream. The accesses—beyond the usual highway and railroad crossings—are there because of extensive public ownership, and also because of landowners' willingness to grant fishing rights to respectful anglers. There are public rights to more than 230 streamside acres, and conservationists are always looking for other opportunities.

The stream also offers much variety, from the narrow headwaters above the village of Cross Plains to the deep and dark meanders below the community of Black Earth. In between, anglers walk atop fertile black earth to find amazingly diverse venues: shady tunnels of flat water, riffle water rushing past brushy banks, and clear, secluded pools harboring nymphing trout. Salmo Pond, a trout, bass, and bluegill pond between Cross Plains and Black Earth, has a parking area, toilet facilities, some picnic tables, and a handicapped-accessible fishing pier. Another fine recreation area, Festge County Park, is located on nearby uplands.

The special regulations section begins at the South Valley Road bridge west of Cross Plains, and extends downstream to the Park Street bridge just east of Black Earth. In this section, only artificial lures may be used and the trout kill is limited by number and size. It's a fine stretch of spring creek water, meandering through rich corn and grazing lands. But fish populations are good above and below this stretch too, even in the recently improved waters below the town of Black Earth, where the increasingly productive slow-moving water holds some big brown trout.

No one lure or method is foolproof, but there are constants. Many Black Earth Creek veterans like to use short, light rods (often for a 2-weight line) for delicate presentations of small drys and tiny nymphs. From late spring to fall, a tippet of at least 5X often is required, even while fishing under the water's surface.

In the spring, mayflies imitated by the Hendrickson and various Blue-Winged Olive patterns are common. So are the Little Black and other caddis. Some of our favorite underwater patterns include the Scud, Cressbug, Leech, and the rubber-legged Girdle Bug. Minnow imitations, including Mepps spinners, will take fish readily. We treasure those early season trips wading through familiar territory, getting our casts back in shape. This time of year often finds us in the upstream portions, nymphing for trout after trout.

As summer approaches, we move downstream and look for the giant *Hexagenia* mayfly, which emerges from gooey silt banks. The Hex emergence is a sometimes spectacular night-time hatch that attracts many anglers—and trout, which have let down their guard. Make sure you have a flashlight, durable waders, and bug dope. Hex fishing on Black Earth Creek can be quite an adventure because of the muck and brush; we've broken rods and gotten stuck in quicksand-like silt on such outings. Pick out a spot, explore it in daylight and wait patiently for nightfall. If the hatch is on, you'll first see the big bugs in the air, with birds swooping over the creek after them. Then you'll see the mayflies, looking like sailboats with their big translucent wings, floating with the current. Sometimes the trout will sip, but often they will slash at the mayfly, erupting out of the water and startling the unaware angler. You'll be casting in the dark, so you need to make short casts and gather your slack line quickly. Remember to cut your leader down, because you won't be able to anticipate the strike as you can during the day. When you feel a tug, raise the tip of your rod. You could have a big one on. We have caught fish in the 20-inch range during this hatch, but we went through a lot of flies doing it; these big ones lie close to the banks under overhanging bushes and trees. We think losing a few flies is worth the chance to tie into a Black Earth Creek monster.

Many anglers head elsewhere after the Hex hatch peaks, but that's when we find Black Earth Creek at its most challenging. Low water and abundant underwater vegetation complicate already difficult casting situations. Stalking is essential. Mayflies, midges, and fluttering caddis may appear all at once in the evening hatch, bedevilling even the most experienced angler. We often go to tiny spinners or midge pupae to fool the trout. During muggy summer days, terrestrials are a good bet. Look for the parts of the stream where tall, top-heavy grasses droop over the undercut banks, and watch for sipping trout. We like Grasshoppers, Crickets, Ants, Beetles, and the slowly sinking Girdle Bug, fished with a twitch now and then. Towards fall, the Tiny Blue-Winged Olives make their reappearance, providing pleasant, but technical, evening fishing. Look for them and for moving fish in the riffle-and-run sections of Black Earth Creek. A #20–24 Parachute Adams, or a tan or light olive Comparadun is a good imitation. Fishing these micropatterns is as challenging as it gets. Fortunately, on many late summer evenings swarms of light-colored caddis appear just before dusk, often followed by trout in aerial pursuit. We've had great luck in those last moments of the day with a #18 Elk Hair Caddis, and welcomed the easier fishing.

When fishing is really tough, experiment. Try different lure colors and retrieves, try traditional downstream wet fly fishing, or try sweeping, down-and-across casts with a Muddler Minnow. Popular nymphs any time include the Scud, Hare's Ear, Serendipity, Pheasant Tail, and beadhead variations of the spring creek patterns. On a particularly slow evening in midsummer, one of our companions used a Scud while we waited for the Hex. He caught a nice 15-incher while we were skunked, except for the little one we hooked while swinging a Girdle Bug. During the summer, you must nymph the troughs between the thick aquatic vegetation. If you're fishing dry, do everything you can to prevent drag. Mending your line properly is essential on Black Earth Creek, where microcurrents can tug the line and ruin your presentation.

Some adventuresome anglers explore Black Earth Creek's lower section near Mazomanie (water enhanced by a recent dam removal and stream work above the Highway 14 span), and its small tributaries—Garfoot Creek and Vermont Creek. Vermont Creek is the bigger stream, but Garfoot has better water quality and more naturally reproduced trout. These are very small streams and difficult to fish with a fly rod. Other nearby streams offer good fishing, too; some anglers place Mt. Vernon Creek (described in the following section) on a par with Black Earth Creek. Elsewhere in Dane County, trout can be found in the upper Sugar River and Story Creek.

We don't often mention shopping opportunities, but we can't write about Black Earth Creek without mentioning the Shoe Box, a growing independent discount shoe store famous for friendly service and good prices. It's located within a long cast of the stream in Black Earth. So if your waders spring a leak . . .

Diverting streamflow from a straightened and degraded section of Black Earth Creek in Cross Plains into a new meandered watercourse with high-quality habitat in 2013. Photo by Steve Born.

The caddis hatches of springtime are anticipated by anglers on Black Earth Creek and across Wisconsin. Photo by Steve Born.

Mt. Vernon Creek

STREAM SNAPSHOT
Mt. Vernon Creek

MILES OF TROUT WATER: 8

SETTING: Spring creek in upper Sugar R. watershed; threatened by development

TROUT SPECIES: Wild browns

REGULATIONS: Categories 3 and 5 in Dane County

BEST FLIES: Hendrickson and Hex (in season), Adams, Scud, Cressbug, Pheasant Tail, Elk Hair Caddis, Hopper

NEAREST COMMUNITIES: Mt. Vernon, Mt. Horeb, Madison

It was late July, hot and sticky. Most trout fishers had stowed their tackle and were looking forward to the cooler temperatures of fall. But one of Dane County's best spring creeks was running cool: the temperature of Mt. Vernon Creek, located about 20 miles southwest of Madison, was recorded in the high 50s, even though the mid-day air temperature was almost 90. The gin-clear stream, with its undercut banks and deep channels through the aquatic vegetation, somehow defied the stifling heat of midsummer. We became energized with the promise of finding feeding trout. But everything has its price, and if you fish Mt. Vernon in midsummer you should be prepared to pay your dues. The dues in this case mean early morning fishing, difficult wading and stream walking, pinpoint casting accuracy, patience and many spooked fish—all before you even get a hook-up. Our ploy was to coax a few trout out from the undercut banks with small Grasshoppers. After a few brief hours of fishing we counted it a successful morning: one or two fish landed for each person, several strikes, many lost flies, and no casualties.

We were captivated by the striking colors of some of the stream-bred browns before their release, and marveled that day at how their beauty mimicked the beauty of Mt. Vernon Creek. But this great resource, so close to Wisconsin's capital city, is endangered by rapid, often-unchecked development that is overrunning quiet little dairy towns and eating up family farms that have been part of the picturesque Sugar River watershed for more than a century. It has us and natural resources managers worried. But there is hope, because people who love Mt. Vernon Creek have moved to protect its vital headwaters through formation of a new Dane County park. We want the next generation of trout fishers to be able to enjoy this vulnerable spring creek in future years.

THE SETTING

Mt. Vernon Creek, 8 miles in length, winds its way through a valley that not long ago was sprinkled with crossroads communities, cheese factories, and

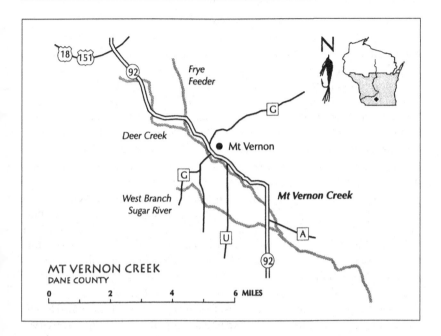

many dairy farms. But the cheese factories are gone, and some of those farms are giving way to secluded homes that have become some private individuals' pieces of heaven. Yet the rural beauty and charm hangs on, even though the valley is under the cloud of development.

Mt. Vernon fits all the definitions of a spring creek. It has a constant source of spring-fed, alkaline waters in the optimal temperature range required by trout, 50 to 65 degrees. Its hard water, which originates from fissures in the dolomite and sandstone bedrock, is rich in alkalinity. The forested slopes overlaying these sedimentary rocks enhance infiltration of rainwater into a groundwater reservoir that constantly replenishes the stream. Mt. Vernon also has a good base flow—the groundwater contribution to stream flow—of almost 20 cubic feet per second.

Throughout its course, Mt. Vernon harbors wild trout, some of them trophy trout over 20 inches long. The Wisconsin Department of Natural Resources used to supplement the wild trout population with the stocking of hatchery fish in the early 1960s, but that has been discontinued. The stream, as long as its watershed is protected, needs little help in the fish-growing department.

MANAGEMENT HISTORY

Today's management efforts are focusing on land acquisitions. Both the WDNR and Dane County are moving land into public ownership to save it from development marching westward from metropolitan Madison. The efforts of these government entities, along with the efforts of conservation organizations such as Trout Unlimited, may help preserve Mt. Vernon as we now know it—a lovely spring creek situated in a relatively unspoiled watershed.

The focus is on the headwaters region, because development there potentially robs a stream like Mt. Vernon Creek of its lifeblood: clear, cold, nutrient-rich water. The Dane County Parks Commission is in the process of establishing Donald Park just upstream from the village of Mt. Vernon. This park, to include trails, picnic areas, and other low-impact outdoor opportunities, will provide an important buffer area for the stream. The park started with a 105-acre land donation from the Woodburn family, which has deep roots in this part of Wisconsin. Conservationists hope the park will eventually encompass up to 1,000 acres of land bordering on Mt. Vernon Creek and some of its feeder streams. The land acquisitions aim to preserve lowlands along the stream corridor, as well as many of the wooded hillsides that are critical for watershed health and aesthetics. Protection may be expanded through negotiation of conservation easements, which prevent development without transferring ownership.

The effort to create a new park builds on many hours of volunteer labor that have gone into the cause of protecting Mt. Vernon. Groups such as the Dane County Conservation League, the Madison School Program, and Trout Unlimited have helped to obtain 20-year easements from landowners, allowing successful projects to stabilize stream banks and limit livestock access. These easements line practically the entire length of Deer Creek, a major tributary to Mt. Vernon; additional easements are located at the confluence of Mt. Vernon and the West Branch of the Sugar River, which some consider a trout stream in the making.

Mt. Vernon Creek long has been on the minds of natural resources managers. It has been the site of many trout stream improvement projects, which became the foundation of much of what is being done to improve trout streams today. Nationally known trout biologist Ray White and then—WDNR area fisheries research biologist Oscar Brynildson developed much of their groundbreaking 1967 *Guidelines for Trout Stream Improvement* while planning and installing stream habitat protection structures on Mt. Vernon Creek. Most of their fine habitat-protection work remains, helping provide trout a better home. The stream cuts a deep meandered channel between undercut banks created by boom covers. These old stream-bank-protection devices still provide excellent cover for trout. As we fish them we can't help reflecting upon the work and the commitment that went before us to protect and enhance this fine stream.

ANGLING OPPORTUNITIES

The crystalline waters of Mt. Vernon are among the most challenging places to fish for trout anywhere. The stream is narrow and deceptively deep, with many undercut banks and a multitude of technical fishing challenges. Stream-side grasses are usually very high by midsummer, and seem to reach out and snatch your fly if you momentarily forget to watch your backcast. Pinpoint accuracy is required to make the right presentation, and the fish are apt to be extremely selective. The deep channels usually mean that most casting must be done from the bank. And wading in this stream will mean that you will spook many trout; in addition it can be downright unnerving. We've heard stories of anglers losing their waders in the silty inside bends of the meanders, so use caution and common sense when fishing this stream.

Access to the stream is plentiful throughout its length because of the large amount of public land that surrounds it, and several road crossings. Several parking areas are located along State Highway 92, which generally parallels the stream.

When spring finally blooms in southern Wisconsin, Mt. Vernon seems to explode all at once. We've had unparalleled early spring fishing on this stream. We recall some fifty-fish afternoons while casting Hendrickson and Sulphur imitations through short wooded stretches of Mt. Vernon. When the season opens in May, Tan Caddis and *Baetis* mayflies are hatching, and they generally continue to hatch through the middle of the month. Hendricksons begin to show within the first two weeks of May, along with the Little Black Caddis. The Sulphur hatch occurs primarily in late May and continues well into June. Midges and small caddis species hatch throughout the season and can complicate the angler's attempts at matching the hatch. In the lower reaches you may find a few *Hexagenia* hatching in late June and July; however this is usually not as dependable as the well-known Hex hatch on other southern Wisconsin streams.

What to use when the trout are not feeding on the surface? Most regulars would opt to tie on a Scud or a Cressbug (#14 or #16)—both standby flies for southern Wisconsin spring creek trout anglers. A streamer—a Sculpin would be a good choice because those fish are abundant in the creek—fished deep in the undercut banks or channels should also yield fish. The same tactic works for fishing a Woolly Bugger or Leech.

As you would imagine, with the extensive meadows that border the stream, this creek has a reputation for fine terrestrial fishing. However, it is by no means easy. Use a quiet approach, and you may be successful some of the time. All the terrestrial patterns should be effective in July and August, but we find that smaller patterns are more productive. This is particularly so for the smaller grasshopper and cricket patterns (#16). Take your time and plan each cast carefully. The fish are there—but they are very spooky. For the spin-fisher, the same rules apply: plan your approach carefully, cast accurately, and try not to frighten these wary fish. And you will do better using smaller lures.

Other streams to fish: Story Creek near Belleville, Trout Creek near Barneveld, and Black Earth Creek near Cross Plains (described in the preceding section).

If you're looking for other sidetrips, the Military Ridge bicycle trail, following the route of the historic Military Road, runs past Mt. Horeb. Blue Mound State Park, preserving the area around the highest point in southern Wisconsin (1,716 feet), has hiking trails, campsites, and an outdoor swimming pool. A nice limestone cavern, Cave of the Mounds, is near the community of Blue Mounds; a tour could be a pleasurable way to cool down on stifling summer afternoons.

Castle Rock Creek
and the Blue River

STREAM SNAPSHOT
Castle Rock Creek
and the Blue River

MILES OF TROUT WATER: 6.5,
Castle Rock; 14, Blue River

SETTING: Two spring creeks with
variety of meadows and woods
in Wisconsin R. uplands

TROUT SPECIES: Brookies, browns,
and rainbows; some stocking

REGULATIONS: Category 5 in Iowa
and Grant counties

BEST FLIES: Griffith's Gnat,
Adams, Scud, Pheasant Tail,
Elk Hair Caddis, Cricket,
Woolly Bugger, Leech

NEAREST COMMUNITIES: Fennimore, Dodgeville, Prairie du
Chien

It was a misty morning in August, a little before the sun had burned off the wisps of steam rising from the dew-laden grass of the pastures. We had arrived in the early morning as night was yielding to dawn. The stream was clear and drew us in as we quickly assembled our gear, stepped into our waders, and hurriedly, yet quietly, got into position to fish. After some cautious scouting from the stream bank, we located several big fish, some exceeding 20 inches. They were feeding on an early morning midge hatch. Before long, each of us was alone on our reach of stream and concentrating on a respectable brown sipping steadily on midge pupae. The crowds of the early part of the fishing season had moved on, planning for hunting, or the UW football season, so we had little fear that our solitude would be disturbed by other anglers. Soon one of us connected, fooling the trout with a #20 olive-green Midge Pupa. We all admired the big fish as it was released and finned back to its position beneath the undercut bank. It looked like the start of another Castle Rock Creek kind of day.

Castle Rock Creek, nestled in southwestern Wisconsin's Grant County, has acquired a reputation as this state's version of a western spring creek because big trout can be caught regularly on tiny dry flies. This reputation has drawn fly-fishing schools from Chicago and both accomplished and neophyte trout fishers from Milwaukee, Minnesota, and Iowa. No matter that some of the big fish are stocked brood trout from a hatchery. The pastoral scene provides the right setting: the old stone Castle Rock Lutheran Church watching over a valley filled with contented dairy cattle; a meandering spring creek bordered by lush growths of jewelweed; ruby-throated hummingbirds flitting from bloom to bloom; a backdrop of rounded, wooded hills that in autumn turn into a palette of yellow, gold, and red; and a relatively open terrain, free of bothersome trees. Things are getting even better at Castle Rock—now, more and more of its big fish are born and grow up in the stream.

THE SETTING

Castle Rock Creek is one of perhaps a dozen good trout streams that flow north from Military Ridge towards the Wisconsin River. Military Ridge, an east-west divide that separates the broad Wisconsin River watershed from those waters that flow south, became the backbone of the historic Military Road. The road, built by the army in the 1830s to connect three Wisconsin forts, ran from Green Bay (Fort Howard), to Portage (Fort Winnebago) to Prairie du Chien (Fort Crawford). Today, the western part of this road is State Highway 18. A state bicycle trail also follows the route, which provides sweeping views of the countryside and Blue Mound, one of the highest points in southern Wisconsin and a landmark for generations of early settlers.

Castle Rock Creek joins another good trout stream, the Blue River, before entering the Wisconsin River at, appropriately, the community of Blue River. Castle Rock is also called the Fennimore Fork of the Blue. Fennimore is an old railroad town known as one terminus for a narrow-gauge train that ran 16 miles between Fennimore and Woodman, on the Wisconsin River, from the 1870s until 1926 (today the Fennimore Railroad Historical Society Museum pays tribute to the "Dinky," the last Class A narrow-gauge passenger train in the state). On their way to the Wisconsin River, both streams cut through emerald-green valleys faced with cliffs that shade grazing dairy cows and meandering trout water. On the uplands are more dairy farms, and rows and rows of corn. When you fish Castle Rock Creek and the Blue River, you're fishing two lovely limestone spring creeks in a storybook setting.

The streams are fed by numerous springs in their headwaters. Castle Rock Creek gets most of its base flow from Swenson Spring. This large spring infuses thousands of gallons of near-50-degree water every minute into Castle Rock Creek, transforming the stream into a highly productive and challenging spring creek. Because of Swenson Spring and other springs, both streams are highly alkaline. These high alkalinities are due to the origin of the spring water—dolomite and sandstone bedrock underlying the nearby ridges and valley floor. The forested ridges allow rainwater and snowmelt to infiltrate into the fractured bedrock and replenish the stream with a constant, nutrient-rich base flow that enhances productivity of trout and the aquatic insects they eat.

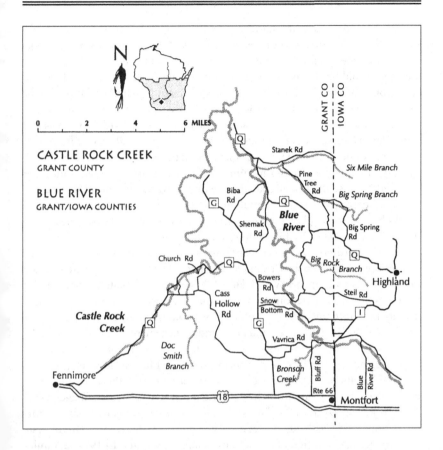

MANAGEMENT HISTORY

The Blue River and its tributary Castle Rock Creek combined are one of the major trout stream systems in southwestern Wisconsin; about 6.5 miles of Castle Rock Creek and 14 miles of the Blue River are classified as trout water. But neither is a trout stream by the time they meet; the trout fishing is on the upper reaches. In these reaches, stream flows are about 10 to 30 cubic feet per second, with the Blue being a slightly larger stream. For many years both streams have been intensively managed by the Wisconsin Department of Natural Resources. Thousands of feet of stream bank have been stabilized with rock and improved with the installation of fish-habitat structures. Although the stream habitat has been improved, the streams still receive regular stockings of trout to supplement the naturally reproducing fish. Most of these stockings will be with browns, but a good number of rainbows are stocked, too.

Both Castle Rock and the Blue are very accessible because of significant amounts of public stream-bank ownership. Castle Rock Creek is easily accessible from County Highway Q, which either crosses or parallels the stream for its entire length. The Blue River is also easily accessible because of numerous road crossings. But in its upper reaches, the Blue River is harder to access and thus offers a high degree of solitude to anglers willing to walk farther from their cars. This section, some of which is included in the Snow Bottom State Natural Area, is a biotic refuge, harboring unusual plant and animal communities that survived because the last glacial advance didn't sweep this part of the state. A proposed expansion of the natural area to 4,000 acres from the current 633 would better protect plant communities such as pine relics. These relics, dominated by white pine, are found on steep slopes and rocky cliffs. They are different from northern forests because there's a mixture of northern and southern species present, and the best examples of these pine relics in the entire state are in this area, according to a WDNR land-buying proposal. State biologists think the natural-area designation also would guard against stream and stream bank degradation from uncontrolled animal waste pollution in the headwaters, poor grazing and logging practices, and poor land management. We've witnessed the animal waste problem and it's of special concern to us, because it has cut the numbers and types of insects and hurt trout in the Blue's headwaters.

It isn't that the WDNR hasn't been paying attention to these streams. Both have received a lot of attention from the agency's area fisheries manager, Gene Van Dyck. Van Dyck in the late seventies pushed for special "fish for fun" regulations, and Castle Rock Creek became one of the few streams in the state with an extensive stretch of no-kill, artificials-only water. In 1977, 2.4 miles of Castle Rock Creek and 1.4 miles of its tributary Doc Smith Branch became catch-and-release waters. The results were fantastic: thousands of brown and brook trout were stocked, and they remained in the stream to grow. Hundreds of the fish exceeded 18 inches, and we all can testify that some of these were lunkers pushing 30 inches. Van Dyck is credited with using the "fish for fun" concept as a stepping-stone to more comprehensive special regulations that are helping to create trophy trout fishing around the state.

ANGLING OPPORTUNITIES

Castle Rock Creek and the Blue River both have an excellent array of similar hatches that will quicken the pulse of any dedicated fly-fisher. The Blue-Winged Olive hatch is usually the first major hatch to appear—if you don't count the midges that appear in February (we call them "snow flies"). Blue-Winged Olives usually appear on cloudy, often rainy, days as early as March. Some of our finest angling days in Wisconsin have occurred during this hatch. One April afternoon following two warm spring days, we arrived at the stream to find miserable cold and rainy conditions. But the Blue-Winged Olive hatch turned that day into a bright memory because we hooked and released many fish 14–16 inches long and a few fish over 20 inches. It seems the heaviest hatches of the Blue-Winged Olives occur on the worst weather days, but if the fish are rising during a legal season, we're fishing. Even in the heat of midsummer a *Baetis* hatch may occur. We've encountered enormous brown-olive *Baetis* hatches on sweltering days with water temperatures in the mid-50s; a #22 olive Griffith's Gnat produced numerous fish up to 23 inches.

Caddis begin hatching in April. When fishing this hatch, be sure to position yourself close to a riffle, because some of the most exciting fishing will take place there as the fish slash at the emerging pupae trying to leave the surface as winged adults. Pupa imitations or dry imitations such as the Elk Hair Caddis skittered across the surface can be deadly during this hatch.

May will usher in the Hendricksons and the Little Black Caddis. You can expect these insects to hatch at approximately the same time, but the Little Black Caddis will hatch over a longer period. The Hendrickson hatch on the Blue is limited to the upper reaches of the stream, because that's where the water quality is best. Towards the end of May and into June, you may catch a Sulphur hatch. Other caddis also will start hatching about this time. As the fishing season goes by, fish often feed sporadically on hard-to-identify minutiae; a #20–24 Adams or Hare's Ear Parachute dry fly is a good choice to fool these wily feeders.

If no hatches are present, there are plenty of other options. Underwater flies are effective on Castle Rock and the Blue. Scuds and Cressbugs are especially effective because the streams are loaded with these crustaceans. Anglers prefer #14–16 Scuds. Weight the fly properly to get it down on the bottom, and fish it with a natural drift. A small "trailer" nymph can improve your fish catching. Do not neglect Leeches and Woolly Buggers. Cast them to undercut banks and drift them through the deeper pools; this technique may entice one of the lunkers. At nightfall in summertime, don't hesitate to tie on a big (#6–8) Madam X attractor. We've had fish—including one 30-inch brown—savage this fly.

Late summer means terrestrials. All of the usual terrestrial patterns will work here, but we've found smaller sizes (#14–18) work best. Present your fly accurately. A matter of inches will separate success from failure; bank feeders rarely move far from protected cover. You can understand their caution after you've caught several fish that clearly have been poked by preying herons.

For those who fish with spin tackle, these streams provide excellent angling

Blue River and Castle Rock Creek offer some of the most picturesque and productive trout angling in southern Wisconsin. Photo by Mark Ratner.

opportunities. Rooster Tails, Mepps, small Marabou Jigs and Panther Martins are tried-and-true lures. Spin-fishers will be successful if they use a careful approach and refrain from spooking these wary fish.

Both Castle Rock and the Blue have several tributaries that are excellent trout streams in their own right. Being considerably smaller, they offer the angler a more intimate fishing experience. Try Doc Smith Branch, which enters Castle Rock Creek in the special regulations waters (Category 5). The Big Green River (described in the following section) is a short drive away.

Big Green River

STREAM SNAPSHOT
Big Green River

MILES OF TROUT WATER: 11

SETTING: Spring creek with variety of meadows and woods in scenic Driftless Area valley

TROUT SPECIES: Wild browns, some rainbows

REGULATIONS: Categories 3 and 5 in Grant County

BEST FLIES: Scud, Cressbug, Pheasant Tail, Elk Hair Caddis, Cricket, Woolly Bugger, Leech

NEAREST COMMUNITIES: Fennimore, Dodgeville, Prairie du Chien

The eastern sky was brightening as we pulled to the ridge overlooking a Montana-like panorama: a spring creek meandering through a broad meadow backed by a silhouette of steep, heavily vegetated ridges. As we left the car and eased down to the stream, wild turkeys gobbled from a nearby ridge, jolting us into a higher level of awareness. We fanned out to our favorite deep pools on the meadow section. Since nothing was rising, we each chose our favorite deep-riding wet fly: one tied on a Cressbug, one a Scud, the third a Pheasant Tail Nymph.

The last man in the party, standing at the edge of the deepest pool, tied on an olive-green-bodied Woolly Bugger. Everybody caught fish that morning, healthy football-shaped trout that peeled off line and bent the rod diving in vain to underwater cover. But our man fishing the weighted Woolly Bugger on a dead-drift came away with the biggest one of all—a 19-inch rainbow that had been recently transplanted into the stream. The fact that it had been stocked didn't diminish the thrill of a fine morning on the Big Green's meadows reminiscent of the West. Nowadays fishing the river is even more exciting because natural reproduction is in full swing. A big hatchery brood fish will be stocked now and then, but wild trout are now the rule in the Big Green.

THE SETTING

The Big Green River runs through one of the prettiest valleys in southwestern Wisconsin, north and west of Fennimore in Grant County. Be on the lookout for marsh wrens and common yellowthroat as you make your way to the stream. These small birds can often be spotted in the low wet meadows, sounding the alarm to announce your intrusion.

This nutrient-rich limestoner flows west, picking up a lot of water from big springs a little upstream from Werley. Then it turns north, taking in the Little Green River before discharging into the Wisconsin River just below Woodman.

Eleven miles of the Big Green are prime brown trout water, managed for the most part as a wild trout fishery.

Many anglers only fish the meadows and cow pastures of the Big Green River valley but they're missing a lot. The wooded sections of the stream, although difficult places to cast, hold many good-sized trout. In these sections, you fish pools and riffles under a verdant canopy. The stream is quite narrow in the high-gradient headwater areas, never more than 10 feet wide. In the lower portion of the trout water, pools will be as wide as 25 feet. The Big Green is typified by long pools separated by big swift riffles. But the stream is never intimidating; instead it invites you to explore its many nuances.

MANAGEMENT HISTORY

The Big Green is one of the most notable trout stream success stories in Wisconsin. In the post–World War II period, state fisheries managers considered the Green marginal trout water because of serious flash flooding and bank erosion, so the stream was heavily stocked for more than fifty years. That didn't necessarily mean the fishing was poor. Old-timers, such as retired Madison postal worker Lowell Gennrich, recalled great success during forays to the Big Green. Now things are getting even better. Modern conservation practices such as barnyard-runoff control and strip cropping have helped to improve water quality and reduce flooding. In addition, many of the slopes that once were heavily grazed or cropped have reverted to woodlands or thick scrub vegetation, which has improved vital groundwater recharge to the stream.

These positive changes opened the way for a grand experiment. In the late 1980s, the Wisconsin Department of Natural Resources implemented large-scale transfers of wild brown trout from nearby fisheries. From 1988 to 1991, more than 2,000 wild brown trout were taken from three local streams and put in the Big Green. The results were deemed remarkable by wild trout advocates: stream surveys in two stretches of the Big Green revealed twenty times more brown trout than had been previously counted. It makes sense: wild trout flourish in a place like the Big Green because they can survive predation, disease, and angling pressure better than the domestic stock. This successful experiment boosted the interest in wild trout that had been percolating through state fish management circles.

Of course, the right habitat must be there. This long has been in the minds of those who care for the Big Green River. The WDNR has acquired about 8 miles of fishing easements along the stream, which provide a buffer for the stream and good access for anglers. Easement areas are usually indicated at

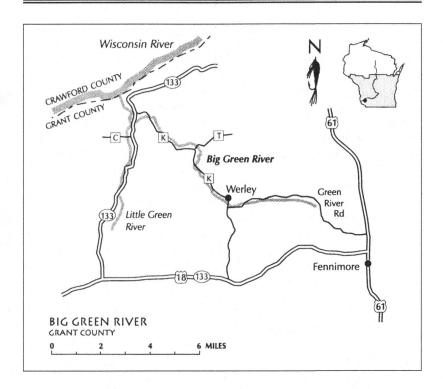

Wisconsin River

N

CRAWFORD COUNTY
133

GRANT COUNTY

61

C   K   T

Big Green River

K

Werley   Green
River
Rd

133 *Little Green
River*

Fennimore

18 133

61

BIG GREEN RIVER
GRANT COUNTY
0   2   4   6 MILES

road crossings and by stiles installed at fences. The Big Green also has an extensive special regulations section in the lower portion of the trout water. The stream is easily accessible from County Highway K and the Green River Road.

ANGLING OPPORTUNITIES

The Big Green is highly productive and provides a wonderful set of hatches that will prompt surface feeding activity. Starting in March, the Big Green's *Baetis* hatch is the spring tonic for many an angler's "cabin fever." A Pheasant Tail Nymph size #16, Blue-Winged Olive Emerger size #16, and dry Blue-Winged Olive patterns are the standard flies used during this hatch.

April brings warmer temperatures and caddis hatches in the upper part of the Big Green. The river has profuse caddis hatches, and we've enjoyed the sunny, 75-degree days when caddis dry flies and nymphs brought in scores of trout. Later on, in May and June, several caddis species hatch. We fish the riffles with a Caddis Pupa, or an adult pattern such as the Elk Hair Caddis or LaFontaine Emergent Caddis. This can be exciting as the trout slash at insects—and your fly, if you're lucky—trying to leave the surface of the water.

With the coming of May, the Little Black Caddis and Hendricksons begin to appear. After the Hendricksons wane, Sulphurs appear. The Sulphurs are usually easily differentiated from the Hendricksons by their smaller size and lighter color. Be on the lookout for both flies to be hatching towards the end of May. These are fun and uplifting hatches to fish after Wisconsin's long winter. The spring sun is warming the earth and green buds are popping out everywhere, lending a chartreuse cast to the entire valley.

When nothing is hatching you can't do better than to use a Scud or Cressbug (#14–16) fished deep through the long pools of the Big Green. A weighted Red Fox Squirrel Nymph, Muskrat, or Hare's Ear in sizes #12–16 can also be dynamite. A particularly effective method is to attach a trailing fly to the nymph. We've found success with these trailers: a small Serendipity or a midge larva imitation (green or red, in size #20). Small Girdle Bugs dredged very slowly through the pools can produce some very large fish. We've also taken many fish over 15 inches by hanging a Girdle Bug downstream in the heavy riffles, working the fly under the many undercut banks. In this vein, Leeches and Woolly Buggers fished deep along the undercuts can be especially effective. The lower part of the stream, which runs through a wooded corridor, is an especially good locale to work these wet flies. Sculpin and crayfish imitations shouldn't be overlooked, because the stream is well populated with both these animals.

July and August mean it's time to bring out the box of terrestrials imitations. Grasshoppers, Crickets, Ants, and Beetles are all effective, especially in the meadow sections. Schedule your fishing time so that you are on the stream in the early morning or at dusk to increase your chances of success; at this time of year, the trout will be more active during those periods of the day. Move slowly, waiting for some signal from a feeding trout. We've had trout over 20 inches rip our carefully presented terrestrials. This terrestrial fishing continues into September. We remember one great season-ending day on the Big Green when nothing was hatching. Only one good feeding fish was spotted, and that beast was looking downstream into a backwater eddy near a farm bridge. A #16 black Cricket floated upstream did the trick, and after a tough fight on 7X tippet, a brawny 22-inch brown trout was taken, photographed, and released.

Other streams in the area that offer fine trout fishing include Castle Rock Creek and the Blue River (described in the preceding section) and the Little Green River.

Jim Bartelt fishes a corner pool on the Big Green River. Photo by Steve Born.

For other sporting activities, there's warm-water fishing and canoeing available on the Wisconsin River. You can launch a boat or canoe at the juncture of the Big Green and the Wisconsin, the site of a small park. And with all those turkeys in the Big Green River valley, a spring "cast-and-blast" adventure may interest you. There are turkey seasons in the fall and spring, but the spring season overlaps the early and regular trout seasons best.

To sample some Wisconsin history, take a little jaunt to the Mississippi River town of Prairie du Chien, site of Villa Louis. This is a well-preserved Victorian mansion built atop an old Indian burial mound. For a look at undisturbed Indian effigy mounds, travel to some nearby Wisconsin state parks—Perrot State Park in Trempealeau or Wyalusing State Park at Wyalusing. Camping is available at both parks. Another Native American–related tourist attraction is in Wauzeka, site of the Kickapoo Indian Caverns, said to be the largest in the state.

Timber Coulee Creek

STREAM SNAPSHOT
Timber Coulee Creek

MILES OF TROUT WATER: 8

SETTING: Fast-flowing spring creek cutting through scenic pastures and coulees

TROUT SPECIES: Wild browns

REGULATIONS: Categories 3 and 5 in La Crosse and Vernon counties

BEST FLIES: Scud, Cressbug, Pheasant Tail, Griffith's Gnat, Elk Hair Caddis, Cricket, Trico (in season)

NEAREST COMMUNITIES: Westby, Coon Valley, La Crosse

Timber Coulee Creek might just be the crown jewel among Wisconsin spring creeks. But it wasn't always so; nestled in the heart of the state's Driftless Area, this stream was once described by state fisheries personnel as unfit for trout because of its poor water quality and habitat. In 1967, an electrofishing survey showed that only 1,098 trout were present in a 5-mile stretch of the stream. Now up to 5,000 fish *per mile* inhabit the 8 miles of Timber Coulee Creek. What once was a wider, warmer, muddier waterway now is a crystal-clear, watercress-lined spring creek meandering its way toward the Mississippi past rugged hills, wooded slopes, and neat dairy farms. The transformation is due to nature and to the loving care given by private clubs, individuals, and public agencies. The most dramatic stream work occurred from the sixties through the eighties, but the care dates back to the Depression. In 1933, the Soil Conservation Service began the nation's first project to combat soil erosion in the Coon Valley watershed, of which Timber Coulee is a part. All the hard work has paid off in ways that couldn't have been anticipated—this former put-and-take fishery is self-sustaining, and Timber Coulee's wild trout are now the primary stock for the state's wild trout program. No wonder Trout Unlimited named it one of the top 100 streams in the country.

THE SETTING

Timber Coulee gathers several smaller trout streams from steep-sided valleys during its 8-mile run through the picturesque coulee country of southwestern Wisconsin. Most of Timber Coulee Creek lies in Vernon County, but it meanders very close to the Monroe County line at one point and then winds for a bit in La Crosse County. Most of the Timber Coulee watershed is agricultural, primarily pasture land for dairy cattle, with hardwood forests on the hillsides and ridges. It eventually joins Bohemian Valley Creek and becomes Coon Creek, both of which are also trout streams.

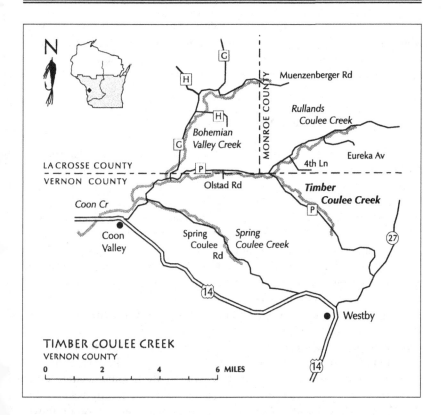

Timber Coulee is very fertile, and has a moderately high gradient compared to other Wisconsin spring creeks. Although the stream is dominated by spring flow, its water level can rise rapidly during heavy rains because of the hilly topography. Be prepared for high, turbid, and often unfishable water. But unlike the old days, the water clears rather quickly, especially in the tributaries.

In the headwater area, a little north of the Norwegian-American community of Westby, the stream is only about 6 feet wide. We don't often fish here, but we marvel at the Snowflake Club's ski jumps towering above us, site of an annual Intercontinental Cup Ski-Jumping Tournament. Spend a few moments imagining what it would be like to jump off one of these and experience the agony of defeat. In the summer, the ski-jump grounds become a golf course. Farther downstream, where Rullands Coulee Creek dumps into Timber Coulee at the Skogdalen Lutheran Church, the stream widens slightly and falls into a delightful riffle-pool pattern. The stream bottom is typically fist-sized stones and gravel. Towards its confluence with Bohemian Valley Creek, Timber Coulee widens to about 25 feet, with deeper pools and a bottom combining rocks, sand, and silt. Intensive stream work throughout is very evident, allowing you to pick out good cover for trout. In the upper reaches of Timber Coulee, flows rarely exceed 10 cubic feet per second; near Coon Valley, stream flow increases to about 30 cubic feet per second.

MANAGEMENT HISTORY

Starting in the 1930s as part of Franklin D. Roosevelt's New Deal, the Soil Conservation Service (now referred to as the National Resource Conservation Service) began the nation's first watershed-wide restoration project, with the help of the Civilian Conservation Corps. A sign commemorating this conservation effort has been erected by the State Historical Society just west of Coon Valley on U.S. Highway 14. The hills in those days were intensively cropped, and countless tons of valuable topsoil eroded into the creek, probably destined for the Mississippi River delta. The watershed project promoted contour farming and other practices designed to curb abusive farming practices. Erosion problems have been significantly eased by projects like these.

The next big stage of watershed improvement began in the early sixties, when local residents and groups such as the Westby Rod & Gun Club installed wing deflectors in a long stretch of the stream. Among these stream-keepers were Kenneth Graupe, father of former Coon Valley fly shop owner Dennis Graupe, and Palmer Olson, a former commercial fly-tier and veteran southwestern Wisconsin angler. A lot of stocking followed, and things began to look better. More recently, the Wisconsin Department of Natural Resources made Timber Coulee one of its showcase streams, demonstrating how stream work and special slot limits could dramatically improve a trout stream. Necessity being the mother of invention, the WDNR, concerned about the extreme flooding which can devastate stream banks and fish habitat structures, developed a three-sided wooden fish crib that would withstand the eroding effects of high water. This structure was nicknamed LUNKER, for "Little Underwater Neighborhood Keepers Encompassing Rheotactic Salmonids." Translation: good, inexpensive trout cover. Hundreds of LUNKERs were installed on Timber Coulee. When combined with rock riprap, they greatly improved the stability of the banks. They proved to be such a success that the fish cribs have been installed in many other midwestern streams. One of the dedicated fisheries personnel involved in developing the LUNKER was Dave Vetrano, the former area fisheries manager based in nearby La Crosse. He has been a leader in making the most of the coulee streams.

This important stream work and the healing power of nature gradually transformed Timber Coulee Creek into a self-sustaining wild trout fishery. There are still a few wild brook trout, but most of the trout in Timber Coulee are wild browns. The last browns were stocked in the fall of 1986. The stream has been such a good producer of wild browns that it provided the brood stock for a WDNR wild trout stocking program begun at the Nevin Fish Hatchery south of Madison. Because wild fish have been found to have greater survival rates and are generally preferred by anglers, the WDNR hopes to greatly increase the number of streams that are predominately wild trout fisheries. In addition, legal-sized Timber Coulee trout are being transferred to other streams, which will help the other streams while allowing Timber Coulee's browns to grow bigger in a less competitive environment. As Vetrano says, "It's quite a testimony, considering that thirty to thirty-five years ago, this was a put-and-take fishery."

ANGLING OPPORTUNITIES

All of that stream work has another advantage: abundant angler access to the stream through easements obtained from local landowners. Drive along County Highway P and look for WDNR pullouts or for stiles that cross the barbed-wire fences. One popular access is Olstad Bridge, the upstream boundary of the special regulations section.

Lots of trout and good stream access; what could be better? How about excellent aquatic insect populations that will provide any angler with challenging, technical spring creek fishing? This stream may have the most diverse array of aquatic insects and crustaceans of any spring creek in southwestern Wisconsin. Several factors are responsible: watershed protection efforts, small dairy farms that don't overwhelm the system with pollution, productive limestone-buffered waters, and extensive riffle areas. For the dedicated fly-fisher, the diversity of insect life and the dependable hatches provide an enriching time on the stream. For some of us, catching trout is just an added bonus.

Let's start with the major mayfly hatches. The Blue-Winged Olives, which appear in early March, are a major and extremely reliable hatch on this stream. The riffles between pools are excellent habitat for these insects, and the trout really key in on the nymphs and duns during the hatch. Hendricksons make their appearance in early to mid-May. Be on the lookout for complex hatches of Blue-Winged Olives and Hendricksons, which can confuse the issue for the angler. Sulphurs are a significant hatch on Timber Coulee, usually making their appearance after the Hendricksons. Blue-Winged Olive mayflies re-emerge in the fall, and we remember one glorious final day of the season, taking twenty or so medium-sized fish out of a lovely riffle-and-pool section as the sun dipped to the horizon.

Timber Coulee is one of the few streams in southwestern Wisconsin with a reliable Trico hatch. Tricos usually make their appearance in early August and continue into September. Be prepared to rise early. Late August is a wonderful time to be on this stream because of the pleasant weather and the glimpses of premature fall color on the ridges. The primary focus for the angler during the Trico hatch is the spinner fall, so carefully select a location where pools and flats are prevalent. After mating in the air after dawn, these tiny insects will fall on the water in great numbers, and can bring out sizable feeding fish. Spend a lot of time searching for steadily feeding sippers and developing a good strategy for the presentation. Don't disturb the fish with unnecessary wading. We prefer to use either spinner imitations with hackle wings, or with wings made of flashy synthetic materials, in sizes #20–22.

Timber Coulee also is well populated with caddisflies. Use an Elk Hair Caddis in size #14 or #16 on these hatches; don't neglect a soft-hackle imitation to take fish feeding on emerging pupae. One of the more easily identifiable hatches is the Little Black Caddis, in sizes #16–18. This is a major hatch, and the angler can expect it from the middle of May until around June 15, but sporadic hatching of this insect will occur after that and elicit good surface feeding activity. Outstanding fishing can be had if you happen to hit a caddis hatch on this stream.

Multi-brooded small blue-wing olive mayflies provide superb fishing opportunities in the Coon Valley creeks throughout the fishing season. Photo by Bill Engber.

Because of the abundant cressbugs and scuds in this clean, cold-water stream, imitations of these crustaceans in sizes #12–16 are particularly deadly. Weight the fly so it ticks on the bottom, at the trout's feeding depth. During the month of August and September, use terrestrial imitations—Hoppers, Crickets, and Ants work well. Fish the lures tight along the banks and at the edges of overhanging vegetation.

If you're looking for new water, try the other Coon Creek trout waters, or go a little east and explore the Kickapoo Valley watershed profiled elsewhere in this book.

Willow Creek

STREAM SNAPSHOT
Willow Creek

MILES OF TROUT WATER: 18

SETTING: Spring creek with classic riffle-pool sequences; flows past farmland, woods, and ledges

TROUT SPECIES: Wild browns, some brookies

REGULATIONS: Categories 3 and 5 in Richland County

BEST FLIES: Scud, Cressbug, Pheasant Tail, Adams, Elk Hair Caddis, Hopper, Cricket, Girdle Bug

NEAREST COMMUNITIES: Ithaca, Richland Center, Madison

It was approaching twilight, that magical time of day that demands to be savored. The fleeting sun cast a golden glow on the rock outcroppings that compose the eastern ridges running parallel to the valley containing Willow Creek. The maple, oak, and basswood on these ridges were just starting to show the tinges of the coming autumn. Earlier in the day, warm winds whipped through the valley, sending grasshoppers and crickets onto the water. The fish weren't too picky, readily taking our imitations. Now we were faced with a tougher challenge. The pool we studied showed dimpling fish beneath the clouds of mating midges hovering over the water. A Griffith's Gnat tied on 7X tippet should do the trick—if we could make the presentation without drag. One larger fish nestled along the bank by the stones and under the big willow tree was the object of the cast. Three tries . . . and success! A strikingly colored brown trout, 15 inches long, was hooked, landed, and quickly released. That last fish capped a wonderful late-season day on Willow Creek, one of the most productive streams in Richland County.

THE SETTING

Willow Creek, which has a reputation for producing large brown trout, is one of the longest trout streams in southern Wisconsin. The main stem of Willow Creek, which flows southwesterly to its junction with the Pine River, contains over 18 miles of classified trout water. The Pine, which holds trout in its upper reaches, then flows into the Wisconsin River near Gotham, in the heart of the state-managed, free-flowing Lower Wisconsin Riverway. Willow Creek lies in a scenic valley typical of Wisconsin's Driftless Area. Forested ridges slope quickly to a valley floor populated by farmers and dairy cattle. Rock outcroppings, such as the appropriately named "Elephant Rock" along State Highway 58, reveal erosion of sandstone and dolomite bedrock. This bedrock usually

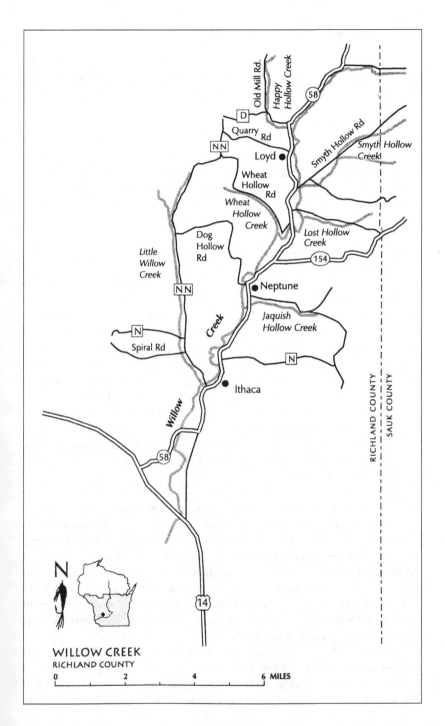

Old Mill Rd.

Happy Hollow Creek

58

D

Quarry Rd

NN

Loyd

Smyth Hollow Rd

Smyth Hollow Creek

Wheat Hollow Rd

Wheat Hollow Creek

Dog Hollow Rd

Little Willow Creek

Lost Hollow Creek

154

NN

Creek

Neptune

Jaquish Hollow Creek

N

Spiral Rd

N

Willow

Ithaca

58

RICHLAND COUNTY

SAUK COUNTY

N

14

WILLOW CREEK
RICHLAND COUNTY

0   2   4   6 MILES

is covered with silt loam, a combination providing excellent conditions for groundwater recharge. This groundwater reaches the stream through seepage and tributary streams; unlike many other spring creeks, no large springs flow directly into Willow Creek.

Willow Creek isn't big water—flows are generally 15–20 cubic feet per second—but it's sufficiently wide for comfortable fly- or spin-casting in its middle and lower sections. In the headwaters, where the creek is fed by a series of springs emanating from hollows, the stream is very narrow, but it quickly broadens to about 15 feet once it approaches Loyd. Farther down, near Ithaca, it broadens even more to about 25 feet in certain pool areas.

MANAGEMENT HISTORY

The bucolic setting can lull the angler into thinking all is well with the Willow, but we've been there on too many rainy days to say that. We've seen five-minute cloudbursts send liquid manure running into the stream from several livestock operations. According to state fisheries managers and biologists, uncontrolled animal-lot runoff—a form of non-point-source pollution—degrades water quality by robbing life-sustaining oxygen from the water, which severely limits the diversity and actual amount of trout food present in the stream. In extreme cases, trout are actually killed during these runoffs, especially when they are already stressed by other factors. Making the situation more difficult is the changing nature of dairy farming. Small farms are being combined, and in some cases cattle numbers are rising in certain problem locations. We hope barnyard-runoff controls can eventually be installed at these sites.

Some steps have already been taken to protect the stream and improve trout habitat. Prior to the late sixties, before comprehensive fishery surveys were conducted, Willow Creek contained only 10 miles of trout water. It now contains 18 miles of trout water, as a result of habitat improvement and acquisition of key pieces of land by the Wisconsin Department of Natural Resources. Land acquisition by the WDNR began in the sixties; more than 400 acres have been acquired since then, including about 13 miles of stream frontage. Habitat improvement is noticeable in the section upstream from Loyd. In 1986 the Willow Creek Fishery Area was established, with the goal of acquiring additional public lands.

The stream has good populations of wild brown trout, although some supplemental stocking of hatchery browns occurs. Small populations of brook trout can be found in the headwaters, and more than a dozen miles of this stream require no stocking because trout are reproducing on their own.

ANGLING OPPORTUNITIES

Variety is one of the hallmarks of the Willow. An angler moving upstream along Highway 58 can experience spring creek fishing in a southern Wisconsin forest, in a pastured meadow, or in a cave-like setting underneath a perpetually damp rock wall. And because the water temperature of the Willow stays cold, fishing is productive all season long.

Willow Creek has a fairly well defined set of hatches. Starting in March, excellent hatches of *Baetis* appear, followed by an early caddis hatch in April. In May, look for the Hendrickson to make their appearance along with the Little Black Caddis. These two insects will usually be found in the upper reaches of the Willow, especially in the Loyd area, because of the better water quality and better bottom habitat. Sulphurs usually make their appearance in late May or early June. By this time the peak hatching activity has switched towards an evening emergence, so plan your fishing accordingly. Midges are likely to be present throughout the season.

Into July and August, the terrestrial insect populations are building and the trout will start taking advantage of those unlucky grasshoppers, ants, crickets, and beetles that find themselves blown onto the surface of the creek. This is when we like to take advantage of what Ernest Schwiebert called "the grasshopper wind." We've experienced great fishing (and great relief) on the hottest days of the year at the Willow by wading wet and casting Hopper imitations near the undercut banks, which are shaded this time of year by tall prairie grasses and flowers. Willow Creek trout seem to prefer smaller terrestrial imitations. We go no larger than size #12 for Hoppers, and for Beetles and Ants the angler should stick with size #18. Don't overlook dry fly attractors such as the Pass Lake (#14–16) or small Royal Wulffs (#14–18); cast to the undercut banks, riprap, and other prime lies. Novice trout anglers we've chaperoned have had some delightful dry fly angling during this time—provided they had the ability to get the fly into position.

When nothing is hatching or terrestrials aren't evident, go underwater. Scuds are mainstays, and Cressbugs seem to work equally well. The most popular sizes are #14 and #16. Pheasant Tails, Hare's Ears, and the popular beadhead nymph patterns are also good producers. Always fish these wet imitations close to the bottom; we and many other veteran anglers like to use a strike indicator to increase our hooking percentage when nymph fishing. Streamers such as Woolly Buggers and Sculpins are always good choices, while Marabou Leeches work especially. well in the deeper runs and pools. The lower reaches of the trout water near Ithaca may not hold as many trout, but they do hold some potential trophies. This would be the place for the big-fish hunter to ply the water with large streamers or nymphs, fishing under cover of darkness. Spin-fishers should find this section of the stream to their liking because of large pools with snags and logs. Mepps, Rooster Tails, and Panther Martins are effective when fished deep and tight to cover.

For additional trout fishing, try the upper Pine River or some of the Willow's little tributaries. If you take the time to explore these upper Willow waters you may find some surprisingly large trout in the small pools. The adventurous angler can take home an intimate fishing experience.

For other recreational pursuits, we recommend a trip to the Lower Wisconsin Riverway, the free-flowing section of the big river. You can take a wonderful canoe trip from Spring Green, past Frank Lloyd Wright's Taliesin and sleepy river towns that haven't changed much since Wright's boyhood days in Wisconsin. Wright's only warehouse design, the A. D. German Warehouse, is located in Richland Center.

Kickapoo River

It's the last day of the trout-fishing season, and we're squeezing in the last casts. One of us slips away to a part of the stream near a dead-end road where few people fish. You have to practically fall down a steep embankment and then fight through dense underbrush just to get into position. By now, it's raining and the slow-moving water is pock-marked with the impact of the raindrops. A dark brown, soft-hackled wet fly is tied to the tippet, and an awkward downstream cast is made just over the edge of the riffles and just before the river takes a turn away from the big brush pile at the corner. In no time, a sturdy wild brown trout is on, allowing the angler to reel in the memories of one more season.

This episode, which took place on the West Fork of the Kickapoo River in southwestern Wisconsin's Vernon County, isn't so remarkable any more. But it wasn't all that long ago that fishing the West Fork or the main stem of the Kickapoo for plentiful wild trout was more dream than reality. Oh, there were trout here and there—those that occasionally dropped down from the clean, cool, spring-fed tributaries. But the West Fork and the main stem of the Kickapoo were more often coffee-colored carriers of topsoil, washed from steep hillsides by the latest hard rain.

There's been a wondrous transformation here in the last twenty years. Trout again are the dominant game fish in the streams of coulee country where the federal government once thought only a dam belonged; and, amazingly, total natural reproduction is within reach.

THE SETTING

The Kickapoo River and its sister, the West Fork, are born of springs in the hills and valleys of the unglaciated region between Madison and La Crosse known as the Driftless Area. These waters and their spring-fed tributaries meet just above Readstown, and drain a 70-mile valley full of apple orchards, Amish farms, and twisty back roads before discharging into the Wisconsin River at Wauzeka, not too far from where the Wisconsin enters the Mississippi. This is a center for organic farming in the state, and it has become a place for people to seek the perfect low-key rural existence. No wonder then, that in 1996 *Mother Earth News* named the Kickapoo Valley one of "The 10 Best Places to Live the Good Life." And they weren't even factoring in the trout fishing!

Kickapoo was an Indian word meaning "one who goes there, then here," local historians say. Getting from there to here can be quite a journey. The watershed of the main stem is 70 road miles along State Highway 131; but the meandering river—nicknamed "the crookedest river in Wisconsin" by its promoters—covers 120 miles. This good-sized river generally has flows exceeding 130 cubic feet per second.

A lot of good Kickapoo Valley topsoil has been washed down that 120 miles to the Mississippi because of the undulating topography, poor farming practices, and ill-timed storms. But that was when this river system was known for its flash floods, which annually swamped poor communities and sent their citizens scurrying for cover.

In 1962 the federal government authorized that a dam, which had originally been proposed in the 1930s, be built above La Farge. But that dam never came to be, although citizens of the valley hoped and prayed for it as economic salvation from their long-standing financial troubles. The government said the dam would contain the flooding and bring a steady stream of recreational tourism dollars to the traditionally poor area. The citizens waited, and waited, and waited. But the dam and its promised 1,800-acre lake were thwarted by several factors: environmental concerns about flooding a beautiful waterway prized by canoeists and populated by various endangered species (warblers, the little Lapland rosebay plants, and the wood turtle, to name a few); changing government and social thinking about costly dam-building; and a mounting cost estimate for the project that topped out at more than $50 million. Part of the dam was built—at a cost of $18.6 million—and the concrete beginnings of the structure can be seen north of La Farge. In the process, the government bought and condemned some 9,000 acres of land on both sides of the scenic waterway, planting the seeds of bitterness for years to come.

In the 1970s, a different way was found to help the people who were suffering from the recurrent floods. The state and the federal government paid to move one town, Soldiers Grove, to higher ground—one of the earliest approaches to solving flood problems by relocating a community, recognizing that the floodplain belongs to the river.

Now the land that was once threatened by the impoundment is a reserve managed by the state and the Ho-Chunk Native American tribe, which has

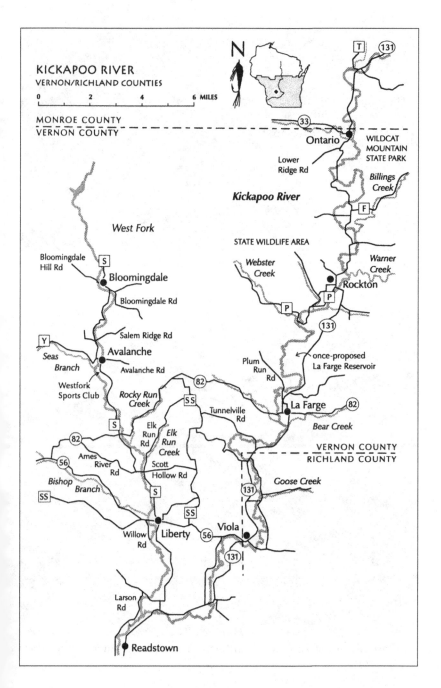

KICKAPOO RIVER
VERNON/RICHLAND COUNTIES

0   2   4   6 MILES

N

MONROE COUNTY
VERNON COUNTY

Ontario

WILDCAT
MOUNTAIN
STATE PARK

Lower
Ridge Rd

*Billings
Creek*

Kickapoo River

F

West Fork

STATE WILDLIFE AREA

Bloomingdale
Hill Rd   S

*Webster
Creek*

*Warner
Creek*

Bloomingdale

Rockton

Bloomingdale Rd

P

P

131

Y

Salem Ridge Rd

*Seas
Branch*

Avalanche

once-proposed
La Farge Reservoir

Plum
Run
Rd

Avalanche Rd

82

Westfork
Sports Club

*Rocky Run
Creek*

S S

Tunnelville
Rd

La Farge   82

Bear Creek

S

Elk
Run
Rd

*Elk
Run
Creek*

VERNON COUNTY
RICHLAND COUNTY

82

*Ames
River*

56

Rd

Scott
Hollow Rd

Goose Creek

*Bishop
Branch*

S

131

SS

SS

SS

Willow
Rd

Liberty   56

Viola

131

Larson
Rd

Readstown

251

The Kickapoo Valley and its coulees seen from Wildcat Mountain State Park. Photo by Steve Born.

An angler fishes one of the many small tributaries in the Kickapoo River drainage. Photo by Jeff Hastings.

located ancestral burial mounds in the region. And the waters of the Kick-apoo are destined to flow free in the valleys between the Ocooch Mountain ranges, as the ridges were called by explorers. During the more than thirty years of uncertainty, the farm economy dropped dramatically. But the silver lining was that the land, abused for years as farmers sought to eke out a living, began to rehabilitate itself. Man's absence and the healing power of nature are revitalizing the land. The riparian farmland began to revert to native grasses and bushes. The hilltops grew trees again. The soil loosened. The rainwater percolated through, not over, the steep hillsides, lessening the threats of flooding. And the constantly cold, nourishing limestone springs replenished. All around Kickapoo country, the trout are coming back. The original native brook trout are even coming back to re-established spring heads. "Many streams in the area are converting, probably to what they were in presettlement," says Dave Vetrano, the former WDNR area fisheries manager. "Scuds. Watercress. Sculpins. Even brook trout are making a comeback. As the water quality improves, they're re-expanding their range."

This revival will be aided substantially by an initiative started by the national Trout Unlimited in late 1996. In cooperation with many local and state partners, TU began a $400,000 two-year program to pull together and accelerate stream restoration and ecosystem protection efforts in the Kickapoo Valley. The money will not only support projects to immediately improve the trout fishery; it will also support a valley-wide ecological education program and fundamental research on the hydrology and biology of the watershed, research which will provide a better basis for future natural resources decision-making in the region. An especially exciting component of the initiative is a cooperative effort with WDNR's Heritage Brook Trout Restoration project in an attempt to restore significant portions of the upper watershed for native brook trout.

MANAGEMENT HISTORY

The national TU initiative is partly an outgrowth of an energetic grass-roots effort on the West Fork of the Kickapoo, where a conservation partnership has been formed for the sake of trout. "We hit the right key on the piano," said Roger Widner, Jr., a native son who ran the general store at Avalanche until his death. Widner led the West Fork Sports Club and a variety of conservation efforts that led some to dub the area "the Montana of the Midwest." Widner's club and its friends have spearheaded much of the good stream rehabilitation work—nearly fifty projects at a cost of about $40,000 by the end of 1995. A Trout Unlimited chapter from Janesville, about 150 miles away, adopted the West Fork after being encouraged by Dave Vetrano. The Janesville chapter pitched in with money and members' volunteer work, while the state council of TU also contributed funding. Other fishing conservation organizations, such as Federation of Fly Fishers, chip in a lot of stream work and funding. The result: more stabilized banks and better trout-holding water through installation of riprap, cattle controls, and in-stream habitat structures.

Since 1990, county conservationists estimate, about 140 LUNKERs— manmade homes for trout—have been placed throughout the county, mostly in the Kickapoo Valley. In addition, government is trading stream bank stabilization work for more public access to the Kickapoo's waters. Meanwhile, the University of Wisconsin–Madison is trying to move the area past the tragedy of the dam by exploring the economic potential of the tourist-angler trade. A new study estimates that annual fishing-related spending will approach $500,000, a number the experts suggest will grow. Overseeing a lot of this is Vetrano, an energetic fish manager who sees great potential in the area. "Fishing pressure will take care of itself, if we can produce more and more of these streams," he says. Better fisheries are being built because of improved water quality from reduced and smarter farming, stream rehabilitation projects, and targeted stocking and transplanting of wild trout. The aim is to increase both the approximately 280 miles of Kickapoo Valley trout water, and the miles of that water that have a self-sustaining, natural trout population, now about half of the 280 total.

The West Fork has at least 1,000 trout per mile, and features many big holdover browns in the 20-plus-inch range. Its entire 24-mile length is classified by biologists as supporting some natural reproduction of trout. In 1996, stocking was ended in the 7.5-mile catch-and-release section above and below Avalanche because the trout population was so large. It could be a sign of significant reproduction. The main stem, cleaning up because of state-county efforts to curb non-point-source pollution, has fewer fish; it was stocked for the first time in 1996. The main stem isn't classified as trout water, but fisheries managers are planning to seek a partial-natural-reproduction designation down the road. Spawning and natural reproduction is taking place in the spring-fed tributaries, but the hope is for significant natural reproduction in the West Fork and main stem in the future, despite the tendency for high water temperatures in the summer. Main stem temperatures reach the 80-degree mark and the West Fork's waters get into the 70s, but fisheries managers say sustained high temperatures appear to be lessening in the Kickapoo Valley and throughout the region. Smallmouth bass waters are turning into trout water, Vetrano says. "We'd like to get all of our

The "pay-off" for a good student of trout and trout fishing—a beautiful wild brown trout. Photo courtesy of Jim Bartelt.

streams self-sustaining. It's an attainable goal," he adds, promoting the kind of public-private partnership that has worked on the West Fork. "There has to be an effort by everybody involved. It also has to be a priority with the angling public. There also has to be an effort by local citizens—local citizens beginning to look at trout fishing as an industry."

ANGLING OPPORTUNITIES

Fishing the Kickapoo requires a willingness to adapt. You'll face an entirely different fishing situation on the upper reaches of the West Fork than you will on the middle third of the main stem. There are times when you think you're fishing a western freestoner, only to round the bend and be staring at the perfect picture of a Wisconsin spring creek.

First, the main stem. None of the main stem is recognized as official trout water, but it's fed by numerous trout-rich spring creeks bubbling from the coulees. Some trout inhabit the main stem above La Farge, but they aren't present in great numbers, so you could spend a lot of time searching. The main stem is heavily canoed below the liveries at Ontario, which is also the site of lovely Wildcat Mountain State Park. The main stem is full of deadfalls and big meanders. If you choose to fish it, the best bet would be a Muddler

Minnow or a Woolly Bugger pattern, but more trout can be found above Ontario.

Most anglers concentrate their efforts on the upper West Fork, a small river with plenty of room to fish. At Avalanche, stream flow during the angling season ranges from 15 to 40 cubic feet per second. Trout often are caught downstream of Highway 82, an area resembling the main stem in character. A good strategy is simply to work your way up and down Highway S, which generally parallels the West Fork. There are many public access spots, including the West Fork Sports Club campground. If you use the campground, and its nearby drinking spring, please make sure you pay at the sports club; it's a very modest fee and fellow campers may give you some good fishing information. We'll pass along one tip: when you're stumped, use the unusual. The Widner family likes to catch its trout on floating Rapalas.

Below the campground the river is broad and twisty, with a lot of cover from fallen trees. It takes some work in this section, but there are big fish to be had. Depending on the time of year there may be a good insect hatch, but in general you'll do better on this section with some of the old reliable wet flies and streamers.

The campground section has the feel of a classic southwestern Wisconsin spring creek, relatively narrow and fast, with riffle-pool sequences. A good bet here is nymphing. Use both standard and beadhead versions of Scuds, Cressbugs, Pheasant Tails, Hare's Ears, and the like with a strike indicator, and you'll find success. Above the campground the river looks like a western freestoner, with big rocks populating rippling water. This may be the place for attractor dry fly fishing. Farther upstream, the West Fork again takes on the character of a spring creek, with some lovely stretches along limestone bluffs and through pastoral grazing land. In these waters, you may use your full arsenal. While you're in this section, take in the surroundings. Northern tree species, such as the yellow birch and Canadian hemlock, are relics from the last ice age. In the spring, these wooded slopes are home to the ovenbird (listen for its *teacher, teacher, teacher* call) and the wood thrush (its call is reminiscent of a flute-like melody). In the summer, you'll often be surrounded by an outstanding display of wildflowers, including bouncing bet and bee balm.

Spin-fishers should focus on lures imitating minnows and other baitfish; the West Branch and the main stem are full of them. Hatches here follow the progression found on most southwestern spring creeks. May and June have the most hatches. The early part of the season is dominated by the Blue-Winged Olive and other small mayflies, plus various caddis hatches. We recommend flies mostly in size #14 and smaller. Clay Riness, a former traveling musician from Coon Valley who has been guiding anglers in this area since the late 1980s, likes the Adams "in all its variations." The Elk Hair Caddis also is a good bet. In June, watch for more caddis, the occasional stonefly, and plenty of midge activity in the evenings. In mid- to late summer, terrestrial fishing is a treat; we favor the #14–16 Black Cricket. In August, the West Fork experiences a good Trico hatch; arrive early and hope for the spinner fall to come your way. When in doubt, we ply the water with big minnow imitations like the Muddler Minnow, and crayfish-like lures such as the Woolly Bugger; fish them deep. We've also found success all season long with a soft-hackled wet fly fished down and across through riffles and the upper parts of pools.

Kickapoo Country offers many nearby streams to explore. Many of the Kickapoo River tributaries are small and require some bushwacking, but there is a reward for those who follow through. On some of these waters, surrounded by high grasses, you may find terrestrial patterns or the Girdle Bug to be the fly of choice; and if you're lucky, you could pick up a native brookie or two. A short drive away is Timber Coulee Creek, a trout paradise that has blossomed because of intense stream rehabilitation work (it's featured earlier in this section).

You have two basic options if spending a night in Kickapoo country: use a campground, or stay in a bed-and-breakfast. Camping is available at the West Fork Sports Club and at Wildcat Mountain State Park. Bed-and-breakfasts have popped up throughout the area; many are quaint and some are rather rustic, and all add to the Kickapoo experience.

Steve Born pursuing trout on Bishop's Branch, a tributary of the West Fork of the Kickapoo River. Photo by B. W. Hoffman.

Appendix
Selected Bibliography
Index

Appendix

Fishing the Web

Vast amounts of trout fishing information can be found via the Web. Sometimes the problem can be too much information, so here we recommend essential websites to help enhance your angling, volunteer conservation work, and general knowledge about Wisconsin's natural resources.

This list is current as of November 2013. Remember that some websites change addresses or missions over time.

State Government and Tribal Sites

Inland trout fishing overview from WDNR
http://dnr.wi.gov/topic/fishing/trout/
Guide to Wisconsin Trout Fishing Regulations from WDNR
http://dnr.wi.gov/topic/Fishing/regulations/troutregs.html
Hook and line record fish from WDNR
http://dnr.wi.gov/topic/fishing/recordfish/hookline.html
Fish eating advisory from Wisconsin Department of Health Services
http://www.dhs.wisconsin.gov/eh/fish/
Great Lakes Indian Fish and Wildlife Commission
http://www.glifwc.org/

Stream Access and Conditions

Trout stream maps, by county, from WDNR
http://dnr.wi.gov/topic/fishing/trout/streammaps.html
Wisconsin Atlas and Gazetteer (in print only; available from bookstores and website below)
http://shop.delorme.com
Map Guide to Improved Trout Waters of Wisconsin, by Todd Hanson (in print only; available from bookstores and website below)
http://www.whereamipubs.com

Managed lands mapping application, for finding public access, from WDNR
http://dnr.wi.gov/topic/Lands/DMLmap/
Current conditions for Wisconsin stream flow from US Geological Survey
http://waterdata.usgs.gov/wi/nwis/current/?type=flow

Trout Fishing and Related Conservation Organizations

Wisconsin Trout Unlimited
http://www.wisconsintu.org
Fly Fishing Wisconsin
http://www.flyfishingwis.com/
Kiap-TU-Wish chapter of Trout Unlimited
http://www.kiaptuwish.org/
Wolf River chapter of Trout Unlimited
http://www.wolfrivertu.org/wolfRiver.html
Badger Fly Fishers
http://www.badgerflyfishers.org/
Arrowhead Fly Fishers
http://www.arrowheadflyfishers.com/
Selected local stream groups
Black Earth Creek Watershed Association—http://becwa.org/
Brule River Sportsmen's Club—http://bruleriversportsmensclub.com/
Friends of the Prairie River—http://www.wisflyfishing.com/friends/
Kinnickinnic River Land Trust—http://kinniriver.org/
West Fork Sports Club—http://www.westforksportsmansclub.org/
Other Wisconsin-based conservation groups
Aldo Leopold Foundation—http://www.aldoleopold.org/
Driftless Area Restoration Effort (DARE)—http://www.tu.org
/tu-projects/driftless-area-restoration-effort
Gathering Waters Conservancy—http://www.gatheringwaters.org/
Mississippi Valley Conservancy—http://mississippivalleyconservancy.org/
Natural Resources Foundation of Wisconsin—
http://www.wisconservation.org/history-mission/
River Alliance of Wisconsin—http://www.wisconsinrivers.org/
West Wisconsin Land Trust—http://www.wwlt.org/our-work
/coldwater-streams/
Wisconsin Conservation Hall of Fame—http://www.wchf.org/
Wisconsin Chapter of The Nature Conservancy—http://www.nature
.org/ourinitiatives/regions/northamerica/unitedstates/wisconsin
/index.htm
Wisconsin Initiative on Climate Change Impacts—http://www.wicci
.wisc.edu/coldwater-fish-and-fisheries-working-group.php

Travel Information

Wisconsin Department of Tourism
TravelWisconsin.com
Local chambers of commerce and visitor information centers
http://www.travelwisconsin.com/travel-resources/visitor
-information-centers
Native American Tourism of Wisconsin
http://www.natow.org/
St. Croix National Scenic Riverway (includes Namekagon River)
www.nps.gov/sacn/
Northern Great Lakes Visitor Center, Ashland
http://nglvc.org/
Fishing guides
http://www.flyfishingguidedirectory.com/Wisconsin.html
http://www.orvis.com/fishingreports

Selected Blogs and Forums

Gary Borger
http://www.garyborger.com/
Seeking Trout
http://seekingtrout.com/
Driftless Trout Anglers
http://www.driftlesstroutanglers.com/
Spinning for Trout
http://spin4trout.tumblr.com/
On Wisconsin Outdoors
http://www.onwisconsinoutdoors.com/FlyFishing

Selected Bibliography

In addition to personal interviews, we consulted many dependable written and video sources that provided useful background information for this book. We've also included in this list our favorite "how-to" books and videos on trout fishing. If you want to know more details than we've included in the book, this is a good place to start. You may also want to look at *Wisconsin Natural Resources Magazine,* published by the Wisconsin Department of Natural Resources, and *Wisconsin Trails* magazine, published by Wisconsin Tales and Trails, Inc.

Becker, George C. 1983. *Fishes of Wisconsin.* Madison: University of Wisconsin Press.

Berrie, A. D. 1992. The Chalk Stream Environment. *Hydrobiologia* 248:3–9.

Borger, Gary. 1979. *Nymphing.* Harrisburg, Pa.: Stackpole Books.

Borger, Gary. 1980. *Naturals: A Guide to Food Organisms of the Trout.* Harrisburg, Pa.: Stackpole Books.

Borger, Gary. 1991. *Designing Trout Flies.* Wausau, Wis.: Tomorrow River Press.

Borger, Gary. 1995. *Presentation.* Wausau, Wis.: Tomorrow River Press.

Borger, Gary. *Shills of Flyfishing* (video).

Born, Stephen M., William C. Sonzogni, Jeffrey Mayers, and J. Anderson Morton. 1990. The Exceptional Waters Approach—A Focus for Coordinated Natural Resources Management. *North American Journal of Fisheries Management* 10 : 279–289.

Brykczynski, Terry, and David Reuther, eds. 1986. *The Armchair Angler.* New York: Collier Books, Macmillan.

Curtis, John T. 1959. *Vegetation of Wisconsin: An Ordination of Plant Communities.* Madison: University of Wisconsin Press.

Dubois, Robert B., and Dennis M. Pratt. 1994. History of the Fishes of the Bois Brule River System, Wisconsin, with Emphasis on the Salmonids and Their Management. *Transactions of the Wisconsin Academy of Sciences, Arts and Letters* 82:33–71.

Gordon, Sid. 1955. *How to Fish from Top to Bottom*. Harrisburg, Pa.: Stackpole.

Hafele, Rick. *Anatomy of a Trout Stream* (video).

Hansen, Michael J., Paul T. Schultz, and Becky A. Lasee. 1991. *Wisconsin's Lake Michigan Salmonid Sport Fishery, 1969–85*. Madison: Wisconsin Department of Natural Resources.

Harvey, George W. 1985. *Techniques of Trout Fishing and Fly Tying*. Belleville, Pa.: Metz Hatchery.

Hilsenhoff, William. 1975. *Aquatic Insects of Wisconsin*. Madison: Wisconsin Department of Natural Resources, Technical Bulletin No. 89.

Hilsenhoff, W. L., J. L. Longridge, R. P. Narf, K. J. Tennessen and C. P. Walton. 1972. *Aquatic Insects of the Pine-Popple River, Wisconsin*. Madison: Wisconsin Department of Natural Resources, Technical Bulletin No. 54.

Holbrook, A. T. 1949. *From the Log of a Trout Fisherman*. Norwood, Mass.: Norwood Press.

Humphrey, Jim, and Bill Shogren. 1995. *Wisconsin and Minnesota Trout Streams: A Fly-Angler's Guide*. Woodstock, Vt.: Backcountry Publications.

Humphreys, Joe. 1993. *Trout Tactics*. Harrisburg, Pa.: Stackpole Books.

Hunt, Robert L. 1988. *A Compendium of 45 Trout Stream Habitat Development Evaluations in Wisconsin During 1953–1985*. Technical Bulletin No. 162. Madison. Department of Natural Resources.

Hunt, Robert L. 1991. *Evaluation of a Catch and Release Fishery for Brown Trout Regulated by an Unprotected Slot Length*. Technical Bulletin No. 173. Madison.

Hunt, Robert L. 1993. *Trout Stream Therapy*. Madison: University of Wisconsin Press.

Koch, Ed. 1988. *Fishing the Midge*. Harrisburg, Pa.: Stackpole Books.

LaFontaine, Gary 1981. *Caddisflies*. New York: Winchester Press.

Leeson, Ted. 1994. *The Habit of Rivers*. New York: Lyons & Burford.

Leopold, Aldo. 1966. *A Sand County Almanac*. Oxford: Oxford University Press.

McCabe, Robert. 1987. *Aldo Leopold, The Professor*. Madison: Rusty Rock Press.

McClane, A. J. 1974. *McClane's Standard Fishing Encyclopedia*. New York: Holt, Rinehart and Winston.

McClane, A. J., and Keith Gardner. 1984. *McClane's Game Fish of North America*. New York: Times Books.

MacQuarrie, Gordon. 1995. *Fly Fishing with MacQuarrie*. Ed. Zack Taylor. Minocqua, Wis.: Willow Creek Press.

Marcouiller, David W., Alan Anderson, and William C. Norman. 1995. *Trout Angling and Implications for Regional Development: A Case Study of Southwestern Wisconsin*. University of Wisconsin–Cooperative Extension, Center for Community Development, Staff Paper 95.3.

Marshall, A. M. *Brule Country*. St. Paul, Minn.: North Central Publishing Co.

Martin, Darrel. 1994. *Micropatterns*. New York: Lyons & Burford.

Meade, Tom. 1994. *Essential Fly Fishing*. New York: Lyons & Burford.

Meine, Curt. 1988. *Aldo Leopold—His Life and Work*. Madison: University of Wisconsin Press.

Moore, Wayne. 1984. *Fly Tying Notes*. Seattle: Recreational Consultants.

Mueller, Ross. 1995. *Upper Midwest Flies That Catch Trout and How to Fish Them.* Amherst, Wis.: R. Mueller Publications.

Nemes, Sylvester. 1981. *The Soft-Hackled Fly Addict.* Chicago. Self Published.

Perich, Shawn. 1995. *Flyfishing the North* Country. Duluth, Minn.: Pfeifer-Hamilton.

Pobst, Richard. 1990. *Trout Stream Insects.* New York: Lyons & Burford.

Rashid, Bob, Bill Stokes, Ben Logan, George Vukelich, Jean Feraca, and Norbert Blei. 1995. *Wisconsin's Rustic Roads: A Road Less Travelled.* Boulder Junction, Wis.: Lost River Press.

Risjord, Norman. 1995. Wisconsin: *The Story of the Badger State,* Madison: Wisconsin Trails.

Rosenbauer, Tom. 1988. *Reading Trout Streams—an Orvis Guide.* New York: Nick Lyons Books.

Rulseh, Ted, ed. 1993. *Harvest Moon: A Wisconsin Outdoor Anthology.* Woodruff, Wis.: Lost River Press.

Schwiebert, Ernest, Jr. 1955. *Matching the Hatch.* New York: Macmillan.

Schwiebert, Ernest, Jr. 1972. *Remembrances of Rivers Past.* New York: Macmillan.

Schwiebert, Ernest, Jr. 1973. *Nymphs.* New York: Winchester Press.

Shaw, Helen. 1987. *Flytying.* New York: Nick Lyons Books. (25th anniversary edition).

Shewey, John. 1994. *Mastering the Spring Creeks.* Portland, Ore.: Frank Amato Publications.

Stanley, Millie. 1995. *The Heart of John Muir's World: Wisconsin, Family, and Wilderness Discovery.* Madison: Prairie Oak Press.

Swisher, Doug, and Carl Richards. 1971. *Selective Trout.* New York: Crown.

Swisher, Doug, and Carl Richards. 1975. *Fly Fishing Strategies.* New York: Crown.

Threinen, C. W., and Ronald Poff. 1963. The Geography of Wisconsin's Trout Streams. *Transactions of the Wisconsin Academy of Sciences, Arts and Letters.* 52:57–75.

Trout Unlimited. *Way of the Trout* (video).

White, Ray, and Oscar Brynildson. 1967. *Guidelines for Management of Trout Stream Habitat in Wisconsin.* Madison: Wisconsin Department of Natural Resources, Technical Bulletin No. 39.

Whitlock, Dave. 1982. *Dave Whitlock's Guide to Aquatic Trout Foods.* New York: Nick Lyons Books.

Willers, William. 1991. *Trout Biology—An Angler's Guide.* New York: Lyons & Burford.

Wisconsin Bed & Breakfasts Association. 1996. *Bed & Breakfast Directory.* Merrill, Wis.

Wisconsin Department of Natural Resources. 1961–1972. *Surface Water Resources of Wisconsin Counties.* Madison.

Wisconsin Department of Natural Resources. 1991. *Evaluation of a Catch and Release Fishery for Brown Trout Regulated by an Unprotected Slot Length.* Technical Bulletin No. 173. Madison.

Wisconsin Department of Natural Resources. 1995. *Five Year Land Plan.* Unpublished report. Madison.

Wisconsin Department of Natural Resources. 1997. *Trout Fishing Regulations and Guide.* Madison.

Wisconsin Department of Natural Resources. *Wisconsin Trout Streams.* Publication No. 6-3600 (80). Madison.

Wisconsin Department of Natural Resources. *Fishery Area Master Plans.* Unpublished reports. Madison.

Wisconsin Tales and Trails, Inc. 1996. *Great Weekend Adventures: Favorite Getaways, Festivals & Events.* Madison: Wisconsin Trails.

Zupanc, Gunther K. H. 1985. *Fish and Their Behavior.* Melle, West Germany. Tetra-Press.

Index

269

About the Authors

Steve Born, a water resources planning and policy expert, is a former chair of the National Resources Board of Trout Unlimited. He has also served on the boards of Trout Unlimited Canada and the Henry's Fork Foundation. He retired in 2005 from the University of Wisconsin–Madison, where he was a professor of urban and regional planning and environmental studies. Prior to that, he directed the state planning and energy offices.

Jeff Mayers is president of WisPolitics.com and WisBusiness.com, online news services based in Madison. He has a master's degree in Water Resources Management from the University of Wisconsin–Madison and assisted in the writing of *Catching Big Fish on Light Fly Tackle* by Tom Wendelburg.

Andy Morton, an expert fly tier, has worked in natural resource management all his life and is a supervisor in the Water Division in the Wisconsin Department of Natural Resources.

Bill Sonzogni is an avid fly tier and angler who serves as a professor emeritus in environmental chemistry at the University of Wisconsin–Madison. He previously served as director of the Environmental Health Sciences Division of the State Laboratory of Hygiene and is the former editor of the *Journal of Great Lakes Research*.